ROMANIA
Before World War II

# The Quality of Witness

*selected and edited by Marguerite Dorian*

*translated by Mara Soceanu Vamos*

*introduction by Michael Stanislawski*

Philadelphia 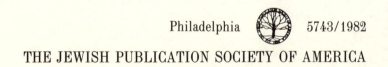 5743/1982

THE JEWISH PUBLICATION SOCIETY OF AMERICA

*Emil Dorian*

# The Quality of Witness

*A Romanian Diary 1937-1944*

Library of Congress Cataloging in Publication Data
Dorian, Emil, 1893–1956.
   The quality of witness.
1. Dorian, Emil, 1893–1956. 2. Jews—Romania—Bucharest—Biography. 3.
Holocaust, Jewish (1939–1945)—Romania—Bucharest—Personal narratives.
4. Jews—Romania—Intellectual life. 5. Romania—Ethnic relations. 6.
Bucharest (Romania)—Biography. I. Dorian, Marguerite. II. Title.
DS135.R73D67313   949.8'004924024 [B]   82–7748
ISBN 0-8276-0211-1

Designed by Adrianne Onderdonk Dudden

# Contents

# *Preface*

At his death in 1956, in Bucharest, my father, Emil Dorian, a writer and a physician, left among other manuscripts twenty-two notebooks containing his diaries. He had started making sporadic entries during the 1920s and they became a regular journal in the mid-1930s. His family and friends knew about this activity as, occasionally, in the course of a friendly argument, he would bring out one of his notebooks and read from it aloud. With time, his journals became the invisible, powerful presence of a work in the making, something that cohabits with its creator and is given proper respect and Lebensraum. The notebooks piled up in the deep drawers of his desk in his study. Perhaps he worried about them when, during the last year of the war, we ran daily to the shelter under the falling bombs and, coming out dazed and drained, looked apprehensively up the street to see if our house was still standing. But by then, too many notebooks had accumulated and they couldn't be carried around in our hand luggage. Besides, during the bombing, the threat of deportation and pogroms had tapered off, death had taken a new shape, and our immediate preoccupation was finding a different way to haggle with it.

I left Romania in August 1948 and in September I saw my father for the last time. We met in Vienna, where my parents had come for a short visit, and we spent a few days together before they returned home. We had been a very close family and now, anticipating our final separation, we walked our pain and anguish through a city still licking its war wounds, amidst camps for displaced persons and an angry population, the traffic barely disengaged from ruins. We tried to play tourists in a deserted Prater and a zoo with animals emaciated by hunger and even rode on the giant Prater wheel from the top of which, in Emil Dorian's antiwar novel for children, *The Vagabonds,* an adolescent wants to call out the end of all wars. We did not speak of meeting again—during the war we had lost the feeling for the future, the trust in it, the habit of planning. We believed in the strength of our past and, candidly, expected it to keep us together. There was no talk about his diaries, no mention of wanting them published someday. At the end of our last day together, in a light summer coat, handsome and suddenly aged, standing near my mother, he receded at the train window.

After his death, the diaries were deposited with a friend in Bucharest and it was through the devotion and perseverance of still another family friend, the late Heinrich Moscovici, who by that time had left Bucharest and was living in Berlin, that the diaries reached me. I had been a witness to their writing, a part of them, but I read them for the first time as an adult in the Western world and the importance and urgency of their publication appeared to me unquestionable. They were not the kind of journal to which writers immersed in their world have accustomed us. They were the notes of a humanist involved with mankind and with the cultivation of the human quality, a work Emil Dorian believed to be everybody's care. They were, above all, a rare document, the kind that endows the factuality of the historical event with the human presence and reverses that grim and inevitable process—time reducing the drama of history to dates and documents.

The street in Bucharest on which my father was born in 1893 was called, appropriately it might seem, Strada Artei (Art Street). It was not the artists' neighborhood. The name could have evolved from some prim bourgeois idea of bohemianism, in which poverty and the proximity of the cheap brothels' quarter were combined. The poor Jewish neighborhood also started nearby so that the two minority groups, the destitute Jews and the desperate and exploited women, lived side by side, more or less tolerant of each other. His street, however, was quite proper with, at its better end, a few wealthy neighbors. It was in the company of their offspring that my father realized the extent and hopelessness of his poverty.

He was born the second child to Herman and Ernestina Lustig—Emil Dorian was the pen name he adopted very early in his publishing career. My paternal grandparents, who died before my time, remained personages of a sepia-colored legend in the family album. One can glimpse his mother in the autobiographical notes of the diary where he writes of her with oblique tenderness and guarded emotion, still hurting: a distinguished woman with a certain amount of education—she spoke fluent German and had read the classics—a tender public to his early poems. His father is absent from the diaries. He had started out as a teacher of German, became deaf early in his career, and was forced to abandon it. For a while he struggled to make a living as a middleman in the grain trade but a total lack of business talent, added to his infirmity, made him give up work altogether. Throughout my father's childhood and adolescence, my grandfather hung around the house depressed, an angry and demanding man, difficult to please, feared and hated by his family. My grandmother took in sewing, my two aunts worked as salesgirls, and my father, barely eight, began tutoring his schoolmates for a few pennies or a jar of preserves. No one knew that the tutor, still afraid of the dark, would wait under a street lamp on winter afternoons for a passerby to cross in his footsteps the terrifying square of the Metropolitan Church at the edge of the Jewish ghetto.

He received his elementary and high-school education in the Jewish schools, which were just then coming into existence. Romania had not yet granted citizenship to its Jews and my father could not afford the tuition the public schools required from "foreign" pupils. The diary recalls the forbidding atmosphere of these first Jewish schools, the feeling of isolation and pressure in which the children were prepared for Romanian universities, where an unofficial but well-functioning quota system had set up a ferocious competition. Most of my father's schoolmates and friends came from needy homes and books and clothes had to be added to the tuition exemption—a dreaded yearly ceremony where my father was called to stand in front of a full auditorium to receive charity under the moist-eyed, benevolent-looking members of the board.

To understand Emil Dorian's "abstract" brand of Judaism, which totally refused assimilation but was not steeped in *Yiddishkayt,* one must remember that he did not receive a traditional Jewish education. Too far south and away from the influence of the Galician cheders and the yeshivas of northern and eastern Romania, Bucharest never was a center of cultural Jewish tradition. The notable moments of East European Jewish culture associated with Romania—the Yiddish Conference of Czernowitz, Abraham Goldfaden's first Yiddish theater, the poetry of Itzik Manger—occurred on Romanian territories under foreign influence, Russian or Austro-Hungarian, where the traditional education of the shtetl formed significant Jewish artists and a flourishing but strictly regional culture.

From 1893 to 1910, my father grew up and completed his education despite his desperate poverty and the anti-Semitic obstacles raised in the way of the education of a young Romanian Jew at the turn of the century. At eighteen, he graduated from high school, having shown a special talent for literature and music. A published poet, he had translated from Heine—an interest he was to keep throughout his adult years—had written an allegorical play in verse for the graduation exercises of the Jewish high school for girls (where my mother, fourteen years old at the time, freckled and skinny, was cast as the "Genie of Knowledge" with gauze wings and silver wand), and had conducted the choir of the Jewish schools.

Literature and writing became a way of life for my father and for a few of his friends during their adolescence. Together, they organized a literary group, Unirea—the Union —which offered a monthly program of lectures and discussions and a lending library. The group, before continuing its own life after the young founders went on with their studies and careers, used to meet at the home of my father's closest friend—Enric Algazi, later contributing editor of *Le Temps* in Paris—in the electric presence of Algazi's mother, a fascinating redhead and an erotic magnet for the young intellectuals "agitated by the highest voltage of adolescence—for we were all writing poetry." In the photographs of the period, the old-fashioned backdrop lending it the sumptuous decor of a private park, my father's family poses modestly dressed and solemn with, in its midst, my father wearing his only suit with grace and elegance. He looks nearsighted and dreamy behind his pince-nez and on his sensual and refined mouth, the half-ironic, half-generous smile of his adult years is already present. He understood, around that time, that he could not afford the literary career he dreamed of and, as among the liberal professions medical work seemed the least subjected to anti-Semitism in the Romania of that period, he arranged for enough teaching and tutoring hours to support his family and registered at the Medical School of Bucharest. Europe was arming.

In the summer of 1916, Romania joined the Great War and my father, in his last month of medical studies, was sent to the front in the uniform of a physician officer. The uniform lacked the stripes indicating his army rank, for a Jew without citizenship was not permitted to wear them. He was, however, permitted to give his life for a country where the civil rights of the Jews were still unresolved. His status—instantly convertible from a simple medic to the physician in charge of the first-aid stations in combat (he was one of the survivors of the week-long carnage of Mără- şeşti)—remained unclear throughout the war and created the absurd, black-comedy situations he later used in his war satire, *Conversations with My Horse.* He spent the entire war on the Moldavian front, where the march of his regiment can be traced on the map by the poems he wrote during this time. He entered them, with date and location, in an old notebook bound in coarse brown cloth, its covers stained and warped by storage in his army trunk billeted in damp peasant rooms. With the signing of the armistice, my father returned home from the front, worn out, infected with malaria, and preoccupied with his writing. From the railroad station, he went to see my mother, Paula Fränkel, the former "Genie of Knowledge" of his allegorical play and, in the garden of her parents, he sat with her on the old peach tree felled to the ground by lightning and asked her to marry him. My mother had been secretly in love with him throughout her adolescence. Without her gauze wings and with her hair up, she had turned into a stubborn-looking, striking beauty. Brought up in a strictly Orthodox family, she was not permitted to cultivate her fine intelligence and talent and to study beyond junior high school. My father's friendship, the books he brought her, their talks as he walked with her for hours along the quays of Bucharest, when he had not enough money to take her on the streetcar, lightened her isolation, fired her imagination. They were married the next year and had the passionate, at times difficult, marriage of two strong personalities, both creative— my mother abandoned a fine writer's talent after having published a first novel—devoted to and admiring each other. In their home, they succeeded in creating the climate of love and stability that permeated our childhood and was magnetic to the circle of friends they cultivated. They had two daughters.

The two-year trip to France he took in the mid-1920s for specialization in ear, nose, and throat diseases also presented my father with the possibility of expatriating himself and his family. His circle of Parisian friends had wanted him to stay and the French minister of education offered his personal help in obtaining for him a French medical license. But we returned home.

Home was for us the Romania of the late 1920s, a country in permanent economical and political crisis—the latest one being the departure of the king, who left behind a regency and a son too young to reign; a country with an ad-

ministrative tradition of demagogy and corruption derived
from Byzantine influence and long years of Phanariot occupation and savage exploitation, a tradition against which
the best parliamentarian intentions could not prevail. It
also meant, at least on the surface, a certain *douceur de
vivre,* an appealing quality of life. That came partly from a
temperate climate with splendid and sharply defined seasons, which dictated a reassuring routine, and partly from
the moderate rhythm of a nonindustrialized society with
servants and time on its hands; and from the simple ambitions and pleasures of my father's own social group where
books, the life of the imagination, the cultivation of friendship, and the art of conversation had leading roles.

Bucharest lent its Balkan charm to all this—a capital of
one million inhabitants and a city of contrasts where opu-
lence and squalor lived carelessly side by side, displaying its
wealth on elegant boulevards and its beggars asleep on the
stenchy quays of the river Dîmboviţa. To its intellectuals
and artists, the city was alive and vibrant, tailored for com-
panionship, with cafés and intimate outdoor restaurants behind green hedges, where the wine was cheerful and inex-
pensive, places that would shelter until dawn your "need to
discuss, to clarify, to revise and agree." Bookshops were
the traditional meeting spot for journalists, actors, and
writers who dropped in to inspect with equal enthusiasm
the latest book or the current stage celebrity blinking se-
ductively under her exquisitely veiled hat. In the middle of
the urban rhythm, the green life of Bucharest's parks offered a zone of intimacy and isolation. Emil Dorian's diaries celebrate in particular the charms of Cişmigiu, a co-
quettish garden in the center of the city, "the rural lover of
every Bucharest citizen," which becomes a personage under
his pen. During the time we lived across from it, my father
would often take me along for a tour of the gardens "to see
what's new" and teach me the art of strolling. He even suggested that we write together a sort of park bulletin in
verse and prose. The project never took off but segments of
it entered his diary, and this first offer of a professional
collaboration in my teens flattered and encouraged me.

With all that *douceur de vivre,* the atmosphere of the
country was strongly conservative and anti-Semitic under

the leadership of the Liberal party. But my father had reasons to look ahead with a certain measure of hope. The last East European country to withhold civil rights to subjects of non-Christian faith, Romania had finally granted citizenship to its Jews. In the eyes of the emancipated Western world, this was a suspect victory. A commission, appointed by the alarmed American Committee of the Rights of Religious Minorities to inspect Romania a decade after the amendment, notes "a wide discrepancy between the constitution and its enforcement by the officials." But in the eyes of an East European intellectual Jew, prepared to put up with a certain measure of anti-Semitism, it meant the beginning of true liberalism, the opportunity to work at its consolidation, a sense to living and creating. Emil Dorian tackled with élan an existence moving between medicine and literature, at times combining both.

Marked by the innovative work of three great Romanian poets, Ion Barbu, Lucian Blaga, and Tudor Arghezi, by the classicism of Romanian modern prose, by the original and independent criticism of Eugen Lovinescu who created a magnetic field of forces in Romanian letters, the 1930s were a particularly active decade in literary Romania. This was also the time when the works of Itzik Manger and Eliezer Steinbarg, both Romanian poets writing in Yiddish, were translated into many languages but remained unknown to the Romanian public. Nor did the Jewish themes expressed in the Romanian work of some outstanding Jewish novelists meet with the attention they deserved. The Jewish experience had to be toned down, bleached. It burdened and embarrassed.

While Emil Dorian contributed to many literary magazines, wrote poetry and prose, and was intensely active in Romanian letters, he could not find a satisfactory spot in it for his work and his convictions. He appeared uninterested in the rarefied air of modernism, which, he felt, eschewed the preoccupations and experiences of a rebellious and lucid Jew living in a hostile Romanian milieu. He was outraged by the political leadership of the time, Jewish and Romanian alike. As a writer, he felt kept at arm's length by the old aggressive nationalism, amorphous at its best but ready to crystallize into articulate anti-Semitism.

The work he published during this period shows the progress of his lucidity and the evolution of an illusion as its themes go from personal to social and the tone from irony to impatience, exasperation, and finally despair. *Songs for Lelioara* (1923), a collection of whimsical and playful verse, celebrating fatherhood with young abandon, appeared before his Paris trip. *Conversations with My Horse* (1928), a series of dialogues in verse between a young Jewish doctor and his proletarian horse, denounces the abomination of war as the two trot together through the landscape of disaster and death. Yet the author's vast reserves of energy are still able to sustain with humor and vitality the profoundly disturbing experience. Original and courageous for the time, the book was attacked for its antiwar feelings interpreted as typically Jewish antipatriotism. His two novels on Jewish life in Romania, *Prophets and Clowns* (1930) and *The Poison* (1939), are at the same time pamphlet, essay, and social criticism—the first an unsparing sketch of the Jewish and Gentile Romanian bourgeoisie, the second a dramatic analysis of Romanian anti-Semitism. The decade between the two books brought him an increased awareness of the absurdity and danger of the times and much personal suffering.

The 1930s were also the time when Emil Dorian raised his children and when he combined a playful mood with an educator's passion to explain the world in two novels for young people, *The Vagabonds* (1934) and *The Cricket's Memoirs* (1936). The cricket's story rehabilitates La Fontaine's cricket and implicitly the tattered reputation of the artist perpetually humiliated by a society impersonated by the capitalist ant who holds the funding purse.

He practiced medicine in an office at home, in the domestic setting of the period, a setting offering less modern conveniences and more human contact with the patient. The writers, artists, journalists, and poets who came for treatment to this humanist physician with a Chekhovian interest in their problems, were often brought to the living room for coffee with the family. The center of his life was at home, where profession, creativity, family intimacy, and his childrens' education intersected, engaged our childhood, leaving both my sister and me with the feeling of its having been unique. The same living room housed for four years the editorial meetings of *Tribuna medicală,* a medical magazine of high professional quality he had initiated in 1933. At his publisher's request, he also found time to write a few books of popular medicine. One of them, *The Mysteries and the Technique of Sex* (1928), in an incident that seems created by the pen of a satirist, brought him a certain fame in the form of a lawsuit for pornography. The book tried to educate while communicating delight in sexuality, but a medical colleague denounced it as "an invitation to prostitution." The entire edition was confiscated by the Public Health office. While the matter was referred to the Ministry of Health and the Medical Association, the Daumier-like characters, moralists, and reformers, multiplied as did the bizarre ways in which they tried to diagnose immorality. The book was praised in court by the judge and the author was finally acquitted of all charges.

This is the man who began in 1937, and continued until his death in 1956, a twenty-year record of Romanian life. He is a complex man, a personality shaped by polarities, which, in less turbulent circumstances, might not have evolved into the dramatic conflicts recorded in his diaries, but might have furthered his generosity and superior broad-mindedness. He was the dreamer, the introvert needing the isolation of his study, but also the dynamic initiator of cultural events to whom group action, education to eradicate the dangers of ignorance, the organization of spiritual Jewish "resistance" were equally important. A *Weltbürger* in the Goethean sense, involved in the culture of other countries, a Jew who identified with a collective Jewish spirit, he was also a committed citizen of his native land, engaged in its problems, deeply attached to its language. But because he inhabited "the eye of the storm of his conflicts," he could remain lucid and composed most of the time. His stable vantage point of values and his warm intelligence that suffers, questions, and rebels made him a witness *par excellence* to an extraordinary time and suggested the title of the present volume.

The excerpts offered here cover the first seven years of Emil Dorian's diaries—a violent, disturbing period in

Romanian history—starting with the installation of the first fascist government and ending with the 1944 armistice. Excluded have been only entries of local interest and some, by now too familiar, information on the war's progress in Europe. Yet his diaries are not a band of monochromatic despair. Reading them, one can certainly go once more through the tragic experiences of a time that already begins to elude us—the drama of a humanist's mind progressively aware of the European crisis of culture, while fighting it with candid humanistic arguments; the question of Jewish passivity in the face of annihilation. Scattered among entries on war, deportation, and destruction the diaries offer us also the logbook of a creative man, a writer's spiritual survival through the discipline of work, the unfolding of a heroic enterprise: his *Anthology of Yiddish Literature* for which he translated four hundred poems while European Jewry was being destroyed. And last, the diarist's provocative and informed mind reveals the kaleidoscopic charm of its escape in notes on "books that go in and out of our lives, leaving trails of marvelous melancholy," on "the colored streamers of childhood," "the musical meaning of love and the symphonic rocking of seasons."

One may best read Emil Dorian's diaries as a triple portrait—of a man, of a country, and of an epoch—and perceive them in their indissoluble, dramatic relationship: a Romanian and a Jew, committed to his double identity; a country under complex and unfortunate circumstances, ambivalent about his provocative presence in its midst; and an epoch that opened on the generous promises of a world concerned with human rights and closed with the degradation and destruction of humanity.

After the war, Emil Dorian held two important positions in the life of Romanian Jews, first as secretary general of the Jewish Community of Bucharest and afterward as director of the documentary libraries and archives of the Federation of Jewish Communities of Romania. Unable to continue public work in the new moral climate, he resigned from both positions and returned to practicing medicine at an outpatient clinic until his death. The story of these years is told in his postwar diaries, which, I hope, will be published at a later date.

I wish to express my thanks to Professor Alvin H. Rosenfeld, of Indiana University, for his support and continuing interest in this work; to Professor Mara Soceanu Vamos, of Fairleigh Dickinson University, for the enthusiasm and devotion she added to scholarship in preparing the translation. The friendship and knowledge of Maier Deshell, editor of The Jewish Publication Society of America, helped both the translator and myself in the shaping of this book. A number of people, all personal friends of Emil Dorian, at some time or other, have played a role in saving this manuscript. I offer them here my infinite gratitude. A few have run out of time and have disappeared quietly, anonymously, trusting that the diaries will survive. Emil Dorian's journals are also their memorial, a common journey told with all the halftones of the detail, a memorial that gives sense and direction to living and connects generations.

*Marguerite Dorian*

# Translator's Note

I first met Marguerite Dorian, the editor of these diaries, at the dingy school in Bucharest, hastily organized in the fall of 1940 when Jewish children were expelled from Romanian public schools. Our friendship lasted a little over one year: after the pogrom of January 1941 my family was fortunate enough to emigrate to Palestine. We met again, over a card catalog at the Brown University library in 1958, and kept in touch. As to Emil Dorian, I know him, unfortunately, only through his diaries. In 1978 Marguerite Dorian sent me her father's manuscripts, asking whether I would like to translate them. I am grateful to her for the opportunity to make available to the English-speaking world a distinguished work of historical and literary value.

The task was both exhilarating and heartrending: exhilarating because of the rare quality of the material; heartrending because the early notebooks, touching personal chords, recreated part of my childhood, dimly experienced at the time.

Two main difficulties arose in connection with the translation of this work. The first, which I note briefly, is peculiar to translating from Romanian. Although a Romance language, Romanian differs from its sister tongues because of Slavic and Turkish influences on its vocabulary and syntax. Many semantic overtones are therefore inevitably lost, even in a rendition into French, a much closer relative to Romanian than English. Moreover, while most Western languages make a clear distinction between expository or narrative style and poetic diction, Romanian, very much like Russian, does not. Finally, mixed metaphors, unacceptable in English, are perfectly at home in Romanian.

The second and more challenging difficulty arose from the author's versatility and complexity. The diaries reflect Emil Dorian's observations on world events, his sadly ironic awareness of developments in his own country, and his increasing realization of the predicament of European and Romanian Jewry. Entries on intellectual and artistic concerns, as well as notes on his personal life, alternate with the unsentimental and therefore all the more shattering descriptions of the creeping degradation and eventual slaughter of Jews. His are the insights and preoccupations of an uncommon "everyman," and of a Jew in uncommon and inhuman times.

Throughout Emil Dorian's diaries the very rhythm of the prose is modulated to fit the subject matter, his many interests, his moods. The translator's main problem and constant concern, then, were to mold the English rendition so as to reflect the author's rich personality, varied styles, and, in particular, the quality of his voice as it echoes the voice of the times.

As the years passed and the months stretched, the writer's doubts about the value of the diary as a genre were superseded by a growing need to bear witness. Indeed, this increasing urgency to record became almost a compulsion that sustained him in his self-imposed task, despite the growing frustration he experienced when faced with the impossibility of chronicling even a fraction of what he felt impelled to preserve. He persevered because he believed that "the spirit must be kept alive if you are to write, and you must write if the spirit is to stay alive."

I wish to thank Liza Soceanu, Boris Porecki, and Fani Grünberg for clarifying the meaning of some of the more obscure Romanian phrases; Mark Vamos, Pauline Lurie, Elliott B. Urdang, and the late Hélène Zahler for suggesting idiomatic or colloquial English expressions; and Ted Fitch, Ruth Pathé, and Ulla Volk, reference librarians, Library of Fairleigh Dickinson University, Madison Campus, for assistance with the English spelling of names and places.

*Mara Soceanu Vamos*

# Introduction

*MICHAEL STANISLAWSKI*

Emil Dorian's diary for the years 1937–1944 is a haunting chronicle of the life and fate of Romanian Jews during the most brutal period in history. Through Dorian's eloquent testimony we are able to witness the gradual but implacable descent of doom: the physical and economic degradation of the Jews, their manipulation by a cynical collaborationist regime, mass murder, and—finally—liberation. But the power and uniqueness of this journal lie beyond its graphic depiction of communal suffering. With Emil Dorian we confront the devastating inner pain of a sensitive "acculturated" Jew denied his hopes, his art, his very identity.

Since the Holocaust, the boundlessness of anti-Semitism and the futility of assimilation have become self-evident to the vast majority of Jews the world over. This is a vitally important realization for the present and future of the Jewish people, but not always an especially helpful guide to the past. Is it possible to avoid anachronistic projection of what seems so obvious through hindsight? In other words, how could Jews like Emil Dorian not read the handwriting on the wall, so blatant in retrospect? How could they retain their faith in progress, in the emancipation of the Jews in such places as Romania, in the face of such manifest evil and persecution? This diary is so compelling precisely because it is so intelligent, so self-conscious, so moving, that it forces us to understand Dorian and many other deceived Jews before we judge them.

In order to understand Dorian and his plight—the plight of his milieu—the reader must be familiar with the bare outlines of the political and cultural context in which he lived. The following observations, therefore, are an attempt at summarizing, in rather bold strokes, the obscure and little-studied history of the Jews in modern Romania—one of the most illuminating refractions of the tortuous, often contradictory, experience of the Jews in the age of emancipation and destruction.

The Romanian state in which Emil Dorian was born was a creature of the late nineteenth century, when the former Ottoman provinces of Moldavia and Wallachia emerged from Turkish suzerainty and Russian protectorateship to full independence as a result of the Congress of Berlin. At the same time as this new amalgam "Romania" was struggling for its autonomy and national identity, its small, centuries-old Jewish population was being enhanced by a large migration of Jews from Galicia and the southern reaches of the Russian Empire.[1] Indeed, these two processes were joined, rather disharmoniously, from the very beginning: the various governments and rulers of the territory refused to consider the Jews in their midst as anything but foreigners, not suitable for inclusion into the nascent "Romanian"

1. For the best survey of the history of the Jews in Romania (except for the voluminous literature in Romanian), see the two-volume study *Romaniah* issued in the series *Pinkas ha-kehillot* by Yad Vashem (Jerusalem, 1969). Although the rather heavy Zionist bias of this work limits its objectivity on ideological matters and rather overplays the role of the Zionist parties, its essays on the history of the various parts of Romanian Jewry and particularly its entries on the individual communities are most useful and thorough. The most concise and informative survey in English is the essay "Rumania" by Nicolas Sylvain in *The Jews in the Soviet Satellites,* ed. Peter Meyer et al. (Syracuse, 1953), pp. 493–556.

nation and its citizenry. This typical East European approach to the Jews was complicated by Romania's desire to be a Western state, and by its reliance—diplomatic, political, and economic—on Germany, France, and England. For complicated reasons combining material and moral incentives, the Western powers all pressed for civil rights for Romania's Jews. In fact, the Congress of Berlin in July 1878 made the very independence of Romania contingent on Jewish emancipation.[2]

Jews in Romania and the West were jubilant, but prematurely so: the Romanian authorities refused to abide by the dictate of the Congress and announced "that there were not, and that there never have been, any Romanian Jews; there were merely Jews, who had been born in the Principality, but who had never been assimilated, either in speech or in custom, by the Romanian nation."[3] For a while, this attitude to the Jews delayed Romania's recognition by the Western powers, but soon economic expediency outweighed moral principles and the alleged influence of international Jewry, and a compromise was arrived at. Jews could become naturalized citizens of Romania, but only individually, on the basis of separate laws judging the merits of each applicant.

This compromise was both duplicitous and fatuous: in the next three and a half decades, only two thousand Jews were naturalized under these provisions, and almost half of these en masse as reward for their participation in the Romanian War of Independence; the other half were rich enough to buy their citizenship papers. Obviously, the stumbling block to the emancipation of the Jews was not their ostensible foreignness, but the xenophobia—or rather, the deeply rooted anti-Semitism—of their hosts.

Indeed, in the last decades of the nineteenth century and the beginning of the twentieth, the foreignness of the Jews of Romania, regardless of provenance, was belied by a very steady process of acculturation. The first Jewish newspapers in the Romanian language were published already in

2. See the fascinating exposition of this drama in Fritz Stern, *Gold and Iron: Bismarck, Bleichroeder, and the Building of the German Empire* (New York, 1977), pp. 351–93.

3. Ibid., p. 385.

the 1850s; the first literary and scholarly efforts soon there-
after (ironically, often pioneering fields such as Romanian
philology and folklore). In Bucharest, Emil Dorian's birthplace, a "liberal" temple was founded in 1867 and became
the chief synagogue of the capital, and at the same time
Jewish schools using Romanian as the language of instruc-
tion multiplied.[4]

But the pace of the Romanianization of the Jews cannot
adequately be gauged by a litany of Jewish contributions to
Romanian culture and vice versa, and not only because that
culture was so young and so unreceptive to Jewish participation. The linguistic and cultural Romanianization of the
Jews in pre–World War I Romania (as in the parallel cases
of France, Germany, even Poland) was entirely a function
of their embourgeoisement. Thus, while many Jews suffered
miserably from the ceaseless limitations on their economic
and educational advance (and approximately sixty thousand emigrated to the United States in the years 1899–1914
as a result of these restrictions), a good part of Romanian
Jews, particularly in Wallachia, found success possible in
commerce, industry, medicine, journalism, etc., and rapidly
adopted the language, culture, and aspirations of Romanian
middle-class life. Of course, this acculturation was neither
paralleled by nor rewarded with an amelioration of their
civil status; on the contrary, the contemporary politiciza-
tion and institutionalization of anti-Semitism rendered
their civil status more precarious then ever. But this did
not dissuade many Jews from identifying with Romania
and its culture or for campaigning strenuously for inclusion into its body politic. Like French Jews who concluded
from the Dreyfus Affair not that anti-Semitism was en-
demic in France but that French justice and the true
French spirit had finally triumphed, the urban, upwardly
mobile Jews of pre–World War I Romania firmly believed
that their emancipation was imminent if the true Romanian
spirit would vanquish its enemies. In the meanwhile, they
abandoned Yiddish, the cheder, and traditional Jewish cul-

4. Theodor Lavi, "Toledot yehudei ha-Regat," in *Romaniah,* 1: 84–91; idem,
"Bucharest" in the encyclopedic section, 44–53.

ture as a whole for the Romanian language, Romanian education, and Romanian mores.[5]

This is the milieu in which Emil Dorian reached adulthood; his life story was paradigmatic rather than idiosyncratic. The cultural aspirations and self-perceptions of this population did not change significantly in the interwar period; only their number grew. The political situation of Romania's Jews, on the other hand, was altered dramatically after World War I. Once more, the victorious Western powers (with the United States now playing the role of Germany) forced Romania to grant civil rights to its Jews.[6] Once more, the Romanians regarded this pressure as unfair interference in their internal affairs and as proof positive of international Jewry's conspiratorial grip on Western governments.

After much maneuvering and negotiation, on May 22, 1919, the Romanian government promulgated a law granting citizenship to all Jews born in the country, those who held no other citizenship, and those who had served in the army at the front, as well as their families.[7] (Thus, Emil Dorian became a Romanian citizen, eligible under all three counts.)

The implementation and scope of this emancipation, however, were vastly circumscribed by the new geographical and ethnic profile of Romania: as the result of its shifting politics during World War I, Romania more than doubled its size and population by annexing Transylvania and the Bukovina from Austria-Hungary and Bessarabia from Russia. These "acquired territories" had substantial Jewish communities: a decade later, the census recorded 206,958 Jews in Bessarabia, 192,833 in Transylvania and adjacent regions, and 93,101 in the Bukovina. The 264,038 Jews of the "Old Kingdom" (*Regat* in Romanian) were now a minority of 35 percent in the Jewish population of Romania, the third largest in Europe.[8]

5. For an interesting selection of translations of works by authors from this milieu, see K.A. Bertini et al., eds., *Shorashim ve-sa'ar: 'antologiah shel sofrim yehudim be-lashon ha-romanit* (Tel Aviv, 1972), pp. 114–24, which, incidentally, includes a translation into Hebrew of a selection of Dorian's writing.

6. See the excellent synthesis of interwar Romanian politics in Joseph Rothschild, *East Central Europe between the Two World Wars* (Seattle, 1974).

7. Lavi, "Toledot," pp. 107–11.

8. Sylvain, *Jews in the Soviet Satellites*, p. 493.

The newly acquired Jews were not only more numerous than those of the Old Kingdom, but also of substantially different mien. The masses were far more traditional, rural, Yiddish-speaking; the elites, either Germanized, Magyarized, or Russified. All had been emancipated in their former states.

To put it briefly and mildly, the anti-Jewish forces, always asserting the alienness of the Jews, received a new impetus and rationale. From now on, in law as in life, a distinction would be drawn between the Old Kingdom Jews, Romanian by default, and Bessarabian/Bukovinian/Transylvanian Jews who could under no circumstances be reckoned as Romanians. The consequences of this taxonomy would prove to be—quite literally—fatal.

As early as 1924, the citizenship of the "new" Jews was severely limited by the Romanian parliament, and the next fourteen years witnessed a steady attack on Jewish emancipation, culminating in the "Revision of Citizenship" decree of January 1938, which deprived over 40 percent of Romanian Jews of their naturalization.[9] But in the chaotic muddle of interbellum Romanian politics, this was only one round in the increasingly volatile anti-Jewish campaign. Center stage in this ugly drama was seized by the Iron Guard, the thuggish Romanian cross between the Russian Black Hundreds and the German National Socialists.[10] The Iron Guard was at times courted, tolerated, manipulated, and traduced by the regime of King Carol; but whether in favor or not, its call for the exclusion of the Jews from all facets of Romanian life was increasingly adopted by all the political parties and governmental coalitions.

Thus, when Emil Dorian's journal opens in late 1937, anti-Jewish persecutions have already become a normal part of Romanian political life, and more and graver problems were feared as Romania inched closer and closer to an open alliance with Nazi Germany. King Carol paid a heavy price for this reversal of Romania's traditional ties to Britain and France: between June 28 and September 6, 1940,

9. See Dorian's entry of January 25, 1938.
10. On the Iron Guard, see Rothschild, *East Central Europe,* and for more detail, Eugen Weber, "Rumania," in *The European Right,* ed. Eugen Weber and Hans Rogger (Berkeley and Los Angeles, 1966), pp. 501–74.

under pressure from the Nazis and the Soviets, Romania
lost one-third of its population and territory when Bessarabia and northern Bukovina were ceded to the USSR,
northern Transylvania to Hungary, and southern Dobruja
(part of Romania since 1913) to Bulgaria.

As a result, in the summer of 1940 the Jewish population of Romania was once more reshuffled in the wake of
world war. Approximately 280,000 Jews came under Soviet
control, 150,000 were returned to Hungary, and 950 to Bulgaria.[11] At the same time, the Jews remaining in Romania
were stripped, for the most part, of their Romanian citizenship: only those Jews and their descendants who were citizens—not residents—of the Old Kingdom before World
War I could retain their citizenship, albeit with severely
curtailed rights; next in line came the residents of the Old
Kingdom; and lowest in rank and status, the Jews in the
remains of the annexed provinces.

The fate of the Jews hung in the air after this counter-
emancipation, and became especially perilous after King
Carol was forced to abdicate in September 1940, yielding to
the "National Legionary State" of Ion Antonescu, based on
the principles and with the firm support of the Iron Guard.
A reign of terror began in Romania, aimed primarily—but
not exclusively—at the Jews: expropriation of property, exclusion from all sectors of Romanian life, and, ultimately,
physical attack. On January 21, 1941, a full-scale pogrom
was launched by the Iron Guard in Bucharest itself, resulting in 120 Jewish deaths, much looting, and the desecration
of synagogues.[12] This pogrom, though, was only one facet
of the Iron Guard's rebellion; the main target was the government itself, including Antonescu. In response, Antonescu, with Hitler's apparent approval, led the army into
a bloody street battle with the Guard; in the end, the Guard
was effectively quashed and outlawed. Clearly, Hitler pre-
ferred a stable "Conservative-Rightist" Romania to an
ideologically fascist but strife-ridden puppet. The new military dictatorship, purged of its radical competitors, pursued an alliance with Hitler that was more tactical than

11. Raul Hilberg, *The Destruction of the European Jews* (Chicago, 1961), pp.
486–87.
12. See Dorian's entry of January 24, 1941.

reverential. Not incidentally, the anti-Semitism of Antonescu and friends was also less extreme than that of the
Guard and Hitler—traditional, based on church and class,
rather than pathological, based on race. The difference
proved to be decisive for Romania's Jews, for they were
now to be a pawn in Romania's war, rather than its target.

The future of the Jews, Romania, and the world as a
whole was altered inexorably by the invasion of the Soviet
Union by the Axis powers on June 22, 1941. The Romanian
army thrust itself with vengeance into the Soviet-occupied
territory, determined to reclaim its erstwhile holdings. The
Jewish population of this region—by now, not surprisingly,
better disposed toward their Soviet occupiers than their
Nazi-allied former persecutors—were consistently accused
of treason and espionage by the Romanian forces. Several
thousand Jews were evacuated on these grounds to the interior of Romania, sent in padlocked cattle cars that suffo-
cated a large number of their passengers. Many thousands
more were murdered in a bloody pogrom in Iaşi, capital of
Moldavia, on June 29, 1941.[13]

As the war progressed, a peculiarly Romanian version of
the Final Solution slowly emerged: a vengeful, cruel, often
bestial but not systematic massacre of the Jews of the "acquired territories"; a more restrained approach to the Jews
of the Old Kingdom, determined by an opportunistic cost-
and-benefit calculus of Nazi favor versus Romanian autonomy versus potential Allied booty.

When the Romanian Army retook Bessarabia and the
Bukovina, its soldiers joined the German Einzatzgruppe D
in "mobile killing operations" of the local Jews. In fact, the
Romanians' fury and lack of order in their killings led to
some tension with the more punctilious Nazis.[14] This tension was exacerbated in August 1941 when the Romanians
tried to rid themselves of some fifteen thousand Bessarabian Jews by shipping them into the German-held
Ukraine. The Nazis had enough to do without this extra

13. Estimates of the dead vary greatly: Hilberg (*The Destruction of the European Jews,* p. 491) cites the figure of 4,000; Sylvain (*Jews in the Soviet Satellites,* p.
505), 14,000.
14. Hilberg, *Destruction of the European Jews,* pp. 199–200.

work and attempted to return the Jews to Romanian-occupied territory. In the confusion and crossfire thousands more Jews were killed.[15]

Soon a more efficient division of labor was worked out. The area of the Ukraine between the Bug and Dniestr rivers, now called Transnistria, was placed under Romanian military control; the Jews of Bessarabia and the Bukovina were to be evacuated to Transnistria and liquidated there, along with the native Jews.[16] In the next two months, 118,-847 Jews were deported to this region and soon placed in concentration camps, where the Romanians themselves began to exterminate them. The technique was less organized than that of the Nazis, but the results were the same: two-thirds of the Jews were murdered. As Raul Hilberg has pointed out, Romania was the only country, besides Germany itself, to implement all the steps of the destruction, from definition of the Jews in law to mass killing.[17]

The tragedy of Transnistria soon became known to the Jews in Bucharest. Emil Dorian reported:

> [W]e Jews have reached such depths of degradation that we are grateful merely to be alive here, whatever the conditions, and not in Transnistria, where hunger, sickness, freezing cold mow down hundreds of lives every day. The news we get from there is shattering. Whatever I do, wherever I am—at the table, at my writing desk—the thought of what is happening to these human beings poisons every moment of my life with its silent scream, its barren hopelessness, its mute rage. [January 25, 1942]

Meanwhile, the lives of the Jews of the Old Kingdom were in far graver danger than Dorian could know. He noted the ruthless expropriation of Jewish property, the mobilization of forced-labor battalions, the dissolution of the Jewish federation of communal organizations and its replacement with a Judenrat-like government. But he could not even imagine that, at the same time, Germany had begun to pressure Ro-

15. Ibid., pp. 492–93.
16. Ibid.
17. Ibid., p. 485.

mania into deporting the Jews of the Old Kingdom to Poland and to death.

In July 1942 Eichmann wrote, "It is planned to remove the Jews of Romania in a series of transports beginning approximately September 10, 1942, to the district of Lublin, where the employable segment will be allocated for labor utilization while the remainder will be subjected to special treatment."[18] At first, Antonescu's government agreed to this plan, but soon refused to carry it out. Historians have offered a variety of reasons for this fateful refusal: the snubbing of the Romanian commissar for Jewish affairs in Berlin; the intercession of foreign governments and the papal nuncio; the efforts of Jewish lobbyists; the activities of clandestine Jewish agents; Antonescu's prescient realization that the Nazis would lose.[19] What seems critical, in the end, was that the ideological gap between Romanian and Nazi anti-Semitism was able to persist because Romania was so loyal and important an ally of the Reich in every other respect. In general, we know that the fate of the Jews in Europe was determined by the extent to which the Nazis directly controlled events in any country, or had to rely on their allies. The Jews of Vichy France, Romania, and Bulgaria (as well as Italy until the fall of Mussolini and Hungary until the fall of Horthy) had a far better chance to survive than the Jews of Poland, the occupied Soviet Union, or Holland.[20] Romania remained a close and trusted ally of Hitler until it was too late to "rectify" its Jewish policy.

Thus, the Jews who remained in the Old Kingdom (and southern Transylvania) escaped extermination; the formerly Romanian Jews in Hungary (northern Transylvania) survived along with the rest of Magyar Jewry until the

18. Ibid., p. 501.

19. Ibid., pp. 501–3; Lavi, "Toledot," pp. 174–99; Lucjan Dobroszycki, "Jewish Elites under German Rule," in *The Holocaust: Ideology, Bureaucracy, and Genocide—The San Jose Papers*, ed. H. Friedlander and S. Milton (Millwood, N.Y., 1980), p. 228.

20. Dobroszycki, "Jewish Elites," pp. 227–30; Michael Marrus and Robert Paxton, *Vichy France and the Jews* (New York, 1981), p. 357; Istvan Deak, "Could the Hungarian Jews Have Survived?" *The New York Review of Books,* 4 February 1982, pp. 24–27.

last months of the war but were swept away in the last wave of Hitler's mania.

As the tide of the war turned, the Antonescu regime attempted to redress its crimes in some small measure. It permitted the Jews of the Old Kingdom to send money, clothes, and medication to the surviving Jews of Transnistria; it began to contemplate allowing the Jews to emigrate to Palestine—of course, for a price; it even began to plan the return to Romania of the Jews who remained alive in Transnistria, fearing that the Nazis would complete the job.

The Jews of Romania were spared the test of Antonescu's penitence: on August 24, 1944, Romania surrendered to the Allies. Three hundred thousand Jews were alive in the Old Kingdom; fifty thousand survived in Bessarabia and the Bukovina; and another fifty thousand in northern Transylvania.

Along with the death of hundreds of thousands of Romanian Jews there died the dream of a peaceful and fruitful acculturation of the Jews in Romania. The believers viscerally witnessed the subversion of their faith. We see Emil Dorian grappling with this trauma throughout his diary, ultimately making his way back to Jewish culture through Yiddish poetry. But there is no uplifting Zionist moral to this tale: Dorian tells us, only half-sarcastically, that his translation of Yiddish poems may "have succeeded in giving them Romanian citizenship." Despite his newfound Jewishness, at the end of the diary Dorian had still not abandoned Romania either physically or spiritually. Along with a substantial minority of Romanian Jews, Dorian elected to witness the emergence of a new, very different, Romanian state. His subsequent fate, personal and ideological, comprises another, equally poignant, story— presaged, perhaps, by Dorian himself in his observation: "New events will keep coming, that is sure. And people are tired of so much history in a single lifetime."

1937

*December 30*

An explosion which has stirred bewilderment and fear: the victory of Goga's[1] government. In the insane tension caused by the elections, nobody anticipated such an outcome. The whole city is fretting and fuming, the politicians have lost their composure. The Jews fear worse persecutions to come. Prepared and then fostered for so many years now by all the political parties, nationalist anti-Semitism in this country has borne fruit at last: between the threat of the Iron Guard[2] and Maniu's[3] party, the pow-

1. Octavian Goga (1881–1938), Romanian poet of the traditionalist school and a politician of nationalist anti-Semitic orientation; from 1931 to 1938, leader of the National Christian party, also known as the Goga-Cuziști (see n. 4).

2. Romanian nationalist party of the extreme right. Its members were known as *legionari* and formed the "Legions of the Archangel Michael."

3. Iuliu Maniu (1873–1955), leader of the National Peasant party. An important figure in Romanian political life, he held significant positions during his ca-

ers that be had to choose the Goga-Cuziști. Both Goga and Cuza[4] have vehemently announced their intention to carry out the racist principle. Immediately following the news, the newspapers *Dimineața, Adevărul,* and *Lupta*[5] were suspended. (In fact, *Adevărul* was bought by the *liberali* last year, but the real owners have not yet disclosed the truth to their readers.) What will happen now to all of us Jews? Will the collapse be total? The majority foresees anti-Jewish measures directly patterned on the ones adopted in Germany after the Hitlerist takeover. The telephones are buzzing—everyone wants news, the latest news, then everyone tries to verify it. The press will be nationalized and the Jewish journalists out of jobs. For New Year's Eve, Goga has announced a detailed speech on the radio about his new program. But right now, the rumors are frightening. There is talk of dismissal, of making survival impossible, of deportation, of concentration camps! Worse than anything is the pity and compassion of the Gentiles, the ones who have not lost their common sense, and the encouraging looks, the reassurances of so many friendly voices muffled by embarrassment. And yet, in spite of the general panic, I have a certain amount of optimism. Within the structure of such a heterogeneous government, some countervailing forces must exist, even though the group consists exclusively of racists. We shall see what the speech of our new premier will bring tomorrow. Until then, the crowds are passionately watching the lists of political turncoats. The odor of power is heady. Difficult to resist.

## December 31

The political agitation and the panic among the Jews continue to suppress any other kind of preoccupations. Goga

---

reer. He was instrumental in the Transylvanian union with Romania, was prime minister from 1928 to 1930, and participated in the political coup of 1944, which brought Romania to the Allies' side. After the war, he was tried and sentenced to life imprisonment.

4. Alexandru C. Cuza (1857–1940), cofounder of the National Democratic party, and later, founder of the League of Christian National Defense, an anti-Semitic group. In 1935, Cuza's party fused with Goga's National-Agrarian party to become the Goga-Cuza party.

5. Three of the largest democratic newspapers in Bucharest.

spoke on the radio. In a way, in spite of the maddening tension with which the Jews awaited it, his speech did not bring anything new. The explanation is simple: the previous government had adopted an anti-Semitic-nationalistic program long before Goga. If you cannot now dismiss all the Jewish officers from the army—for there are none—or fire the Jewish judges, the Jewish university professors—nonexistent—Jewish lawyers in the state service, Jews holding administrative jobs—because there never have been any—if you can't prevent the Jewish students' admission to graduate studies[6]— what is there left to do, beside suspend a few Jewish newspapers . . . which are owned in fact by the *liberali?* You may pick a quarrel with the Jewish village innkeepers (but how many of them are there left today?) and decide to review the citizenship of the Jews who have settled here after 1920. How many there are Goga must know quite well, for he was minister of internal affairs at that time and thus implicitly the beneficiary of the bribes taken from the Jews who had "sneaked into the country" illegally!

As to the promised price-cutting on several products, there is a lot of poetry in Goga's view of the economy and little understanding of the technical aspects of price controls. Generally, the speech sounded as if it had been revised in haste at the last minute, and—along with a few difficulties in delivery (the poet suffers from high blood pressure)—was read without the élan of the unbending force that everyone expected.

But that does not mean much, of course. The violence might still appear later; the government isn't even properly installed. One cannot make predictions at this point. Yet there is nothing of a dictator about Goga. He shows, rather, the hesitancy and mediocrity of a dictator's flunky. Let us see what the new year will bring us. The old one closes upon a balance of struggles and collapses and the tragic anticipation of a time of humiliations. The night is full of snow.

Today, in a freshly published right-wing magazine that considers itself "free" (!), I read that "as we do not have a

6. Romanian universities had strict admittance examinations, designed mostly to achieve a traditional, unofficial, but very effective *numerus clausus* (quota system).

government program where one can fight for the national cause, a group of *uncircumcised* intellectuals is working at organizing such a program.''

The emphasized word proves that the above-mentioned intellectuals have undertaken this work not with their heads but with their foreskins.

In the special school group created for the heir-apparent of our throne, King Carol has brought together students from all social classes and all minorities: Saxons, Hungarians, and so on. Why not also a Jew? How else is the future sovereign going to learn anti-Semitism?

Scene in front of a bookshop in the center of town. A map of Spain hangs in the window. A father and his little boy stop to look at it.

"See? This is the map of Spain," the father explains. "Here are the rebels, see—and over there the government forces."

The little boy gazes at the map, musingly. Then he asks, "But where are the kikes?"

1938

## January 2

It snows night and day, an exuberant snow such as we have not had in years. B. asked me over to his place to "discuss urgently" one of his latest projects, a memorandum a few Jewish writers would like to submit to Goga—from one creative person to another. The idea stems from B. as well as from a few other writers, and its springboard is our prime minister's firm decision to consult with the leaders of our minorities. Yet I see a few obstacles. To start with, the official status of the Jews in this country is not at all clear. What are we? We are not accepted as Romanians and, officially, we are not a minority. Nor are we *heimatlos*—stateless persons. We are . . . a target for stones. We might possibly not even be important enough to be discussed. And should a political decision declare us a minority after all, surely the poet Goga is enough of a politician by now to prefer dealing with our Jewish businessmen and politician-lawyers rather than with our Jewish writers. And another thing: my feeling is that, in our government, the group in charge of the Jewish question is Cuza's party, which has on its agenda nothing else than legalizing a few acts of violence. These laws are going to be implemented as soon as Goga is forced to reverse his foreign policy. At any rate, now we must wait calmly and see how events develop. B.'s memorandum—which should be composed with extreme dignity and sobriety—cannot do any harm, but then it might not have any salutary effect either. And for the moment, I doubt that he will write it. B. is attractively spontaneous, ready for self-sacrifice, full of original, revolutionary ideas, but these ideas do not survive the daily humdrum and die in an embryonic stage.

It snowed so beautifully on this street today. The snow settled layer upon layer, high and opulent, as if intent upon showing how substantial oblivion can become, how necessary the calm it spreads. So many years, so many people, so many ideas buried under the drifts of so many snows.

Streitman[1] tells me: "I like the idea of anti-Semitism, but without anti-Semites."

## January 4

A sad observation, reconfirmed every day: people do not need freedom any longer. They have no use for it. Freedom troubles them, isolates them from the context of current life, sterilizes them—while submission to a collective discipline with a supreme chief gives them substance and serenity.

## January 7

Sometimes I am able to experience loneliness to its very limits—which verge upon nothingness. It is a state similar

1. H. S. Streitman (1873–1950), Romanian-born Jewish essayist and journalist.

to a breakdown and can be traced through its finest shad-
ings into the twilight of consciousness. The moment comes
when I give up reading because, along the pages of the
book, my daydream begins to unfold and then to unravel,
making confused patterns. There's no one at home. I feel
the first intimations of solitude within the confines of this
room, like the indistinct murmur of a far-off river. Books
and objects lose their contours, dissolve into the walled-in
gray afternoon. Very slowly, this outer layer of loneliness
disappears and I begin to hear the loneliness inside me, like
a faint musical rumble; muted echoes of years and seasons,
fragments of old images flash through my mind. A vast
questioning smile hovers over them. This phase does not last
long. There remain a few scattered thoughts whose meaning
fades, while disconnected words strain yet a moment longer,
then melt away, too. Their shaky ghosts flicker one more
time, then vanish into a limbo empty of memories and
sounds. And I am weightless—a snowflake that could float
anywhere—Greenland or Transvaal.

*January 11*

The "Program of National Compensation," so named by
Goga, begins to be furiously applied. The less concrete the
reality upon which this program must operate, the more extreme the zeal of those who carry it out. The speeches and
the interviews tell of equity, promise that Jews born here
will not be deprived of their rights (diversion!), but right
now, unable to find immediate fault with this category of
Jews, the government satisfies its thirst for nationalism and
electoral publicity with any kind of Jews. There is an impatience, a rush for action in all this, and it smells of trouble.
Today—the official decision to dismiss all the Jewish physicians working for the state medical services. The new government declared that "this institution has been taken over
by the kikes." What are the real facts? Out of five hundred
physicians employed by its offices in Bucharest, fifty are
Jewish. At the same time, thirty percent of their clients are
also Jewish. Consequently, all this furor is caused by those
fifty physicians born and raised in this country, educated at

Romanian universities, and veterans of war! Poor country, taken over by the kikes!

Advising, questioning, consulting, telephone calls. Fear has caught on like an epidemic. One must have nerves of steel to be able to deal with all these panic-stricken people. The idea of expatriation grows more enticing. The names of the most exotic countries are on everybody's lips: Chile, the Congo, Mexico, Australia . . . Fear sends you searching for the most absurd solutions. I tell someone I am going to stay right here, in this country, and he looks at me pityingly. The Jews want to fold their tents once again and wander through the world, they know not where. The temptation of sonorous names and faraway horizons. And wanting to forget the present persecutions, they forget that once they are settled somewhere else, their presence will provoke new ones.

## *January 13*

A. and B. came to discuss with me the present political situation. A. is preoccupied with the idea of publishing a daily Yiddish newspaper as soon as possible. He believes that the Yiddish language alone can be the galvanizing element uniting all Jewish energies for passive resistance. All Jewish writers should start writing in Yiddish at once! He sees Yiddish as the Romanian Jews' only hope of salvation. My objections could not move him. If we really need a daily paper now for the Romanian-Jewish population—a population that has always been lied to, cheated, and misled by government promises—then why not a newspaper in Romanian, the language that the new generation of Jews speaks and writes, in the Old Kingdom as well as in the annexed territories?[2] At any rate, that might be less of a sacrifice than forcing writers who do not know Yiddish to learn it. And should they have to learn a new language

2. The old Romanian territories of Moldavia and Southern Romania or Wallachia are referred to as the "Old Kingdom." Greater Romania was created after World War I by the annexation of Transylvania, Bukovina, Banat, and Southern Dobruja.

after all, why not Hebrew rather than Yiddish? In Germany, after their total disaster, the Jews did not resort to Yiddish but put out that marvelous newspaper *Jüdische Rundschau,* written in German. And if there is no other way out, why not two newspapers, one in Romanian and the other in Yiddish, for their respective readers and writers? The truth is that nowhere among the Jews does one find a diversity of tradition that results in such dramatic conditions as in Romania. We have Hungarian Jews, Jews from the Bukovina, Bessarabian Jews, and Jews from the Old Kingdom—all of whom, due to their own regional traditions, do not see eye to eye. Their merging into a single group in order to defend themselves against persecution, according to A., would be possible only through the adoption of Yiddish. A.'s is a very personal point of view which I can well understand, just as I ask his understanding for my own attitude—mine as well as that of so many other writers like me. This position is by no means a humiliating abdication, but the honest conviction that the unifying element among all these categories of Jews should be the Romanian language, precisely if isolation—as A. himself agrees—is definitely to be shunned. B. can detach himself more easily (if, of course, only theoretically right now) from my position because of the alluvial deposits of Yiddish in his background, accumulated while growing up in Bukovina and among the special traditions of Moldavian Jewry. But the important question for us all might still be this: suddenly, the government forbids you to continue writing in Romanian. What then?

### January 14

What I have been waiting for during the last few days has come to pass: I have been dismissed from my position with the state medical services, because I am a Jew. Today's papers carry lists of colleagues fired for the same reason. The streets resound with the call of newspaper vendors: "Jewish doctors fired!" Victory! Nationalism is satisfied.

*January 15*

I have talked to many Jews in despair over the situation, which is indeed very serious both because of the present policy and because of future dangers. Everybody asks, "What will become of me?" I haven't heard a single Jew ask, "What will become of *us*?" At any given moment of their history, in favorable as well as in adverse circumstances, the Jews have acted and reacted individually. What Gentiles call "the great collective spirit of the Jews" is a sinister anti-Semitic joke.

*January 17*

*Monitorul Oficial*[3] has just published the government's decision forbidding Jews to hire maids under forty years of age. The reason given is abominable: "The Jews are white slave traders." But no less revolting is the lack of reaction on the part of the Jews. Not a handful of us dared gather in a home, in a synagogue, at a street corner, to protest against this medieval calumny, even at the risk of the police descending upon us or of the whole thing ending in bloodshed. I'm disgusted with ourselves. It is a sin to say it, but I must.

*January 21*

Good Lord, how many initiatives, meetings, discussions. Invitations to participate keep pouring in. I see everyone and go everywhere. I listen. Daily I give myself shots of history. Daily, wherever I go, I observe the same fact: the Jews are a people of multiple initiatives and total intransigence. Last night, a meeting of about twenty writers and journalists at the house of the lawyer and writer, S. The object: publication of a daily Jewish newspaper. The Jewish journalists dismissed from *Dimineața* must be helped, a purpose which, to many of those present, seemed too trivial

---

3. The official government publication of the time.

to arouse their enthusiasm. They understand the need to help the Jewish unemployed, but not the need to give priority to journalists!

A.'s idea of turning such a paper into a battle flag is naive, and naive also is the hope that this newspaper could become an organ of Jewish defense; in fact, it will represent only a means to earn a living for the journalists hurt by the present political circumstances. At any rate, the Yiddish language is no miracle cure and actually, under the circumstances, it might even be inopportune. Useless, too, were the debates over the format of the newspaper: no one could come up with a practical suggestion. It is indeed difficult. A newspaper cannot be improvised just like that, and with such diversified objectives from the start, it cannot turn out successful.

Besides, the expectation of raising the money (there was talk of ten million lei) appears strangely naive for people who should by now know the niggardliness of our Jewish bourgeoisie when it comes to promoting culture.

*January 25*

Filaret, the TB hospital, has only one Jewish patient, a young man who has been fighting the illness for several years. The Gentile patients, at the suggestion of a former clerk of the newspaper *Universul,* [4] have revolted, and have signed a petition to the chief physician demanding the immediate discharge of the "tubercular kike." For the moment, the physician has reacted with dignity. We shall see how things develop, for, I am told, they eventually will develop. Incredible!

Of all the steps taken against Jews, none seems to me more insulting and underhanded than the latest decree: to reevaluate their right to citizenship. I never expected persecution to take this form. If the Jews had any courage and dignity left, not a single one would go through with it. Citizenship was granted once and for all. It is an historic act

4. One of the largest dailies in Bucharest.

meant for all eternity. How can one conceive such an inept thing as a reevaluation of this law, which created for the Jews moral, political, and socioeconomic realities? If a government suspects that there was fraud in some cases, it should start investigations of those cases. Isn't that the function of authorities, magistrates, and police? After the peace treaty, no retroactive law can be applied to citizenship. And yet here are one million people insulted by an arbitrary decree and forced to travel far and wide through the country, searching for documents to meet a ridiculous deadline of twenty days. Were I not afraid of repercussions for my family, I would not comply for anything in the world. What value can be attached to citizenship when it can be withdrawn at any minister's whim? What guarantee is there that other governments will not imitate this shameful action? If the fact that I was born in this country of parents who were also born and raised here, that I fought in the war and have written Romanian poetry—if all this does not entitle me to citizenship, which would be unconditionally granted in other countries, then I ought not to lift a finger to establish my rights, even if, as a result, I were forbidden to practice medicine. There would be more dignity in my becoming a shoeblack at a street corner. No word can express the turpitude of our political leaders who first deprive us of our livelihood because we are Jewish and then attack our citizenship. After having systematically seen to it that we starve, they will grant some of us the honor of citizenship! And to think that no one, Gentile or Jew, has reacted against such knavery! If at least, on the day when the decree was issued, the Jews had closed their shops, as they did in Poland when Jewish students were expelled from universities!

*January 27*

I cannot find a single peaceful thought, a single image to dream over in these pages where once I used to record other kinds of events than today's horrible ones. I recall beautiful books of poems bound in blue and red, the pleasure of touching them, of opening their silky pages to pore over them with friends, to discuss them for afternoons and evenings on end. But it must have happened in another existence.

A moment's healing touch: I stopped in front of a florist's window. Behind me, the screeching and throbbing boulevard vanished. Gone, too, were the voices of newspaper vendors selling their daily poisoned flowers. Facing me, behind the glass curtain, a fairyland. Shining, plump carnations, with the pink voluptuousness of women about to reach maturity, poised for the first step of a sprightly dance; shamelessly lascivious gladioli; virginal branches of white lilac; roses lost in pure meditation, undecided between the metaphysical white and the unreal yellow of a sky after the rain. Peace and harmony among creatures born in different climates from such a variety of seeds smiling at each other in the improvised country of a show-window under an electric lamp imitating the sun.

### January 29

Today I spent two hours at the *Monitorul Oficial,* going through the 1917–18 collection, looking for a royal decree. Moments of grim sadness as I relived the whole war period. In its dry style, lacking the details proper to a chronicle, this newspaper brings vividly to life a powerful segment of pure history. Each issue spreads out vast cemeteries with the names of those dead on the battlefield. Every two or three pages, yet another endless list of casualties. At one point I reached list number three hundred. And then the long list of discharges, of all kinds of arrests and trials, containing many names of many people, known and unknown at the time, but playing key roles in our current public life. It takes only a twenty years' plunge into the underground of history to realize how many lies there are at the origin of so many glorious careers!

## February 2

Our king has given an interview to the foreign press, the third this month. He has always expressed himself quite clearly about the Jewish question. This time, he was more forthright than ever: he reassures us that there will be no pogrom, that our country is struggling with the Jewish problem it must solve—but his answer doesn't clearly tell how this is going to be done. He adds that some of the Jews might simplify matters by leaving Romania of their own accord.

I sincerely confess that I dread attempting once more what I have so often and so unsuccessfully tried in the past: to organize Jewish writers, artists, and journalists in a group whose purpose today appears more justified than ever. By definition, such a group should stay clear of political involvement, and yet today hardly any activity can take place on such ideal grounds, untouched by the imperatives of our political present. Still, in spite of its diversified objectives and the contradictory personalities within such a group, its existence would bring the prestige we lack in these difficult moments. The objective would be the collaboration of all these people in a cultural and social mission: to work at bringing the Romanian and Jewish populations closer to each other through a better knowledge of their respective cultures and traditions. (I know, the Romanians do not want us, but as long as we are alive we must try to achieve this kind of contact.) We must try to educate the poor Jewish masses; and finally, we must initiate and collaborate on studies supporting the Jewish organizations that are now struggling for the rights of the Jewish population. Much could be done to accomplish this. Starting, for example, with the little magazine *Adam,* which could be transformed into a weekly. It could carry substantial and meaningful messages that would have a much needed echo in political circles, Romanian and Jewish alike. In the midst of this disorder of our Jewish life, of this dissolution and total disorganization of old strata, such a concentration of Jewish men of letters, writers, and scholars would be an example of harmony, bringing a wave of vitality and trust in our moral endurance. Yet the thought of having to deal directly with so many writers, with their obtuse feelings about collective action, their destructive attitudes, disarms me again. Last evening I talked to L.S. late into the night about our old disillusionment with the publication of a Jewish daily. As I expected, the pettiness of a few journalists brought the project to a ridiculous end. How should one go on attempting new projects if the past and present are full of so many obstacles and so many disappointments?

*February 4*

At the Jewish hospital Caritas, over the door facing the main stairway, on a marble plaque, you can read the names "Peppi and Jancu Goldstein." This gentleman, a wholesale dealer in flour, is the president of the Jewish Funeral Society of Bucharest and the satrap administrator of the fat business called the Jewish cemeteries. At the same time, as a board member of the hospital, he made a donation to have a room elegantly appointed and a door on which his name is inscribed in marble. The room serves both as a conference room for the board and as a synagogue: that represents two gifts for the price of one. It has a large table with oak chairs on the left and a cupboard with the holy Torah on the right. Friday evening services are held here every week.

I opened the door and came in at the end of the service. Who was officiating? The cantor of the cemeteries and of the Funeral Society. For what public? The clerks of the Funeral Society and of the undertakers, plus a few ghosts, men and women, patients of the hospital and future clients of the same cemeteries. Someone familiar with the secrets of the institution informed me that as long as the donor—president of the dead—was alive, prayers for his life and blessings upon his name were strictly required at Friday and Saturday services. Also, after his death, at specified dates, certain prayers must be said for him forever. If one considers the cost, these free services represent a third and fantastic bargain—for you cannot really tell how long *forever* lasts in the case of a man who dies and is buried with all due religious process. But ah, the end of the prayers: the first sexton, a gaunt face, bloodshot eyes, hoarse voice, closed the book and suddenly shouted at the patients, "Up, get up! Service is over! Out! Get out of here!" And the old wrecks submitted, shuffling their shadows back to their hospital wards—the antechambers of the huge business headed by the philanthropist Mr. Jancu Goldstein, who on his walk through the paradise of immortality will take along his spouse, Peppi.

*February 7*

Last night, three hours of debate over the prospective group of Jewish writers and journalists. My home was transformed into a convention hall, filled with endless speeches seasoned with coffee and tobacco.

M.S. still wants to hold on to certain "positions," which he cannot abandon by slamming doors, even though he knows he will lose them anyway. S. sees the present situation through the rosy glasses of his political party. He objects to a distinction between *Romanian* and *Jew* (which has never been our purpose), even though in his literary work he does express himself as a Jew. F., who recently joined the Zionists, sees this prospective group as a cultural group in which all kinds of professionals should take part. The others lack true enthusiasm and are not yet aware of how serious the present situation is for the Jews—a situation that cannot be reversed by future political changes.

Strange, this phenomenon observed only in Romania: the fear of calling yourself a Jew. Under all circumstances, and especially the present ones, the Jewish writer, quite aware of reality, clings to an imagined integration into national life, while knowing that actual integration has been denied him. His acceptance as a Romanian was, at best, only a polite and relatively generous formal act, cancelled by the slightest incident. In other countries, Jews do not know this kind of cowardice. To call yourself a Jew is not an act of aggressive, nationalistic delimitation, but a kind of freedom that doesn't warp the sincere feeling of kinship with the place of your birth, with its language and its culture. France has its Jewish writers who call themselves Jews, who write, when there is a need, on Jewish themes, and who are published by Jewish publishing houses; the same situation holds in Italy or Switzerland, where nobody seems to fear the ghost of isolation. Call yourself a Jew in this country, and you have committed a criminal act of betrayal. A group of Jewish writers produced by this very soil means only a group of alien elements, their association with their particular tradition, and nothing else. But this tragic problem has no solution. The Jews will never achieve collective action here, least of all the Jewish writers blinded by their huge vanity. One thing is certain to me: under any kind of future regime, the Jewish artist and writer will remain an alien species whose isolation or even elimination will be carried out systematically and unanimously.

*February 11*

Between last night and today, the pace of history has quickened to a tragic intensity: one could feel every human being shiver at the intimate contact with the essence of historical events. Suddenly the Goga administration has collapsed, right after the speech in which the premier dreamed of a ten-year government. What then was the sense of this dreadful parenthesis, of forty-four days of vexations, of ridiculous spasms, of dissensions and crass incompetence, bringing anarchy and economic disaster? Nobody can explain it. Strange rumors keep circulating. Some of them are confirmed by the foreign press. We have come to the point at which we are forced to resume the old custom whereby, at great crises of history and faced with danger, the ruler would call upon all the available bearded sages for help and counsel. Thus a new government has been assembled in haste to correct the mistakes of the previous one, as the king himself has declared. This explains how our patriarch[5] has also become the premier of this new group of high and

5. Title of the head of the Romanian Greek-Orthodox church, at the time of this entry, Miron Christea (1868–1939).

experienced counselors! The Jews are generally optimistic, but their optimism is mostly the effect of their temporary relaxation, a vitally necessary reaction. The show goes on; only the actors have changed. The former aggressive Cuzist in charge of Internal Affairs has been replaced by an aggressive Vaidist;[6] and Goga himself, by his uncle, the supreme head of the Church, whose speech six months ago described Jews as "the parasites who squeeze the poor Romanians, suck the vigor out of the Christians' marrow, forcing them to leave the home of their ancestors and wander away." The new administration has left unchanged the old repertory of policies: the Jewish question, revision of citizenship, jobs for Romanians only. All measures taken so far remain irrevocable. Most important: the constitution is being amended and the parliament dismissed. How long this new administration will last cannot be foreseen. But one feels that its basic structure is shaky. Meanwhile, the waves of foreign events rush in. Everything depends on the situation in Germany. If—as rumors have it, or more precisely, as rumors would have it—Hitler is now playing his last card, Europe (and implicitly our country) might be saved.

### February 13

Started working again on my abandoned novel, *Marta Granet*. I've discarded everything I've written up to now and have the feeling that this time it will get going. The need to escape everyday life, the longing for a trip forever unattainable, have reached their peak.

### February 21

I have been practicing for a whole week on the first pages of the novel, which is to be a psychological study of an ugly girl. The first sketches seemed interesting and I was carried away by a kind of facility of writing, mainly because I wanted to tear myself away from everyday life

6. Member of the Vaida Voievod party, named after Alexandru Vaida-Voievod (1872–195?), a politician of nationalist anti-Semitic orientation.

and all the people pathologically concerned with the latest news. The only noteworthy event might be the new constitution, conceived by the king and submitted to the people for a nominal and obligatory plebiscite, that is—unanimous ratification. At first glance, this new constitution seems inopportune. It was not well received, naturally enough, since it was put together in haste and in an atmosphere of panic. It seems rather a disproportionate step for a country to change its constitution merely in order to correct a political error. For it was devised as a weapon against the Iron Guard. What an honor for them! To think that they could not be subdued by less extreme means!

## February 23

I went today to the infantry regiment in which I served as an officer during the war, in order to find confirmation of my status in my dossier. I was not listed among the officers. Nor had I ever been listed, according to a major who looked very serious, no doubt because he was a member of the draft board. Yet my honorable discharge as an officer was issued by this regiment. Another despicable example of the disorder prevailing in paperwork. Finally, a sergeant found an older dossier containing my file. Mere oversight: six years ago I was transferred to Buzău, without being informed about it. But that is not the important thing. In the middle of the sheet, in large letters: "Suspect—Jew!" I asked the major for the meaning of this. He stuttered a confused answer. No use to protest. Here is the result of my lifelong devotion to this country, attested to by another major who happened to be passing by and stopped when he recognized me. We played together as children in the streets of Bucharest and later were war comrades.

## February 26

I have finally given in and joined the efforts to organize the Cultural Foundation of Romanian Jews. Writers, artists, newspapermen are to join in an effort to bring about social rapprochement and cultural exchanges with Romanian Gentiles. We have composed an appeal which all participants are to sign. Let us see what develops. Even the most extreme individualists, it seems to me, should find this point in common: their exclusion from any participation in Romanian cultural life. Because it is obvious that, whatever the changes for the better in the character of the legislation, Jews will continue to be segregated. In other words, the problem is not with legal measures but with the old, stubborn antagonism pervading all levels of Romanian society. (The revision of citizenship is undoubtedly unconstitutional, yet it caused wide public satisfaction.)

The greatest danger is, however, the short memory of the Jews. There are many particular dangers related to the activities of the Cultural Foundation of Romanian Jews. One of them is already evident: the antagonism between partisans of Yiddish and those of Romanian. This antagonism has long been a stumbling block. Some Jewish-Romanian writers are in almost physical pain when they hear Yiddish. Strange, how they appreciate almost any language, be it Kirghiz or Ukrainian, and find justification for the existence of any culture—but when it comes to Yiddish, they cringe in disgust. I gave much thought to this problem when I had to decide about practical steps. Because I, too, have no great affinity for Yiddish. Which did not prevent me from translating many lovely Yiddish works. But like or dislike should not become a prejudice. I know writers born and bred in Romania who are sorry they cannot express themselves in Romanian because they did not learn it in time; and I know Jewish writers who write in Romanian and who regret they cannot express themselves in Yiddish, because they spoke only Romanian both at home and in school. At any rate, the use of Yiddish is not an exclusive proof of an authentic attitude toward Judaism. An interesting case is that of P., who claims that when he realized he was a Jewish and not a Romanian writer, he resigned from the SSR[7] in order to maintain his integrity. Beyond affinities and affection, one must take into account the powerful objective reality of a language created by a long his-

7. Societatea Scriitorilor Români, the Romanian Writers' Association.

torical and cultural development. Of course, to speak the language of a minority is inconvenient. Still, Yiddish is no different than the languages of other minorities—for instance, the Sashi,[8] Hungarians, Ruteans.[9] But then Yiddish should be considered in the same way as the languages of the latter, and should not be subject to prejudice and political suspicion. The Cultural Foundation of Romanian Jews must not become a forum for nationalism. Its aim ought to be the balance of cultures, their equal value in human terms, an improvement of behavior through the spiritual impact of the arts, and the practical possibility of cultivating them after years of unjust neglect.

## *March 3*

D'Annunzio[10] is dead. For most people he died long ago. He himself announced a while back that he would melt and become a mysterious chemical element. But it didn't work out that way. Only his work, which wasn't even passionate but merely emphatic, has melted away. I remember the influence exercised over Europe during my adolescence by two famous baldheads: Rostand[11] and d'Annunzio. Rostand, however, had lyrical pathos and a fame he did not exploit like a ham, while d'Annunzio kept his fame alive by all sorts of vulgar means. To fan public interest, he exploited his bald head and goatee as well as his long affair with Eleanora Duse. But one can't make a lasting career as a lover. And so, some twenty years ago, d'Annunzio figured he might crash the gates of immortality by becoming the hero of Fiume. Thus he created that most tasteless of concepts: the "soldier-poet." But as no one showed the slightest interest, he withdrew into solitude to await his chemical liquefaction. When this phenomenon did not occur quickly enough, he made one more splash: during the war on Abys-

8. A German-speaking minority established in some regions of Transylvania between the thirteenth and fourteenth centuries.
9. A Ukrainian-speaking minority from the former Austro-Hungarian territory.
10. Gabriele d'Annunzio (1863–1938), Italian novelist and poet.
11. Edmond Rostand (1868–1918), French poet and dramatist.

sinia he sent Mussolini a golden cigarette box filled with cartridges. Now the great lyrical poet rests dressed in the uniform of a squadron leader, no doubt awaiting a flight into immortality.

## March 20

Two weeks of a premature spring brought exhausting awakenings. Science has written in large letters its diagnosis on these moods of sadness and mental turmoil: vitamin deficiency. This is supposed to explain everything. . . . And once again the clanging of weapons was heard over Europe. The occupation of Austria by Hitler's Germany (according to a plan previously outlined in all its details) has jolted the world. A new martyrdom, following the recipe tried out in Germany, is inflicted on the two hundred fifty thousand Austrian Jews, one hundred eighty thousand of whom are in Vienna. The most insensitive people have been shaken by the wave of suicides which swept away, among others, prominent university faculty. But there has been no official protest anywhere. The civilized West and the so-called generous America voiced no objection against the Hitlerist bestiality which did away with the intellectual cream of Europe unable to escape from Vienna—Jews, indeed, but also thoroughly Austrian. That human solidarity on which the Jews persistently count is nothing but a myth. If in 1933, in the heart of Europe, the Hitlerist takeover could lead to crimes and atrocities unparalleled even in the Middle Ages, with no intervention from abroad, how can any nation be expected to show courage and dignity? This is not merely a Jewish problem. England has hardly any interests in Europe and it could not care less about the fate of anybody, whether Czech, Jewish, Polish, or Lithuanian. As to France's sluggish protests, they are probably prompted more by self-interest and expediency than by generosity. Yet it is already clear that the Jewish question, although it still serves as a political diversionary tactic, is becoming a secondary concern. The world is slipping toward the end of an era.

*April 1*

The question of the Cultural Foundation of Romanian Jews has reached a point of no return. No delay is possible: either I give up or I get it launched. I realize that everything depends on me, which is an advantage, but may also be a drawback. For I am not free of sadness and doubts, knowing what lies ahead. . . . Of course, it is quite possible to undertake certain things while one is unsure of oneself and of the undertaking. But there are other things that require a firm foundation of certainty and confidence. I have started the tedious and thankless task of laying these foundations, and have approached writers, artists, and newspapermen in an attempt to get unanimous endorsement. I spoke to many. Everyone has a different point of view, a personal slant, everyone wavers when it comes to joining. Indeed, I understand their difficulty, for to acknowledge your Jewishness here is tantamount to becoming an exile in your own country. "But what are you giving up?" a writer may well ask. He is perfectly aware that he is not giving up anything. No one understands that to assume and acknowledge your Jewishness is not desertion, for you cannot abandon your own background the way you can jump over the fence from one yard to another. Nor does the foundation require it.

Some of them are cunning and think that no one will see through their hypocrisy. They tell themselves: "After all, my secret thoughts are my own. Now that the going is rough, I can go along with this idea. Who can stop me, when the opportunity comes, from jumping back over the fence?" Poor people! They are so deluded, so at a loss, that they overdo their neophyte expressions of support.

The majority, however, has shown real understanding for the gravity of the problem. But the many nuances in their reactions are psychologically instructive. A promising young essayist and novelist has sent me letters and memoranda, and then finally declared that he cannot see how his name can appear alongside those of unknowns. A painter finds that the foundation is a most worthwhile idea, but he is afraid of being drawn back into Jewish sensibility. He would therefore like to modify the text of the prospectus. A lawyer and newspaperman with strong leftist views makes a basic demand that an epithet modifying the word "politics" should be changed. A doctor inquires about retirement provisions. A venerable reporter and essayist, although fully proficient in Yiddish, protests against the inclusion of Yiddishists. One of my colleagues denied us his signature on the grounds that he is against Jews. But he is still a member of the UER,[12] which he recently joined, as well as of the association of Jewish professionals, Unirea, and other Jewish societies. Another painter maintained that there is no real anti-Semitism, but only a temporary opportunistic reaction. Very many thought that the foundation was a philanthropic organization and submitted requests for funding. A philosopher spit on the signature of a fellow philosopher whom he considers a fraud, a scoundrel, and unworthy of membership. And so on and so forth, with all writers and artists, aged anywhere from twenty-six to seventy, who constitute a gallery of an infinitely sad variety: ridiculous and egocentric, naive or conceited, destructive and materialistic. And one must manage to fish out some point they have in common. The only consolation is that, although one cannot make an omelet without eggs, it is possible to form a cultural foundation without writers.

I never mistrust people, I only mistrust my ability to adapt to them.


*April 3*

The Cişmigiu[13] is all decked out. Nothing new. The same bushes in bloom in the same spots, the same babies, like flowers, drinking the spring out of their bottles. The magnolias have shed their petals, broad-shouldered George Panu[14] bends over the graceful young people seated at his

12. Uniunea Evreilor Român̂i, the Union of Romanian Jews, one of the principal Jewish organizations between the two wars. It promoted the integration of the Jews in Romanian political and cultural life and cooperated with the main Romanian political parties, especially the Liberals.

13. The main public park of Bucharest.

14. The memorial of a figure prominent in Romanian public life.

feet, the peacocks cry out their desolation. . . . There is a heartrending sadness in this repetitiveness. Maybe each spring is only the memory of the first one we lived long ago? To experience it really, we should be granted the sight of spring only once in a lifetime.

Between the strict brain of Moses and the generous heart of Jesus there is room for a new divinity.

Finally last night there was a meeting of Jewish writers, artists, and newspapermen to set up the time and place for launching the Cultural Foundation of Romanian Jews. All of them behaved well; that is, there were no speeches.

The idea aired today was to get Jews to petition for a hearing at the next session of the League of Nations. Although fragmented, wounded, dying, this institution still matters, it seems. And, it also seems, news about our prospective foundation has reached the League. How? Spies? An indirect invitation? Who knows, perhaps some politicians are already watching us? Perhaps they hope, not that we will sell out, but that we can be seduced? I shall have to be on the alert. Of course I may be wrong. But I want to jot down these thoughts now so I can rejoice later when they prove untrue. It is a prudent act for a candid man who lacks political flair.

Civilization has profoundly altered many concepts: it has turned birth into baptism, love into marriage, and death into funerals.

## May 3

Again, a stifling fog over Jewish life. We have tried, for obvious reasons, not so much to disregard as to forget for a moment the impending tragedy. Now, the abuse and vituperation in the patriarch's speech have revived our pain. The old prime minister has shown himself unswerving in his hate and anti-Semitism. The power of the Iron Guard, it seems, is rising throughout the country and can no longer be stemmed. The government is taking a suspiciously long time for a so-called preparation of public opinion. This preparation consists of issuing data known to everybody for many years. Concern is widespread and increasing. Both Romanian politicians and Jews await with mounting panic the implacable march of events. The situation can be summed up thus: the Jews would not oppose the Iron Guard's program if its principal point were the extermination not of the Jews, but only of the politicians in power today; and the politicians would have no objection to the Iron Guard if its main target were merely the Jews and not the politicians. For the moment, the politicians will adopt extreme anti-Jewish attitudes so as to satisfy so-called public opinion. Be that as it may, this second outburst of the patriarch since he became prime minister is a bad omen.

Even optimistic Jews have lost hope in the chivalry of the great Western powers, England and France, and in their intervention in the tragedy of East European Jewry. But they still have one hope: America! The United States will take over the role of knight in shining armor who, they dream, will rush to their rescue at the eleventh hour.

## May 6

The suffocating atmosphere created by increasingly ominous news and suspense thickens like dense smoke, clouding everything. We have reached a point when any news seems plausible. As events tumble over each other, logic vanishes. Hope is construed as callousness, and the Gentile friend has lost the courage to console us. Indeed, disasters are piling up: burning hate is rising in Germany; anti-Semitism is government policy in Poland; in Austria, Jews are exterminated; Hungary is passing anti-Jewish legislation tantamount to methodical starvation of the Jews. What will happen here on the day—perhaps nearer at hand than we imagine—when the Iron Guard's justice will become the law of the land? And even if this does not happen, what is in store for us with a prime minister who keeps harping on "the invasion of our country by foreign heathens and Jewish scum?" Some seeds of logic and compassion seem to sprout in the new constitution, only to be trampled upon by the devils of absurdity who have overrun the whole land.

All the Jews endlessly chew over the one preoccupation: leaving Romania. But this is merely an obsession, a neurotic symptom of powerlessness and despair. For in actuality, nobody moves—since there is nowhere to go, there is no salvation in sight. It has always been impossible to flee in time once a country has become aggressively anti-Semitic. And we are talking only about people with means, for the mass of the Jewish people is held down by its struggle for daily bread and shackles of fear. (In Germany, a Jew who emigrates may take along 8 to 10 percent of his property; in Austria, all his property is confiscated.)

There is no way out. We scream, we groan, blood mixes with earth, we die, and a whole generation is destroyed. Then there is silence, while waiting for history to open a window to salvation at the moment when the whole world is choking to death.

## May 15

Another meeting with B. and D. to set up a program for the Cultural Foundation of Romanian Jews. We worked for about three hours—comments and amendments of the points I had drafted.

## May 23

A bitter joke, beloved by Jews, tireless consumers of topical jests. A Jew's prayer: "Dear God, for five thousand years we have been Your chosen people. Enough! Choose another one now!"

Today, S. showed me an article in *Universul,* quoting the opinions of a high-ranking German officer that had been published in an essay entitled "Air Raids and Racial Selection." As I read it, I felt a chill wind of madness blowing through my brain. Here are a few lines, written down because I fear that some day I myself shall not believe that I ever read them:

"Air raids will affect in particular overpopulated districts, that is, those inhabited by poor people, people who are the flotsam of life and who, through extermination, will escape their misery. The explosion of one thousand tons of bombs and the large number of dead will drive many people crazy, for individuals with a weak nervous system will be unable to stand these bombardments. Thus, thanks to air raids, it will be possible to unmask neurotics and remove them from society. As soon as they are unmasked, they will be sterilized so that the race can be cleansed of sick elements."

The author is alive and well and unsterilized.


*June 29*

The gesture of that popular Jewish speaker who, talking in a synagogue about the Jewish massacres in the Ukraine, walks to the altar, angrily jerks aside the velvet curtain, throws open the doors hiding the Torah, and cries out, "Lord, are You asleep?"


*July 2*

What interesting emotional experiences there are all around! In a large shop window on Calea Victoriei[15] I saw splendid, colorful posters, some three-dimensional, that blinded me with a torrid sun, an ultramarine sky, bronzed shores. In each of them, like a statue, an upright impressive female figure dominates the view, beckoning, "Come to Corsica!" I cannot resist this temptation. I stop, stare at the poster, and go on a voyage.

---

15. A main street in downtown Bucharest.

*July 12*

All is not lost while the hope of writing a poem is still alive.

In the cemetery there are patches of old graves lost among weeds. Lit by the sun at noon, they reminded me of my childhood gardens. There was something of a cemetery in the large yards on the outskirts of Bucharest—abandoned, fenceless, with weeds scorched by the summer heat. You could scream your lungs out and nobody would hear you. Over the yellowing grasses, I suddenly saw my mother returning home in the evening, taking shortcuts through one of the gardens. She wore dark glasses with a cord tied to a button or to her belt. Because she had trouble with her eyes she used to go to the military hospital to see Colonel Petrescu, an ophthalmologist famous at the time. The hospital is still there, but then it was on the outskirts of town. You could reach the end of the line by horse-drawn streetcar (two horses up the hills, and one on flat streets). But Mother went there and back on foot, for she rarely had money for the fare, and even if she did, she saved it for more urgent needs. (And what a long way it was from the ghetto to the hospital!) In the course of her visits they put some very powerful drops in her eyes (perhaps silver nitrate), which blinded her for a while. But as household duties claimed her, she did not have the time to wait for the effect to wear off and so started back immediately, stumbling into lamp posts and walls. How often she lost her way, having made a mistake herself or having been misdirected! When she appeared in our yard, I would run toward her to lead her. But by then she had recovered and could see better. She never let me go with her to the hospital; I was too little.

Perhaps these memories were brought back today by the funeral of a wealthy bank director's mother, arranged by her son lavishly but discreetly (no notice to friends and colleagues). For the first time in my life I saw a coffin of polished oak lowered into the grave.

No, that's not it. Mother was somewhere there, and I thought of her the moment I crossed the gate of the cemetery. While clods of earth sounded on the coffin lid, I felt my face suddenly smiling. An old, a very old memory. I was barely eleven. Mother sat on a small couch by a window overlooking a large yard surrounded by many apartments. I went over to her to read her my first poem. I no longer recall its title or its contents, but I still remember the first stanza:

> *Now I leave torment and sorrow*
> *Oh, what bliss not to exist.*
> *Tie the logbook of my boyhood*
> *With a bit of blackest twist.*

Mother broke out into a soft chuckle, so as not to offend me. To my question, she answered that the suffering expressed was so disproportionate to my age that it could only make one smile. Then, with a sigh, she added, "My darling, what do you know about life that can make you so sad?"

Actually, just a few days before, I had witnessed something very sad. The owner of our very large tenement building, the now famous E.B. (who had taken over the business of his father, tailor and usurer), had thrown out into the snow-covered street the belongings of a poor family who had failed to pay the twenty lei rent for the previous month. That was the future banker's first step up the ladder.

## July 13

The conference presently convened at Evian under the auspices of President Roosevelt, where several nations are to discuss a solution of the problems of Jewish refugees from Germany and Austria, boosts morale and trust in the future of humanity. It would have been a sublime effort if the participants and, in particular, the initiator of the conference could have shown the courage to disregard political expediency and set up norms for dealing with the Jewish situation in general. In other words, rather than wait for the successive unleashing of persecutions in country after country and only then seek a means to help, they should establish an international code for these unfortunate Jews torn between various nationalistic conflicts. Rules of conduct should be established, once and for all, for times when some country or other, seeking so-called national self-determination, exercises bestial power against its Jewish inhabitants. Only thus can one avoid some of the most horrifying occurrences of the century, such as the one consigned to a magazine coverage describing the life of fifty-one German Jews floating aimlessly on the Danube in a dilapidated boat. They were refused asylum by all neighboring countries after being forced to declare that they earned their living by theft. All their property had been abandoned to the Germans.

Will the day come when people will drift on the Black Sea or the Baltic Sea, begging for asylum up and down the coast, their lives depending on the good offices of some new conference?

## *August 2*

I have made my final decision about the Cultural Foundation of Romanian Jews. At the first opportunity I shall call together all the writers and artists and, under some pretext or other, inform them that I withdraw completely from this undertaking. My growing conviction that no help is forthcoming either from the prospective bourgeois sponsors or from the proletarian writers has been confirmed once more and in definitive circumstances. What I had imagined is too beautiful and altogether unsuitable to the Jewish condition here and now. Let it remain a dream I dreamt for fifteen years of useless waiting.

## *August 4*

I met again a gentleman with whom I played as a child before I started going to school. He is now a comically small man with a large head like a lopsided melon, with little eyes pushed deeply into orbits behind an old-fashioned pince-nez attached with a cord to the buttonhole of his lapel. (I believe this is the last pair of glasses of its kind in Bucharest. Except for those you see occasionally on stage worn by a spinster with a hair bun, in a plain blouse and skirt.) My

former playmate used to be an important businessman selling timber after the war, and owned a one-horse coach. I
don't know what he is doing now. Once every two or three
years we run into each other on the street and each time he
stops me. In a tone of tender and respectful envy he tells
me, "Ah yes, *you* have done very well!"

I never understood why he should think that, nor did I
quite want to ask him. Then he takes up the old refrain, "Do
you remember?" But I never quite dared ask him what specifically I was supposed to remember. The other day, having
to cross a forgotten street in the old Bucharest ghetto and
walking along a fence bordering a garden, I suddenly remembered . . . this was the place where the house of his parents
stood a long time ago. A wealthy house, spacious, with seven
or eight steps leading to a little veranda enclosed by small-
paned windows and an impressive living room with a set of
grave-looking high armchairs protected by white slipcovers.
The thick rugs made my step hesitate. (He was not permitted
to bring his friends in through the front door.) Six huge
rooms crowded with mahogany furniture and gold-leaf woodwork, Venetian lamps, a china cabinet with expensive knick-
knacks, a grand piano, and a separate children's room (my
playmate had a younger brother) stuffed with toys, picture
books, and all kinds of marvels that stunned me. But the most
fascinating place was the garden: vast, taking up an entire lot
between two streets, with flower beds near the house but wild,
covered with high grass farther down under the cherry, the
walnut, the apricot, and the mulberry trees. Under the trel-
lises and pergolas heavy with vines, you embarked on exotic
voyages with all the bugs of the earth, with the garden's
freshly stirred odors. You knew the most secret nests, the
best hiding places. The boys' father had his front teeth covered in gold, their mother wore gold-rimmed glasses and
spoke French. (Her German did not impress me, for my own
mother spoke it quite well.) For my friend's mother I was a
sort of case in point that served to demonstrate educational
issues. Around four in the afternoon we were called in, and
she would serve cocoa with bread and marmalade or cake and
soda water. Of course I was included, but later I realized that
I was used as a stimulant for the lazy appetite of her children.
She would sit down with us and go on talking to her brood:

"Look at this little boy [meaning me], look how nicely he

eats, and he never tastes such goodies at home. . . . Look
how clean he keeps himself, and his mother can't afford to
buy him a suit every season. . . . We buy you four suits
every year. . . . Listen how beautifully this little boy speaks,
and his mother can't keep a governess for him as we do, his
mother is a very poor woman. . . . See how smart he is? And
he certainly doesn't hear at home all you can hear and learn
here with us. . . ." And on and on.

The list was long. Sometimes I had the impulse to run
out and I remember how, one day, I could not take it any
longer. I dashed out into the garden, food still in hand, unable to decide if I should throw it down. The older boy ran
after me, crying. He asked, desperately:

"Where are you going?"

"I am going home."

"No. Don't. You must stay."

I said, "If you lend me your whistle." He owned a huge
whistle he was wearing on a white cord tied to the buttonhole of his shirt. I longed for it, but my fantasy never
dared go beyond the thought of holding it for just one
whole day.

"Wait here." He raced in and returned to take me by
the hand and bring me back in to confront his mother.

"Is it true you asked him to lend you his whistle?"

I stood speechless, fists clenched, my eyes wet.

"He's all right," his mother decided. "You can give it to
him. He deserves it. Give it to him. He isn't one of those
street tramps who'd grab it and never return it." And she
pierced me with her eyes. "You wouldn't do that, would
you?"

So now I remember. Yet I still do not know why my
former playmate believes I have done so well. Today we
both speak French. And I did return his whistle. I never
owned another.


*August 15*

Twenty-two years ago, on August 15, the sea of time
parted and never have the two halves come together again. I
wandered through the forests and fields of my country

devastated by warfare, at the very time when I myself, bewildered and harassed by personal problems, had just emerged from an adolescence ridden by material hardships and torn between poetry and reality. I have often thought about those times, whose echo lingers to this day.

I am a creature of the Great War, my soul rent by fear and revolt, my thoughts darkened by awareness of death and the uselessness of all endeavor. Between my home-coming, then, and this moment, now, the years have fallen like snow—and this is what is called the fullness of a life-time. The past sways like a figment of the mist. I have waged another kind of war: to make a decent living, for I was determined to escape the poverty of my tormented childhood and adolescence. Today, almost a quarter of a century later, I am back in an even worse situation. Year after year I have anticipated ever new catastrophes. They were postponed, but now the storm is about to break. There are wars, millions of soldiers in training, demented arma-ment races. Any day now the world will become a mad-house, a hell ruled by wild beasts. The love song will be mangled forever.

While I am writing this, my daughters, young girls in full bloom, thirsty for life and trusting it, are dancing next door to music from the same station where, only ten minutes ago, a girl's crisp voice gave precise information about all the horri-ble deaths occurring in two of the world's cardinal points.


*August 28*

Anesthesia: flirtation with eternity.


*September 8*

The imminence of war has stretched nerves to their lim-its. People talk about nothing else. It is a matter of days, if not hours. Everybody awaits Hitler's Nuremberg speech. When you think that life and death depend on the word of a single man—you feel like screaming with helplessness and wild despair. And once again we catch a glimpse of British perfidy in European politics. For, actually, everything depends on England and not on Hitler who, if he unleashes a calamity, will do so only because he is familiar with the psychology of the English. So great is the horror of war that there are people who rejoice at the mere thought that it may be postponed for six months.

## September 14

We can't even begin to guess what went on in European political circles last night! According to this morning's news, only a momentary illusion separates us from the outbreak of war. The cabinets of several countries held meetings with their chiefs of staff. A state of emergency has been declared in Czechoslovakia. At this very minute troops are probably massing on the frontiers of those countries that will be the first target.

I still find it impossible to imagine this horrible possibility. Since this morning I'm in the grips of images from the Great War, which my overstimulated imagination projects onto the black sky of tomorrow's disaster. But people are still joking. Some expect the war to be a universal solution to our problems. Others let themselves sink into moral disintegration. Tomorrow. What will tomorrow bring?

## September 16

The world is going mad. We live only to devour news reports and rumors. They say innumerable Russian planes flew over our country toward Czechoslovakia. Special bulletins begin to sound like those of 1914.

An unexpected bomb: the British prime minister, Chamberlain, flew to Berlin in a last attempt to mollify Hitler. He was expected to stay three to four days, but he returned almost immediately, after barely having had tea with the mass-murderer. A bad sign, according to some, a good one according to others. Chamberlain promised to return to

Germany in a few days. A mystery to which optimists attribute great importance.

Chamberlain claims he is ready to sacrifice himself for the sake of world peace. A pity he didn't do it. He is seventy years old, a ripe enough age to be willing to give up everything. Therefore, he could have put a gun in his pocket and during the hour he spent alone with Hitler he could have, with one bullet, won peace for all Europe. In Austria, great septuagenarians—spiritual, political, and financial giants—committed suicide when the Nazis marched in. They felt they had lived long enough. Chamberlain lost a unique historic opportunity. One gesture could have rendered him immortal—as well as assured him of at least one statue in every country for all time.

## September 21

Tension is at its peak. The whole world awaits breathlessly Czechoslovakia's answer to Hitler's demand for its dismemberment, a proposal subscribed to by the French at England's insistence. No one knows what the talks in Paris and London amounted to. The cabinet in Prague works day and night. It seems the Czechs want to resist to the bitter end even though they have been abandoned by France, their ally and guarantor. The Czech army has been mobilized in its entirety. What will happen before nightfall? Everything has stopped. People do nothing but talk and wait. They voice indignation, they sigh, they make preparations. Panic is increasing. Groceries are swamped for supplies. Children's faces look worried. The thought of disaster is riveted in your brain as you walk in the street. Unwittingly you say goodbye to a host of little things: a stroll, some flowers, a bookstore window. . . . But of course the unfortunate Czechs will give in. They have no choice. The Russians cannot come to their rescue, and they will leave the Germans free to do as they please in the West. And even if they do give in, that is not the end of it. This is the thought that poisons everybody: the war is merely postponed! For how long? Whose turn will it be after the German boot has stepped into Bohemia? How long this day is.

Countries such as Liechtenstein, Monaco, Estonia, etc., however tiny, have nevertheless a head of state, a parliament, an army, in a word—all the paraphernalia a leader uses to make his people happy. It seems that in one such country, the president opened a window and instructed his commander-in-chief, "General, kindly lead the army under a tree, it looks like rain."

## September 24

Fright and despair have suddenly increased. The second meeting between Hitler and Chamberlain took place at Godesberg under bizarre circumstances. In this little village they resided at two separate hotels from which they sent letters to one another. Only at nighttime did they eventually meet for three hours. Nobody is particularly heartened by this news. Hitler must have set new conditions and the English prime minister's phlegm is about to burst. Alarm has increased all over Europe. Dictatorship is the greatest of misfortunes. In any country which has political parties and a parliament, if the head of government proves ineffective in a political maneuver, he is dismissed and replaced by someone else, who can retract. But Hitler cannot retract. There is no way for him and his followers to be replaced by a leader who might eventually make concessions. And this is what could roll the world toward destruction. It seems that centuries go by before we find out the real contents of political talks. Right now, we are in the dark. And in the meantime, we mobilize.

## September 27

In the midst of all these worries, Marguerite's[16] illness struck a blow that has dwarfed everything else. It is just an ordinary pleurisy, it seems, but involving many other problems, of long standing. In the privacy of my thoughts, so often crossed by mad imaginings, I used to be complacent in

16. Marguerite Dorian Taussig, the author's younger daughter.

the belief that the danger of illness for my children was past. But here is a new danger. Marguerite is oversensitive, and this makes it harder for her to bear with a lengthy illness. Her suffering shatters me.

## October 7

Days of sickness, worry, sadness.

The war has been postponed in an atmosphere of regret, disgust, and restlessness. Every human being is a participant in the invisible defeat of a great dream. Because of this, and possibly because of the general feeling that the great confrontation has merely been postponed, peace did not bring the expected relief. In the course of these great European upheavals, the Jews suffer new wounds beside the scarcely healed old ones. In Hungary and Poland—greedily swallowed after Czechoslovakia—the Germans will impose their famous ethics which they have raised to the status of a political doctrine. And perhaps, sooner than we know, it will be our turn. New events will keep coming, that is sure. And people are tired of so much history in a single lifetime.

## October 20

I have forgotten all about this notebook for many days. Marguerite's pleurisy kept me bent over every hour of her suffering. Luckily, so far things are progressing well. Her temperature is back to normal. But all that is left of this child, too thin even before, is a shadow returning slowly and with difficulty to normal life. The big worries are just beginning. And she is so good and understanding.

## October 31

A delicious afternoon, steeped in poetry, daydreaming, and luminous communion with Professor A., during a long walk along the Jianu-Băneasa lake. A sweet autumn, silky and calm. We discuss, clarify, revise, agree. I keep postponing the urge to write about him and his brother, my colleague. A lasting friendship which has developed slowly, touching in its brotherly affection, its depth expressed only through delicate vibrations. What surfaces is the secure knowledge of our harmony, our total understanding of one another, and constant appreciation. There is between us a continuous exchange of enthusiasm and sadness, which halo our conversations like a golden dust of reserve, respect, and shy reticence.

## November 7

The days are spent writing poetry. I hardly read anything, and the few pages I do read are for relaxation. I have been working on a fairly long ballad, an attempt to tell the tragedy of the fifty-six Jews expelled from Austria who, turned away by all neighboring countries, floated on the Danube in a derelict river boat. I felt I suggested, beyond the actual fact, the historic destiny of the Jewish people. Of course, 265 lines should be enough, provided that they convey both the drama and the satirical overtones. I have always been afraid of writing poems in this nonchalant and simplistic manner, of the danger of merely skimming the surface of things, of turning verse into a frothy game, and not reaching the stirring complexity of that poetry which reflects the profound meaning of life.

## November 16

Impossible to keep regularly to these pages, although thoughts and events gather every day. I waste all my spare moments on my "Divertissement" poems. It has been a long time since I last was so caught up in a fever of work. So far I have collected some thirty poems and I feel I could write as many more today. This is indeed a marvelous diversion from the ceaseless stress of everyday routine. Often, when I think of a new piece I'd like to write, two others come to mind, then I am tempted by a third one on which I start work immediately. I am no longer as interested in the quality of the accomplishment as in continued inspiration.

Another episode in the Jewish tragedy. A young Jewish boy thoughtlessly killed a member of the German embassy in Paris.[17] The repercussions in Germany, according to some commentators, have been unprecedented, medieval in their brutality. Actually, this is merely one more step in a series of similar atrocities: mass arrests, destruction of Jewish stores, a fine of forty billion lei extracted from the whole German Jewish community and more laws leading to the murder of the unfortunate German Jews. This absurd and inhuman cruelty has aroused, it seems, unusual indignation throughout the world. Unfortunately—to no avail. The strong and unanimous protests of the press will not alleviate the plight of the half-million Jews doomed to die. A new conference will be convened; there will be many speeches; solutions will be put forward—some even in the honeyed voice of the cowardly Chamberlain—then everything will be forgotten. No outstanding statesman in any country has dared to take the bull by the horns and initiate a practicable program to rescue the Jews.

If the sympathy of European people could be expressed by every concerned person donating a coin as homage for the Jewish gift of the Bible to humanity, the sum collected could change the lot of the Jews and buy them a secure future, somewhere in the world, once and for all.

Not out of this metal-gray day, nor out of thoughts, nor books, but out of the depth of my being arises this refusal to go on, to pick up everyday living with its hollow sound. A sudden drop into deadly weariness, a total paralysis . . .

17. Deeply affected by the sufferings of his parents and other deportees from Germany in a no-man's land on the Polish frontier, Herschel Grynszpan (1921– c.1942) shot Ernst vom Rath of the German embassy in Paris, on November 7, 1938. In revenge, the Nazis subjected the Jews of Germany to the persecutions of *Kristallnacht,* the "Night of Broken Glass" (November 9–10). Grynszpan was killed by the Germans during World War II.

*November 27*

Last evening I accompanied Lelia[18] to a tea where she was introduced to . . . social life. With her new hairdo (touchingly funny, this mixture of a budding lady's impatience and a schoolgirl's preoccupations), the young woman, eager to discover life in the excitement of the dance, was charming and a pleasure to watch. But the gap between dream and reality is hard to fill, particularly at her age. The noise, the stifling heat, the hubbub, the exhaustion, everything leads to disappointment, unacknowledged as yet.

As for me, I had the feeling of a ghostly slip in time, and the bitter taste left by meetings with certain people of one's own generation. With superb stubbornness, we keep picking up our lives. All that matters is immediate magic. There is only one truth: the first time around.

*November 30*

Throughout the crawling misery of days, new events confirm the rumors started last week about burned synagogues and other upheavals in Romania. Within two days: Ştefănescu Goangă, rector of the University of Cluj,[19] was assassinated; bombs exploded in a Timişoara[20] theater during a performance by Jewish actors; finally, Stelescu's assassins, Zelea Codreanu[21] and ten of his followers, were shot down. According to the official communiqué, they had "tried to escape last night while being moved from Rîmnicu Sărăt to Jilava,[22] and were fatally wounded because of the fog."

The uproar in the city must be enormous, judging by the number of telephone calls I received. The worst uncertainty

18. Lelia Dorian Lazarovici, the author's older daughter.
19. Capital of Transylvania.
20. Capital of Banat, province in southwestern Romania.
21. Corneliu Zelea Codreanu (1899–1938), leader of the Iron Guard from 1924–38, also called *Căpitanul,* "the Captain." Stelescu, one of Codreanu's comrades, attempted a split of the party and was savagely punished by the Iron Guard's Death Commandos: he was shot while recuperating in the hospital from an appendectomy, after which his body was hacked to bits with an axe.
22. Main Romanian political prison.

is expressed in the Jews' query, "What next?"—since previous tragic experiences have taught them that they will be the ones to pay, in one way or another, for this kind of event.

## December 5

I gave in and attended yesterday the festivities "to honor the retirement" of my former high-school teacher of the Romanian language, B.K.

The festivities were led by the president of the funeral society Sacra (a coincidence or a direct connection to the notion of retirement?), surrounded by cultural and political exponents, all of whom felt obliged to make speeches and jokes, in that steambath of bodies with wilted souls.

Daring and self-confident, with a high opinion of himself, selfish, lacking charity, and a master schemer, B.K. was never a shining intellect. He produced a naive dissertation "bon pour l'orient"—good enough for the East—in which he discussed some aspects of the Junimea[23] influence on Romanian literature, beating a horse dead thirty-eight years ago, after which he achieved nothing else in his field of specialization, the French and Romanian languages. A poor teacher, out of touch with his students' aspirations, he spent his bitterness and resignation at being a mere high-school teacher in the sport of whipping the palms of children. But he was, it is said, a good administrator. For me, the first contact with him in my first or second year of high school was decisive. Being poor, I could not buy the necessary textbooks, at least not as fast as required. My French teacher, S., used to supply me with his reviewer's copies. Though I had no Romanian language books, I knew the lessons perfectly. Still, one day B.K. gave me a deadline, shouting that those who have no money for books should not attend school. At the next session I arrived with my lessons prepared to perfection, but again without a textbook. He called me to the blackboard and I answered all the questions faultlessly. Yet he swelled my palms with some twenty lashes "so you remember you must bring your text-

23. A Romanian literary group, active during the late nineteenth century.

book to school." I cried with shame and indignation, and I also cried—I remember well—because of the pain, such smarting pain that throughout the morning I was unable to touch anything with my hands. Help came again from the kind S., whose father was as poor as mine and in the same profession. He quarreled with K., and swore at him like a truck driver in the teacher's office (I happened to overhear them), then supplied me immediately with a "teachers' complimentary copy."

Perhaps it was this occurrence which led me a year later, if I am not mistaken, to make a gesture of revolt I have kept secret to this day. There was at the time another believer in whipping: Professor A.S.G., who introduced me to the elements of modern Hebrew. He was an intelligent man, with sound knowledge in his specialty, an author of good textbooks, and master of an elegant Romanian. (I believe he was also a journalist.) But the rod must have satisfied some complex, for he whipped with undisguised pleasure. One spring afternoon I convinced two schoolmates that we must abolish the whipping system. We returned to school that evening. One of my schoolmates kept watch in the school yard and the second in the hall, while I slipped into the office where the switches were kept. I gathered them all, together with the reserve supply, a bunch of a dozen tied with willow twigs. Nobody saw me as I went out into the yard where we threw them down a manhole grating. As we were three conspirators, the work went very fast.

The next day there was an enormous uproar in the school and its main office. G. and K. were desperate. But we were not apprehended. The boys stood their ground despite all the investigations and reprisals. Now I realize that one moment of weakness on the part of any one of us would have changed our lives disastrously. I could have been expelled and, lacking financial means, unable to attend any other school, I would not be a doctor today.


*December 6*

Is this the end of an era or the beginning of an ill-starred, new one, an era of terror and upheavals? Every day—surprises and new events. This rhythm is becoming unbearable. For years now, we have been living history intensely. In fact, the problem is simple, unchanged, if you look at it in a broad perspective. But human beings cannot make the effort of living permanently in the perspective of a broader scheme. They fall prey to details which resonate with the force of major political events. Their nervous systems lose resilience.

## December 12

Happiness and success don't need to be analyzed. No explanations can be found, however hard you may search for them. Everything seems natural. Pain and defeat, on the other hand, require long and repeated analysis.

A diary satisfies, mostly, the need of unhappy people, or rather, of those who are not successful in life. Active conquerors of the material world do not feel tempted by a monologue without a public. It may be an interesting situation at times, but it is almost always a false one. To indulge in polemics with life is not only absurd but futile as well. Life must be forced down to its knees, slapped, and spat upon.

## December 15

The shooting of Codreanu and his Iron Guards has finally led to the implementation of anti-Jewish regulations intended to appease public opinion. The cabinet devoted special time to this issue and today a clear program was outlined, a program which is to settle "pitilessly" the emigration of "unrevised" Jews.[24] Nobody bothered to specify to what country and how they were to emigrate. No Jewish refugees are accepted anywhere.

In view of Romania's special circumstances—the almost

24. The decree of January 28, 1938, had reexamined the rights of the Jews to Romanian citizenship and classified them into "revised Jews" (who retained a few rights) and "unrevised" (with no rights).

traditional impossibility of matching action and decree, the specific economic need for Jewish contributions, the technical impossibility of mass exportation of "undesirable Semites," the socioeconomic class to which the "unrevised" Jews belong, and finally, the complexity of the problem of a worldwide resettlement of Jewish refugees—I don't see how any substantial change can result from the decisions loudly and categorically announced. But my opinion is no more valid than anyone else's. So many illogical things *have* happened that anything seems possible, even in this country.

A rumor confirmed by several sources: the Jewish financier B. has confronted several prominent Jews in the Bucharest community with a plan that would allow the 250,000 "unrevised" Jews (how many are there? why are there no official figures?) to emigrate from Romania over a period of five years. The government would favor such a program if the Jews would contribute the necessary funds: twenty thousand lei per person. Mr. B. indicated that this was not his idea but that it came from higher up. In other words— 5 billion lei would be needed. One billion lei a year to partially delouse Romania of its Jews; and since it would be only a partial solution, it will be a fruitless one, for the remaining "unrevised" Jews would still be seen everywhere and stir up the same resentment. Now we have a new problem: what is better? To be "revised" or "unrevised"?

## December 26

Melancholy and romanticism, predictable patterns, old clichés people tirelessly revive every Christmas. At times you feel stifled by this repetitiveness, sick of your perennial delight in a few snowflakes, a fir twiglet, or a touching Christmas carol. You dream of a new Olympus with a fifth season which would speak to you through more than the five senses, with a new memory, other legends, fresh associations. And yet, looking at it objectively, you realize that Jesus is the greatest event in the history of the world.

1939

*January 2*

The government's expressed stand on the Jewish question has warped the love Jews felt for Romania. "A certain
number of Jews must leave the country" is the political slogan, with its very special meaning, repeated on all festive
occasions. Which Jews are supposed to leave, and how
many, is not specified. For the time being, all Jews share a
feeling of disappointment and fearful anticipation of those
measures applicable to all categories of Jews. Obviously
anyone of good faith knows the meaning of the words *an
unrevised Jew*. Within one family there are "revised" and
"unrevised" Jews, war orphans unable to lay their hands
on documents proving they are the offspring of veterans,
and so many others who, because of a typographical error,
two different numbers in two documents, have been rejected
and classified as foreigners. Of course, it is technically im-

possible to expell one hundred fifty thousand Jews. There are, unfortunately, quite a few Jews who are looking forward to such an emigration, expecting to stay here and fare better. But who can guarantee that domestic policy will not be opportunistic and will not lead to the sacrifice of one hundred fifty thousand or more Jews? Who knows if the proposed policy is in good faith? For the time being, discord is creeping into the relationship of Christians and Jews. It is much like a crumbling marriage, in which the spouses still share the same roof but no longer feel anything for one another. Therein lies the tragedy. For as to emigration, it does not seem very likely. (Right now, the most hospitable countries stubbornly refuse to allow Jews in.) Actually, staying here may be the more horrifying alternative, since economic destruction seems certain. If within the next two years political and economic problems are not solved through the downfall of fascism, a peaceful solution is hardly likely to occur.

There is an anecdote about two flies, one a pessimist, the other an optimist. B., who told it to me, suggested I write a fable. It is tempting. It seems that the two flies fell into a glass of milk. The pessimist flapped its wings a couple of times, gave up the fight, and drowned. The optimist kept flapping its wings with all its might, firmly hoping that it would escape. And indeed, after a while, the milk was churned so vigorously that it turned to butter and the fly was saved. More often than not, when I tell this story, the listener is likely to ask: "What if they had fallen into a glass of water?" Those who ask this kind of question are pessimists who don't deserve an answer.

When addressing the Crown in his capacity as prime minister, the patriarch,[1] too, used the problem of the medical profession to illustrate graphically how disastrous the ethnic situation is. He underscored the fact that there are over forty-six hundred non-Romanian doctors in Romania as against forty-two hundred Gentile Romanian doctors, and viewed this phenomenon as a paradox which must not be allowed to continue. It logically follows that measures

1. See "1938," n. 5.

will be taken immediately to reestablish an ethnic balance, one which is acceptable to nationalist sensibility and which is doubtless necessary for the people's health. Optimists, while accepting as unquestionable the statistical data, nevertheless maintain that, since the past cannot be changed, practical steps can be taken only with regard to the future. Were this the case, what was the point of airing such tragic and paradoxical views within the echo chambers of the royal courtroom? Steps to affect the future have already been taken: there will be no new Jewish doctors, for non-Gentile students are no longer accepted by medical schools. How, then, can the "paradoxical" situation be corrected? Should we wait twenty years for a new crop of four hundred Gentile doctors to even out the statistical balance? And how are we to cope with the urgent, immediate needs?

Things are progressing rather fast. A single party, of a fascist nature, has been constituted. It alone will submit candidates for parliament. A uniform, too, has been designed—neither brown nor black—which only cabinet members are to wear for the time being. The Roman salute has been decreed obligatory. All the rest will follow.

The opinion of the man in the street seems to be: "Well, what do I know? Maybe it is better this way!"

## January 8

Rainer Maria Rilke is not an ethnic poet in the sense in which so many others are. He belongs to a supercountry, the country of everyman's eternal poetry. True, he wrote in German, but there is nothing specifically German about his poetry. Of course he forged a language of his own which lends new power of expression to the inner voice, creates unknown verbal associations, and he has invented new rhythms and rhymes which have radically changed lyric orchestration—but the same phenomenon occurred when he wrote in French.

I have two notebooks with Rilke's French poetry (copied one winter from a rare book) in which the French language is handled in the same manner as the German. That is, he made it pliant and brought out a new musicality to express, unfettered, everything that is poetic in the world: God, love, loneliness, death—themes of universal human interest, disconnected from anything specifically national. Born in Prague, having lived in Switzerland and France, Rilke never found language a problem. Had he lived in England, he surely would have written in an English cut out to suit him. His poetry, like music, is untranslatable. It is interesting to note that the reader can switch from Rilke's German to his French poems without feeling disturbed by the kind of effort usually needed when switching from one language to another. He remains within the same lyric climate, Rilke's climate. Below is one of his French poems, which I do not find in the two notebooks containing over one hundred twenty works:

*Parle, ô source, toi qui n'es pas humaine,*
*chante, ô source, tes pleurs;*
*rien ne console autant de la trop indigène peine*
*qu'une peine d'ailleurs.*
*Est-ce de la peine ton chant? Ô, dis-moi,*
*est-ce quelque état inconnu?*
*En dehors de ce qui nous aide et ce qui nous blesse,*
*peut-on être ému?*

## January 12

I have been obsessed of late by the idea of a satirical novel, or at least a sad one, based on the present life of Romanian Jews. Its tentative title would be: *Wanted: Homeland,* or *For Rent: One Homeland, All Facilities Included.* I have as yet no clear picture of the characters and the plot, just a vague outline. But I think it might make a book of black humor which would pinpoint some interesting moments and original aspects of contemporary Jewish experience in Romania. To insure anonymity, the action might take place in a large Polish town. It would center on the acute problem of Jewish emigration. A wealthy businessman, active as a Jewish leader but without ever giving up his business, feels his economic position threatened and figures that he can make a tidy sum out of the tragic Jewish circumstances. He is the owner of a cemetery, has fearlessly fought many an ideological battle with his competitor, and, as a prominent leader in the Jewish community, picked many a fight for high principles. Since he has important connections in leading political circles, he becomes the founder of a large Society for Semitic Salvation (SSS). He finds a newspaperman-poet who once favored assimilation, then became a Zionist, then converted to Christianity, then reconverted to Judaism, and who is now an unemployed opportunist. With his help, the businessman sets up a newspaper, *The Emigrant,* intended to propagate a new doctrine, spearhead his activity on behalf of Jews, and help organize emigration. Thanks to his connections in leading political circles, the businessman manages to set up a kind of monopoly which can bring in ten thousand lei per head for each Jew he saves. And as he has the right to help in the emigration of some five hundred thousand out of a total of five million Polish and Romanian Jews, he stands to gain a nice profit of five billion, to be eventually deposited in hard currency in a safe bank abroad. This impressive business proposition, backed by the government, draws considerable foreign capital—and the project is greeted with overwhelming applause by Jewish leaders, who bestow upon him the title of "real savior of the Jews." The action plays out against the backdrop of an epic fresco, highlighting the tragic and ridiculous aspects of today's Jewish life at all social levels. The Jewish expeditions head for various parts of the world. But a major center for landing Semites saved by the SSS is the Bushkiland island in the Equatorial Pacific, where the small population of primitive natives has been forced to accept them. The society acquires two large ships. After a couple of shiploads are lost on some unknown exotic shores, one group is unloaded in Bushkiland. Several weeks go by without any news about the fate of these first colonizers, after which a most enthusiastic second group sets out. Upon reaching the coast, they set eyes on a horrifying spectacle and refuse to disembark. What has happened? The natives of Bushkiland, though cannibals, are decent human beings. They don't eat only Jews, but any people. According to the agreement reached with them, ten Jews out of each thousand were to be for their consumption. The president of the SSS, philanthropist and businessman that he is, figured that many more than ten Jews per thousand were sure to die if they remained in their country, so he considered it a good deal to save 99 percent. The second load of colonizers happened to arrive at the very moment when the ritual sacrifice of ten Jews was being performed, by the seashore, under a full moon. The leader of the expedition gets off to investigate and returns to report details of the happenings. The newly arrived Jews refuse to disembark in Bushkiland. The ship leaves. But the condition for emigration imposed by the country of origin and accepted by the SSS was that no emigrant could return home. Scandal. Jewry protests. The press is in an uproar. The president of the society is forced to flee. In the meantime, the ship wanders from sea to sea, unable to find refuge for its cargo. Finally, world war breaks out—and that is a time when all human flesh is nationalized.

I would like to write this book in collaboration with someone. But if this is impossible, I shall start by myself. Will I, actually?

## January 16

It is useless to grasp the world lyrically. To see life through the veil of a song means to perceive it falsely. For the transparence of a song is still a fog, even though it be golden.

## January 30

After listening on and off to Hitler, I got bored with history in the making and throttled his voice with a flick of the radio switch. He doesn't contribute even a drop of sensationalism any longer. Conceit inflated by the stupidity of neighbors and a political program summed up in one word: "Germany."

## February 3

Coincidences which can occur only in ghettoes on the outskirts of town: a young woman pushing twins in a baby carriage, then another woman, her belly in its last month, pulling an infant barely able to toddle, and behind her yet another woman, belly just as pregnant, carrying in her arms, under her shawl, a baby still too small to walk.


## February 9

The Hungarian prime minister, Béla Imrédy, is the protagonist in a minor drama. After devising a racist law, he discovered there were Jews in his family, on both the paternal and the maternal side. People are touched by the personal tragedy of this anti-Semite, and naturally sympathize with his plight. The Jews are amused. But the joke will be short-lived. Soon another anti-Semite will be found, this time an untainted one or one whose impure blood cannot be detected, and he will implement the program devised by the "heroic" Imrédy. (The Hungarian prime minister earned this epithet because he suffered the consequences.) If at least this case, which might happen again and again, would shake a little of the racists' bad faith and blind obstinacy! For it is a glaring proof that the Jews are Europeans, raised on this continent at the same time as the Huns, Teutons, Piedmontese, Slavs, etc., and that their home is here, in Europe. And if things are carried too far, some prominent figure will be beset by the ghosts of his Jewish ancestors who will disprove all contentions to the contrary.

Not joy, but the delightful feeling that joy is possible.

A pure and spontaneous love for the Jews is extremely rare. At best there are honestly rationalistic attitudes of non-anti-Semitism, or anti-anti-Semitism, or indifference. Philo-Semitism is not a permanent stand. Therefore, initially, an effort at objectivity, not love or real understanding.

The death of the patriarch who for many years condoned and propagated hatred and injustice has overshadowed the news of the death in London of another patriarch,

Gaster,[2] exiled to England also by hate and injustice, but of another kind and another era. He passed away, old and blind, but surrounded by esteem, clothed in glory, and, above all, full of love and working intensely for Romania. Interesting to note that Goga himself invited Gaster to Romania years ago, on a speaking tour of many cities, where he appeared as the veritable ambassador of the Romanian language and folklore and received the homage of civil, military, and religious leaders as well as of an enthusiastic public.

## March 11

Special news bulletins announce the takeover by German troops of Slovakia and of the Transcarpathian Ruthenia by Hungarian troops. After a respite of a few months, a new chill freezes the heart of mankind. The spark may well start in this corner of the world, and what we have feared all along may come to pass in March.

## March 17

Although it was barely two months ago that Hitler hysterically roared to the world his sincere intentions—"Wir brauchen keine Tschechen [We don't need any Czechs]"— he has just annexed Czechoslovakia to the Reich. And still Europe has not awakened. Within twenty-four hours, a country with its own culture and democratic institutions has disappeared from the map.

Sooner or later, Germany is likely to suffer the consequences of this action. The Sudetenland was as easy to devour as a soft piece of meat, but Czechoslovakia is a bone that will stick in the throat. For the people will no longer

2. Moses Gaster (1856–1939), a Romanian-born Jewish scholar and humanist of international reputation. He made valuable contributions to the fields of history, philology, Judaism, and Romanian folklore. He also played an active part in the controversy over the Romanian Jews' citizenship at the time of the Congress of Berlin and was expelled from the country. Invited later to return, he refused and made London his home.

listen to the stale slogan: "Our brethren are in chains, we must free them." The repercussions in our country may be more serious than we think. Right now, however, Hungary's appetite cannot be satisfied. Germany cannot penetrate here without first preparing the climate of opinion. Might the knot be tied in Ruthenia? We are in the dark. Rumor has it that two battalions are stationed at our frontier with Hungary. Consultations, unrest, spreading panic.

## March 19

The pressure of political events is growing from day to day and reaches unbearable proportions. So much terror in the world has disrupted life's simplest rhythms. People are again driven crazy by news, by threats, by uncertainty. The West seems to be moving somewhat less sluggishly, and Russia, which so far has stayed in the wings to avoid playing the capitalist game, is willing to act should the English and the French commit themselves to decisive sacrifices. As the hostility created by the annexation of Czechoslovakia increases, the consultations, conferences, and rearmaments have been stepped up.

I read the news dispatches somewhat absentmindedly, because living through massive doses of history in the last years has left me bone-tired. I don't allow myself to be influenced by the scaremongering that predicts war not merely within weeks, but within days. Speculations about foreign policies touch me perhaps much less than they should, but still, sometimes, I am overwhelmed by forebodings of catastrophe.

All great nations have been motivated by capitalist considerations and the resulting thirst for domination that has never shrunk from the worst crimes, so I cannot share their indignation on idealistic or moral grounds. Having quietly digested their own infamous deeds, they self-righteously protest against the infamous deeds of others or even mere intentions to commit them. It's an old game.

Crossroads of history, epoch-making ideological clashes during which adversaries overbid their hand to win human happiness, are interesting only in the perspective of time. In living reality, they destroy those whose individual aspirations are to escape material contingencies and enjoy freedom of thought and the beauty of dreams. Only to the extent to which a generation is able to dream and think can it be said to have lived. But we?

### March 21

Returning home just now at midnight, I found a sheet of paper on which Lelia has jotted down phone and visitors' messages bearing alarming news—an ultimatum, unrest caused by Hungarians at Tîrgu Mureş, mobilization. It is too late to find out anything. It's raining as if it were an autumn night . . . Cold shivers run through me . . . What will tomorrow bring?

### March 22

The feeling of alarm is spreading. Events are typical of the eve of war: break-ins at the savings bank and at shoe stores, rising food prices. It seems that two thousand *setebişti* [3] have left, and their flight has caused bottlenecks. More and more of my friends and acquaintances are leaving. Absolutely nothing is known with certainty. Two army corps are stationed on the Hungarian border, another one has been dispatched toward the Bulgarian frontier. Have there been any incidents, I wonder? There is increasing speculation that Hitler has delivered an economic ultimatum—might it be true? It still seems impossible that Hitler will unleash the war. He is not a military dictator and does not rely on war. His system seems to be based on intrigue, panic, and the nervous exhaustion of those he wants to conquer. So far his successes have been neither diplomatic, nor economic, nor military. They are the strikes of a gangster

3. Employees of the Societatea Tramvaielor din Bucureşti, the Bucharest Trolley Company.

who terrorizes his neighborhood. But what is the use, now, of this profile in political psychology?

## March 25

A sudden return to poetry. I wrote two short pieces and have been working on some of the unfinished poems of last fall. Lyric creativity is an enchanting consolation, no doubt. Diving into the pure depths of inspiration, the surprising flowering of solitude, the magic which transforms each moment into a musical sound—this has often given me the strength to overcome much suffering and injustice. Then life contains a truth which swells inside you like a sky ready to shower songs.

A young journalist wrote, in a conceited tone that brooks no contradiction, a miserable little article summarily dismissing the works of Julien Green[4] and Jules Renard.[5] Yet another proof of the misunderstandings surrounding a writer's notebooks. His hurried jottings made me laugh, but not all his readers will have the same reaction. Most of them still believe that a diary is a form of revenge against people and events. It is the interpretation of the average man, who loves gossip.

A diary is not composed of two parts, as is too often, too simplistically, and too sententiously maintained—part pamphlet, part chronicle. At least, that is not all it contains. A politician, who goes through ups and downs and knows glory and regret, may indeed write such a diary. This is the prototype of a sensational diary in which people expect to find revelations. But what is still called "the inner life" is something quite different. Only those people can grasp the full impact of a diary who know what loneliness is—not just the common feeling of isolation, but the irreductible knowledge that we are alone, no matter what we do or where we are. The significant events as well as the minor

4. Julien Green (1900– ), a French writer of American origin, is the author of novels and several volumes of diaries.
5. Jules Renard (1864–1910), a French novelist and playwright best known for his *Journal*, which was published posthumously by his wife.

occurrences in our life stay with us even after they have been spent in action, while sadness—and I mean sadness, not boredom—inserts them into different scales.

Love, with the effort to grasp its musical meanings, books that go in and out of our life leaving trails of marvelous melancholy, questioning destiny and one's conscience, childhood with its colored streamers rooted in the first sensations, small harvests of the poetry of daily life, and time, time with its symphonic rocking of seasons, and, finally, jottings on the progress of artistic work—this is the chronicle a diary records.

Actually, the published diary is not necessarily identical with the original. We cannot know what Madame Renard left out of her husband's journal. All we know is the selection that was printed. In it we find naked honesty, daring dreams, biting irony unsparing even of the writer, and, above all, ineffable poetry.

### March 27

We are paying today for the events of 1918. At the Versailles peace talks Clemenceau was prompted not so much by lucid understanding as by vengeful anger. Mankind's tragedy: at a crucial moment, its destiny was shaped not by a man but by a tiger.[6]

### April 7

In the midst of rainy, autumnal weather and a continuing military campaign—an unexpected outbreak of spring. Languid heat, paschal light, scenery like an immense, unreal lake in which someone is stirring up the mud of melancholy.

Again, grave events. A while back, when I learned that Hitler was going to take a two-week Easter vacation, I was

6. Georges Clemenceau (1841–1929), the French politician who negotiated the Treaty of Versailles, was nicknamed "the Tiger."

sure that something new was brewing. And so it is. The surprise is that this time it was Italy's move, a preestablished one, no doubt. Newspapers report that the Italians are bombing Durazzo and Valona and that airplane squadrons are attacking Tirana. It seems that a famous French woman reporter predicted this invasion for the month of April, an invasion which is to spread to Salonika. Chamberlain, if he condescends to return from his fishing trip in Scotland, will tell Parliament that his latest manly decision applies both to Germany and Italy, with whom his country has a treaty, and that his foreign minister will ask the Italian government for an explanation, naturally after Albania has been occupied. Mr. C., poet and professor, who happened to be visiting me, rejoiced and explained with his customary rotund optimism the general trend of events: England and France are in perfect agreement with Hitler and Mussolini in their decision to turn against Russia. Each territorial conquest is a link in the logical chain which leads to the breaking up of the structure of today's society. No country can react in any other way. By fall, Japan will collapse, there will be civil war in Europe, everything will lead to the unavoidable outcome. Surprises? They cannot be foreseen. In the meantime, Easter brings new bloodshed and petrifying thoughts.

I have reread the fifty completed pages of my novel to see if I can continue. To be sure, I could, but the question is: should I? Not because of what is to come, but because of what I have written so far. I have analyzed everything with the utmost lucidity; I can be ruthlessly honest with myself. It reads like newspaper reporting, interesting at times, lively and with the power of a documentary, but it does not reach the depth that constitutes art. Ingenuity, even rich, poetic imagination, mastery of form, a superficial skillfulness—these are not the elements of real creation. Intelligence, even if sparkling and studded with novel associations, succeeds in creating only the illusion of artistic reality. I know all this. I know it and I carry it within me. I have the same opinion of other works I have written. Perhaps in some poems I have expressed my feelings better.

But this is not enough; in fact it is nothing. Are there other abilities that would allow me to penetrate the hidden core of things? Or that would convince me that I have done it? Useless questions. The facts are what they are. I have always been conscious of them. That is the truth. There can be solace in elegance of form, in an imagination nourished by verve and tenacity, but that can never jell into what makes a genuine literary and artistic personality. Reflected light, yes—fire bursting from the depths, no.

A feeling first experienced during adolescence and which has recurred quite often: fragmented, torn apart, floundering in a mire of hopelessness, disoriented, you stare at people around you and at yourself in particular, and then all of a sudden, one night, you discover the stars. The vast distance, the solitude, and the quiet are breathtaking. That eternal blinking high up where life has reached the height of a cold, indifferent light, overwhelms you. A cool wave flows over your pain, a silver brake halts your thoughts.

## April 25

The movie *Alexander Nevsky* is interesting because of its unique, graphic vigor. Its director is the Russian Jew Eisenstein. A good opportunity to evaluate the problem of national and racial incompatibilities. To my mind, this Jew has brought to life perfectly the atmosphere prevailing in Orthodox Russia in the thirteenth century. His visionary power has penetrated to its very source, its authentic, historic, psychological, and artistic roots.

## May 12

Any writer wishing to become a contributor to the leftist weekly *Today* must fill out a form, to be eventually forwarded to the Office of National Security, stating his actual name, military status, status as a citizen, status according to the Census Bureau, and so forth. (Authentic!)

*May 31*

It is Lelia's last day in high school. She spent yesterday evening in my study, while I worked. She was studying for a final exam. I took a fresh look at her as she sat in a pool of light. Her features are showing definite signs of growing up. Almost all childish traits are gone. On her attractive face the thoughts brought on by life seek expression. She knows nothing yet of her fate on her chosen road, but forebodings of the difficulties ahead are beginning to shape her. She is adamant in her decision to study medicine. Who has the right to stop her? There are no options any longer. I keep thinking of the years of exhausting labor this profession devours and of the disappointments and difficulties she will meet with in this career, and in between I see her tired youth, its colors growing drab and its sap full of sadness. . . .

*August 22*

Beginning of the grand intermezzo between summer and fall, a time to draw the balance sheet of sorrow.

*August 24*

Once more mankind has stopped breathing. The most unlikely of all probabilities: a nonaggression treaty between Germany and the Soviet Union. An electric shock of surprise and madness has coursed through the world. A moment of disbelief, a morning of bewilderment, one restless night—and here we are, the deed is done. The hope that war can be averted fades with each passing second. This time, most people believe, the collapse is but a matter of days. And yet, perhaps, the possibility of war has receded. No one understands as yet the Soviet Union's action. Has it turned its back on European problems to settle its affairs in the Far East so that, after Asia becomes Communist, it can concentrate on a Communist takeover of Europe? It is certain that Germany has escaped the trap into which it had fallen. It is possible that a *deus ex machina* (Mussolini or the Pope) will appear at the last moment as a friend of Poland to mediate the Danzig dispute, after Germany will have increased her demands precisely in order to facilitate an agreement. In this case, should Poland have to give in on this point only, England would not have to intervene. Can Hitler afford to go to war? After all, for him rearmament is only a political weapon and not a military objective. He will, as he has declared, take Danzig without a war. Perhaps at this very moment he has already annexed it. But of course intransigence must be exercised to the limit, with its tough speeches, mobilization, and other bureaucratic moves. At any rate, this is the end to chaos. The mad game is now centered on a point. The beast grins with satisfaction and is getting ready for new bounty.

## August 31

A whole week of torture, with deadly downs and sparks of hope flying, during which all Europe has been mobilized while embassies went on holding secret talks in between calls and letters. History is being lived at fever pitch. Nerves are ready to snap, and disgust with life has reached inhuman levels. Nothing is known as yet. We are waiting, day and night, ceaselessly. People say that Hitler's decline has begun, that he is no longer the master of negotiations. All sorts of rumors dreamt up by optimistic fantasies keep feeding this joy over Hitler's presumed loss of power. People expect Italy to defect from the Axis and, eventually, Stalin, whose actions resulted from calm and wise deliberation, to support the Allies.

The standstill of the last couple of days is perhaps due to efforts at overcoming the impasse without bloodshed. At any rate, Hitler no longer roars, issues warnings, or sets up deadlines of days or hours, but sits down with his friends and writes letters and reports. Armies, however, are on the alert everywhere. The machinery of war is ready, and this knowledge keeps our terror alive. Over the gnashing at the frontiers, over the strain of universal madness, a single gesture of last and sublime consolation: the baton of Toscanini in Lucerne, at this very minute, sending skyward the offering of music.

## September 1

War has broken out after all. During the night Hitler issued orders to attack Poland. In the morning he convened his so-called parliament and after a few demagogic barks annexed Danzig, declared himself a soldier, and appointed a successor in the event of his death. This is the détente we waited for so long! Emotion and indignation are intense; death is drawing closer. People got easily used to the crimes in China—it all happened somewhere there, somewhere far away. . . .

Italy remains neutral following a violent popular reaction against war. Mussolini has been defeated, but, curiously, this breaking up of the Axis did not bring forth the response it deserved, at least not one comparable to the reaction to the nonaggression pact between Germany and Soviet Russia. England and France are mobilized and will be forced to take action. Where and how is hard to tell as yet. In Poland people begin to die, and children are among the first victims. It is hard to believe. It still seems an attempt at intimidation, propaganda, pressure. And yet, there are official communiqués. In one night, the last night of August, with a full moon high in the enchanted sky, the earth and its last flowers asleep, a few brutes have plunged the world into darkness, blood, and pus. Where is the protest of those who have lived once before this shame? Will it be like this to the end of time? I cannot believe it.

## September 3

The last hope is dead. The deadlines for Germany's reply, set by England for 11:00 A.M. and by France for 5:00 P.M., came and went without any change of attitude. France and England are "in a state of war with Germany." Still, all the terms they use to qualify Germany's behavior are cautious and sparing. They don't speak of "lies," but of "untruthfulness," not of "savagery," but of "disregard for civilized behavior." And they keep repeating that they "are determined to . . ." or that they "will be forced to adhere to the agreement," etc. Hitler attacked immediately. The English, after almost twelve hours, have done nothing yet. The world expects an air attack by Germany, at the very least. The English, it seems, are waiting for the first German plane to appear in the sky over London before retaliating. There is probably everywhere great hesitation at the prospect of slaughter. No doubt the same is true for Germany. It is impossible that the people, though lacking political understanding, should finally accept a struggle with the English and the French, who will certainly find ways to explain to German civilians and soldiers that the fight is not with them but only with their regime. Even the "memorable session in the Reichstag" (as they themselves called it) gave me the impression of a complete lack of following among the people. The loudspeakers howled, the representatives applauded, but everything seemed unreal, out of touch with the terrified and mute multitude. The Italians managed to spill out into the streets shouting "Down with war!" only because of the distance between Mussolini and the crown, but the Germans lack this advantage. They will surely find another one, soon.


## September 4

New stylistic devices unfamiliar to us, veterans of the last great war: "The German air force controls the Polish skies." A new concept, this "national sky."

People seem to be drained of their personalities. They all speak in the same way about the same things, ask the same questions, ruminate on the same problems. A haven must be found not only for bodily safety but for the soul's salvation. It may be healthy for me to start writing some autobiographical notes. Childhood memories, memories of adolescence, faces from the past and peaceful old places may build a shelter for the spirit, for the soul can subsist only on the crest of an ebbing wave.

Being a neutral country today is a far cry from what it was during the last war, when wheat turned to gold and the joy of living rose to an almost shameless paroxysm. Today, most neutrals are armed. Although untroubled to all appearances, they are undermined by permanent pressures and dangers. Propaganda is at work a hundredfold harder in neutral countries. The daily, poisonous broadcasts, suffocating legislation, restrictions, the unchecked stream of rumors, the feeling of progressive economic asphyxiation—all this creates the illusion of intense participation in the boundless madness of war.

## September 19

It was rumored that when the German armies would come close to the Romanian border there would be an uprising among the Germans of Bukovina. It seems there was some truth to this rumor. The Russians' quick takeover of Galicia, however, upset the apple cart. Moreover, Romania took military steps in Bukovina a few days ago. This made it possible for Polish refugees to remain there unmolested. Their only complaint is that they must reside in an area overpopulated by Jews. However hard to believe, it is a confirmed fact: even in their homeless wanderings they are benighted by anti-Semitism. They reject any hospitality or help offered by "kikes."

Our prime minister, Armand Călinescu, was shot by a band of Iron Guards. The news, interrupting a Strauss waltz, has just been broadcast, probably by an Iron Guard who forced his way into the radio station. Telephones are ringing. The streets are teeming. It is a moment of panic. A German plot? Merely a belated act of revenge? Endless rumors and fear. Who will be his successor? No one knows, nothing is known. There is nothing but music on the radio.

## September 24

Some things are clearer. For the moment, it seems, we have escaped the war which, just yesterday, appeared imminent. The occupation by Soviet troops of the Polish areas along Romanian borders has thwarted the uprising of the Bukovina Germans. They had planned to riot when the German army drew near. According to the reports of Bukovinans, some very serious incidents occurred. Arrests and executions. Many see a connection between Călinescu's assassination and the Bukovina plot. It is believed that his assassins took over a radio station and broadcast the news of his assassination as a signal for uprisings in designated locations. It seems that the leader of the group had just returned from Germany and that large, unaccounted-for sums of money were found in the possession of his followers. In the last few days, in this atmosphere of stunned disbelief, there seem to have been innumerable executions besides the ones we know about. Throughout the country, the corpses of Iron Guards were displayed in city squares. With unrestrained curiosity, the shaken population of Bucharest filed by the seven corpses exhibited on the spot where the prime minister had been assassinated. An eleven-year-old girl, on whom I had performed surgery that very day, made her father promise to reward her not with an ice cream but with a trip to see the corpses spread out on the pavement.

The pressure is slacking somewhat. Everybody watches the Soviet Union, whose foreign policy promises to be ruthless. People have finally grasped that a very serious change is taking place in Europe. Even the bewildered and the skeptics are at last making an effort to understand the situation. Some go so far as to accuse Stalin of straying away from . . . Stalinism. And yet, no one knows anything for sure.

## September 29

A woman friend who understands Polish overheard a Polish doctor, sitting at a table next to hers in a café, console his refugee friends: "So we lost our country, but at least we got rid of the kikes!"

## October 8

I have submitted to the Cartea Românească publishing house Dr. Mihail Prunk's[7] manuscript entitled *A Complete Manual of Sexual Education.* It is a selection of published papers which I have revised, summed up, and edited. I wonder how the book will fare in this new version. Georgescu-Delafras did not reprint it because of the German-sounding name "Prunk," which was precisely the book's main appeal for Cartea Românească. That's how it goes . . .

## October 12

The first issue of *Jurnalul* has come out, with Teodorescu-Branişte as its editor-in-chief and with the former staff of *Adevărul.* Great excitement among journalists whose pens had been rusting for the last two years. I saw some of them: eyes aglow, believing that the new paper will be a smash hit. Branişte asked me to become a permanent contributor to the medical column. Am I going to take Dr. Panus Pantor[8] out of the mothballs in which he has lain hibernating for almost a year? "Medicine and Life" . . . It doesn't overly excite me. I always imagined a different kind of future for my journalism. An attempt to keep a dream alive. I don't like medical journalism very much. But perhaps it is only a new beginning. How many times have I begun anew?

7. One of the pseudonyms under which the author published articles on social medicine.
8. Another pen name the author used for his work in medical journalism. The name was taken from a character in one of his books for children (*The Cricket's Memoirs,* 1937).

*October 19*

I spoke briefly to I.S., university professor and reader for Cartea Românească, about my manuscript, which was accepted for publication. He told me blithely: "You can discard the chapter on Freudian psychology. Freud is dead and so is his psychology."

*October 25*

Strong people alone know how to organize their suffering so as to bear only the most necessary pain.

*October 30*

Lelia was admitted to medical school. Apparently this was an extraordinary feat, since out of 255 candidates admitted, only 7 Jews made it. There were 620 applicants, of whom 250 were Jewish—a very large number, but understandably so, the frontiers being closed, study abroad impossible, and other fields of higher education restricted. Thus, less than 3 percent got into medical school. (One more achievement for nationalist protectionist policy.)

Lelia is very glad, but she seems bewildered, wavering between satisfaction and bitterness. As to myself, I don't know whether I ought to be glad. The disappointments the medical profession brought me make me hesitant and sad as I look at the beginning of this career that still appears to her so sunny and full of boundless hope. Still, I am refreshed by the confidence and persistence with which her youth dashes onto this road, where success is not always commensurate with one's preparation, good will, and dedication. But she is wise, hard-working, and modest. With her joyful nature, her capacity for work and her willingness to adapt, her clear, natural intelligence, and her kindness, perhaps she will succeed. I hope the good Mrs. K. was right when she told me that luck often skips one generation. Because it is indeed a tragedy for someone who is unlucky to become a doctor. But social and economic conditions will also play a decisive part in Lelia's life. Who can foresee what will happen in eight years? Perhaps by then medicine will be socialized and its assured practice will endow it with value for the community.

Now when I embrace my frail, blonde daughter, whose eyes are smiling at the prospect of her first flight, concern for her future is foremost in my mind.

## November 1

A slow walk under the sun's lingering tenderness. The quay is glassy, purple-gray, full of noontime traffic.

If one could only shake thoughts off, discard them at a street corner and walk away, free of their burden which obliterates the sun. Still, meeting so many other troubled people who pass you by silently, mutiny in their eyes, holding back unuttered curses behind clenched teeth, lightens your own burden. Because of the huge amounts of human suffering it carries, the street dilutes individual pain.

Some workers dressed in rags unload enormous crates. One of them stops and rolls a cigarette: "Take a break, Ionică, let me light up." "The boss will be mad if we take too long." "Don't be silly! The longer we take, the more expensive the crates. Why should he get mad?"

A tiny woman, almost hidden by a black woolen shawl, a rolled-up paper held tightly in her hand, asks where the town hall is. Probably she has an application for a free funeral or for a problematic ration of wood.

Strung out along the sidewalk, waiting to cross the street, several girls with wilted cheeks and wide eyes, in thin clothes and scuffed shoes. They must be going home, hungry, after school.

And the street stretches out ahead, gathers behind you, scatters, then winds up again around your heart, throbbing with your own worries, now softened by the sun and the suffering all around you. You stop for a moment, at a loss whether to go on or go back. But at the end of each street, a new street opens.

## November 7

I managed to conclude a contract with Georgescu-Delafras for a layman's guide to medicine: *Medicine for Everybody*. I am already disgusted by the idea of writing this sort of dictionary. G.-D. is now a prominent man: secretary of the National Resurrection Front[9] in the Bucharest Department of Trade and Industry. He had admitted that, although interested, he was afraid, because of his position, to publish a work by a Jew. Publication would be possible only if the book were signed jointly with a Gentile doctor. My old, devoted friend Marius Popescu was kind enough to lend me, in a most unassuming manner, his authentically Romanian name. And this is why, shielded by his foreskin, I can come out with a book published by that great conquistador. In his new capacity, G.-D. now puts into practice all the nationalist ideas he expounded years ago, when he was a *valachist*[10] and wrote for a weekly with the zeal of a great reformer.

While I was signing the contract, he declared in pompous tones:

"I am about to publish one of my works in which I simply destroy you members of the minority."

"Dear me! And what do you say in it?" I asked, smiling.

"I tell about the policy of the Front and what we're about to implement."

And my old friend, who is a political conqueror as well, explained to me the plans for "ethnic proportionality." Then he added, benevolently:

"I am a humanitarian. All middle-aged and old Jews will be allowed to keep their jobs. But no young ones will be hired for any work. We are done with them forever!"

"And what will all these Romanian *citizens* do?" I asked.

9. Frontul Renașterii Naționale (FRN), a single political body replacing all Romanian political parties. It was created in 1939 by the king.

10. That is, pro-Wallachia.

"Since you won't let them work, according to your proportional rules that have no mathematical basis, are all of them to starve?"

"They can do whatever they please. I don't care. Let them go wherever they want. They won't be let in here. No trade permits will be issued to new Jews. As for clerks, only Gentile trade-school graduates will be employed. The others must get out!"

"Where to? Other countries, too, are closing their doors to foreigners, to take care of their own citizens, but of *all* their citizens!"

"They'll find a place somewhere!"

"As for myself," I concluded, "I hope you will rise to an even higher position, so you can negotiate with the British and talk them into opening wider the gates of Palestine."

It was in this atmosphere, with the self-satisfied, anti-Semitic economist spouting his incoherent and inconsistent views, drunk on "humanitarian" visions, that I had to sign the contract. I had to. I fought down the temptation to throw back at him the fistful of money he had doled out to me (thanks to the warranty of the foreskin). And now, back at home, remembering all this, I despise myself.

*November 12*

Regret, the scar of desire.

*November 16*

It is not possible that the hands of the pianist Wilhelm Kempff should belong to a Hitlerite. They brought out of the piano keys the sound of genius long before Hitler brutally pushed Germany into infernal darkness. What is perpetrated by the criminal hands of those hypnotized by Hitler can have no connection with the angelic light of Mozart's soul, resurrected whenever Kempff plays him. Kempff's political affiliation is a discordant note or is due to an artist's naiveté. I am sure that if he and Vladimir Horowitz met, they would embrace each other and clasp hands in celebration of a shared dream.

## November 20

Today I typed for twelve hours straight, except for brief interruptions for meals.

Old objects, like old monasteries, give you the feeling of the permanence of the past, of material reality, while the modern style, with its simple lines, utilitarian and efficient, seems ephemeral, as if existing in an atmosphere without depth. The old lawyer's waiting room suggests the layering of time, none of its echoes lost.

The large, tall mirrors in their broad bronze frames seem to have retained all the old reflections. Grandfather clocks in rich casings of ebony and mother-of-pearl, tall vases with garlanded columns, lamps covered with sculptures, Louis XVI armchairs with moldings and ornaments in relief, paintings in large gilded frames, metal candlesticks with hand-painted porcelain inlay, all covered by a dust of peace and daydreams and lulled by the tick-tock of the clocks and the silent reflections of crystals. The big carpets, heavy with the footsteps buried in their woof, the long, pleated drapes held up by silk cords with enormous tassels, absorb the moments falling like an invisible rain. I am waiting for the old Flügel piano, covered by a brocade cloth, to start playing a minuet while the people step down from the enormous picture frames and sit in the armchairs covered in silk gnawed by the teeth of years. I sit still in a deep armchair and inhale time like a live, unaltered aroma, my mind furrowed by fragments of poems and prayers.

## December 8

A strange urge to revisit the distant past, due perhaps to the cruel nature of the present era, which seems to create the need for a refuge: I looked over my translations of Heine. It may also be a reaction of protest against the injustice done him in his country, the second time around.

I translated his poems when I finished high school, and then forgot them, intentionally, because I was dissatisfied with my work. Of some I even grew ashamed, after they were published. My having been an adolescent is a sufficient excuse for certain imperfections, the lack of style, the lack of a fresh, forceful, poetic language. In time, I became convinced that Heine's simplistic sentimentalism could not appeal to a mature poet shaped by a different tradition. Furthermore, he was crushed by Rilke's overwhelming lyrical universe, whose appearance in German poetry is like a revolution, a change similar to the geological ones the earth underwent in its formative era. A return to Heine would entail a concise presentation of his work in our language through an interesting selection of poems. All the more so because there is no such anthology to date and the random translations which have appeared in the works of a few Romanian poets are far from perfect and rarely faithful to the text. I think *Biblioteca pentru toți*[11] ought to have in its collection a translation of the best of Heine. Whatever the motives that prompted me to glance at his work, I ended up by becoming more engrossed in it than I expected. True, Heine verges upon sentimentality. The excessive use of diminutives (which he culled from folklore but rendered annoyingly simplistic), the superficiality and cheapness of his moods, and his obsession with sufferings so petty as to be ridiculous, can be laughable and even irritating. But if you go beyond these things, you discover an authentic lyricism, so masterfully crafted that it survives the test of time. The very spirit of folk poetry emerges clearly in some of his stanzas, like a melody played on an old lute. Intimacy and humor, nonexistent in the somber, formal poetry of his time, still maintain their flavor of novelty. And then, his nonconformism, his political lucidity, the daring to be totally sincere, run through everything he wrote. Perhaps his fame after so many decades is explained more by his origi-

---

11. "Everyman's Library," a popular paperback series publishing the best of world literature in Romanian translation.

nality, suffering, and personal revolt rather than by the value of his creations. Still, all these elements are echoed in his poems, written in a fever of sincerity lending them throbbing life, passionate color, and, at times, immortal artistry. I think I will become, at my age, a translator of Heine.

## December 24

Days and nights, but especially nights, are all spent on this feverish digging into Heine's world. I am not so much interested in the poet as in the poetic process, the struggle to find the closest approximation of his meaning, while knowing that the better the equivalent in another language, the more remote it is from the original. There are, to be sure, no major discoveries in his lyrical work. But a valuable melody emerges quite frequently, especially when irony enriches a mood, an inner experience, or a stylistic device not particularly complex in themselves.

Many difficult problems face the translator. As a youth, my basic aim was to be faithful to the text, even at the expense of form. Today, rendering the precise meaning is no longer an impediment to style. I have translated a poem, and not a minor one, in three different styles. The game itself is interesting, but it will soon be over. I have translated several new poems, and now there is a little left to polish, although the possibility that I will make new discoveries, as has happened several times before, is always there.

This Christmas season will be entirely devoted to poetry. It promises to be quiet and full of gentle sadness brought on by the same recollections. Of course, there is downy snow, with its halo of a mysterious legend, with carols and the thrills of preparation, but over all this, images of childhood's wasteland: an unreal Christmas tree in the home of a wealthy neighbor, huge snowdrifts by the locked door, the cold in our room, torn shoes, the disillusion of eating the same boiled beans for three days in a row, while somewhere, far away, in the huge core of the city, the temptation of the fairyland in shop windows with their colorful toys and warm boots spread out on mothflake snow.

*December 27*

The holiday has gone by like an island of oblivion. I am not reading anything, not even a newspaper, as I ought to. I have discovered a few of those songs Heine called *Schöpfungslieder,* have translated them with pleasure and, I think, fairly well. But I am beginning to sober up. A wave of futility, of meaninglessness, of pointlessness—not only in poetry but in life itself. As if I were waking up from anesthesia. Fatigue? Without a doubt, poetic labor inspires the highest, the most interesting, and the most complete feelings, but only on condition that you go on sleepwalking. But life lets out a piercing scream and wakes you up. Your soaring is halted. Tomorrow daily life begins. And between Christmas and New Year, daily life sometimes puts in dramatic appearances.

These are the tired gasps of a year filled with defeats and crucifixions.

*December 31*

End of year, almost all hearts stand still. Not so much because of what was as because of the fearful days ahead, of the new year we have come to consider a crucial one. All sorrow is justifiable on this night of snow as we hang over a chasm of hopelessness, sick of life and people. The seasonal feelings, cheap and trite, suddenly gain dramatic depth. For the first time, truly, the worn-out question "What next?" reverberates with real meaning. What next? What next?

**1940**

## January 4

I don't know why I left one page blank. We go on living with yesterday's news, but there's one difference: some of our calculations of probabilities have changed. Strange how quickly so-called public opinion can shift. Last spring, anti-German propaganda created a feeling of anticipation uniting all social classes. I overheard peasant-soldiers say: "I won't go back home before I've killed me at least three Germans!" Now anti-Russian propaganda grows stronger every day, instigated by the English and the French. Will they push us into a war against Soviet Russia? No one is inclined to look at things impartially any longer. We ought to stay neutral to the end.

There are many thresholds to suicide. That is why so few among those who want to kill themselves actually die. To succeed, one must reach the last threshold.

## January 5

The translations from Heine are in finished form and clean copy. I have entitled them "Songs and Romances." This time, I think they are good. At any rate, I am no longer ashamed of them. The effort put into this new Heine adds up to about one hundred nights, if I include day and evening hours. I make this tally in order to find a material equivalence between work and fee, assuming I can get the volume published. I submitted it to Fundaţiile Regale[1] where Professor Rosetti, elegant and affable, rejected it for the time being, claiming he had to cut by half his commitments to writers. And he told me to try again next year. So it will have to be published by *Biblioteca pentru toţi.*[2] O., still its director, might be persuaded to accept it in the end. Heine's bad luck: to be Jewish, translated by a Jew, and published by a Jew as well! I remember how O., that ridiculous character, was looking for a "rightist" (!) to supply Romanian translations for the eightieth anniversary of Heine's death. And now, alas, what a downfall!

To stay in training, I have picked up Eliezer Steinbarg[3] again. I think it may be possible to publish a monograph, although his widow is most difficult. Perhaps the publisher will persuade her. The anthology, which I have completed, together with an introduction, can make a fairly interesting little volume, representative of Steinbarg's work. I will add the final touches to a few more pieces on which I have started working. Having reread them I feel I can make good progress. So I still have my refuge. The lyrical spell, its circle broken for a moment, is intact once more.

---

1. Fundaţiile Regale pentru Literatură şi Artă, the Royal Foundation for Literature and the Arts, a cultural institution endowed by the king. It had its own magazine and publishing house.

2. See "1939," n. 11.

3. Eliezer Steinbarg (1880–1932), a Romanian-born Jewish poet who wrote in Yiddish and Hebrew, best known for his collection of fables.

*January 19*

Human kindness can seep through life's smallest chinks. Last night I didn't feel well, an upset stomach had been bothering me for several days. The girls and Paula[4] had gone to bed. Cook had finished her work long ago. The maid, a gawky, thirteen-year-old girl, loose-tongued and energetic, was the only one awake. Knowing I had eaten nothing, she came into my study and told me she wasn't going to bed, she was staying up in case I needed something. A few minutes later she came in again: "Be sure to ring when you want me to go to sleep." She was very proud that, of all the people in the household, she was the only one left to serve me. She owned the whole place. The kitchen with its hot stove was entirely hers. When I asked for boiling water to sterilize some instruments, she went to work with the intense zeal of someone entrusted with the highest mission. Then she served tea with particular care, like a religious ritual, revealing her total devotion. "Why don't you take something else?" she asked, with a pained face. "You have eaten nothing for so many days!" Her voice, usually harsh and gruff, had maternal modulations. When, later, she brought a cup of cocoa to my bed table and I thanked her, her face suddenly blossomed into a wide smile, and she left happy.

*January 23*

The other day I was reading on the streetcar when two men, seated next to me, apparently headed toward some administrative office, started talking—in lowered tones, presumably not to disturb me:

"They're kikes, I gather, aren't they?"

"Yes, they're kikes. Know what I worked out? Ten grand: five for you, five for me."

"And these people pay good money for such a small favor?"

"They pay for anything. That's our luck, that we can

4. Paula Fränkel Dorian, the author's wife.

still cash in on them. Otherwise, what would we do?"
"That's fine, old man, that's fine. Let's go, then."

At my lecture on "The Fable," in a dreadful hall in Văcăreşti[5]—a lively, dynamic public, passionately interested
in the topic and well informed: writers, reporters, actors,
and many students, wonderfully alert and thirsty for information. One ought to address them more often, rather than
the bourgeois circles of dull people who meet you with
vapid eyes and a wilted soul.

I have finished, completely, the volume of translations
from Heine. It will be published by *Biblioteca pentru toţi*. I
have received for it the fantastic sum of 8,000 lei, without
any rights to royalties, and that is all, forever, no matter
how many reprints or new editions may be published. I still
have a month to reread and revise. It seems to me I will
always find something more to correct.

## January 24

Dear R.,
I am terribly sorry for the pain you felt today because
of me, or rather, because of both of us. I hasten to offer you
consolation, which I can do not only because you are very
dear to me but mainly because I do not suffer, or, to be
more precise, I *no longer* suffer.
You came out of the world war with impaired hearing: a
bombshell burst your eardrums. Since then you have been
sick, and you haven't even asked the state for your due veteran's compensation. Over the twelve years since I met you
and grew fond of you, you have been under my medical
care. In a manner of speaking. Every once in a while I look
into your ears and see the same thing. And when you feel
worse, I soothe you. Unfortunately, our medical science is
helpless before the misfortune brought upon you by the
scourge of war.
Now you have been called up for military duty and were

5. Main street in the Bucharest Jewish quarter.

sent to a military doctor. You showed him a medical certificate I issued and my medical report. The doctor immediately asked you whether you were a Romanian. Why did you jump as if scalded? The fellow was right, as he clearly explained: "If you are Romanian, why did you go to that kike Dorian?"

You got up, you wanted to leave, but you had to stay and you were mortified. Why? For such a small matter? My poor, dear R., what's the use of having your hearing so seriously impaired if you were able to hear those very words uttered by Captain Georgescu, M.D.? I myself have become literally deaf to such remarks. Why did you get mad at my young colleague and hasten to assure him of my competence, of which even he himself may be fully aware?

Poor fellow! There may be quite a few things he does not know. For instance: that Europe, drunk on the industrial revolution of the last century, supplied machines and technology to Asia, which became industrialized by using the labor of poor and undemanding workers; it produced cheap goods and threatened the economy of the Old World, where labor is expensive and workers have needs that cannot be denied. How is he supposed to know that the Jews had nothing to do with this, or with any other equally radical and historically unavoidable process, whatever the explanation for it, or at least, that the role they played is neither smaller nor greater than that of any other people alive today? He was given an explanation based on brutality, which is only one of the means of temporizing prevalent today, and this explanation suits him because it requires no effort of thought on his part. Poor Georgescu (whose father perhaps was called Georgief or Georgevici—these farcical situations are quite common), having reached the height of knowledge, so that, by looking into an ear he can diagnose a perforation, believes that such farsightedness is an act of "national dynamism": a hole in a Romanian eardrum must be examined only by a retina which is pure Romanian. It is a patriotic gesture—small, parochial, limited if you will, but then, supreme sacrifices are not everybody's lot—still, a patriotic gesture nevertheless, since it aims at integrating into the national patrimony all the eardrums perforated by German shells. What am I to think if you rebel against it?

Don't be upset, dear R., you have heard the insult only once—I feel it all the time. Lack of humanity aroused your indignation. But that, too, is useless and naive and almost leads me to believe that you are afflicted by moral deafness as well. Brutality has been raised to the status of governmental doctrine, it has created a new morality of so-called collective heroism—and you want to stop its progress with a romantic view? What a kind man, what an old-fashioned angel you are!

Elementary duties? Today, neither individuals nor organized bodies can be bothered with such trifles. Cruelty—whether prompted by selfishness or under the cover of creativity and dynamism—is, when all is said and done, nothing but cruelty. For instance, dear R., at Sulina there are barges with some two thousand Jews from Czechoslovakia and Germany (countries converted to Georgescu's way of thinking a while back) waiting to go to Palestine. Shipowners are asking an additional twelve million to take them there. But as the poor fugitives (enough to make up a village) have no more money left, they are rotting in a box called a barge, in temperatures of below thirty degrees, without food, without beds, without fire. (You probably remember from your days on patrol what a barge is like.) They are so crowded that, at night, they take turns sleeping. Many have been killed by the cold. Do you think any state has provisions to extend the most elementary humanitarian assistance to them? Well, our country displayed its elementary humane duty by doing nothing—because those involved are Jews. What would you say if some two thousand Romanians left America to come here, ran aground in some frozen port, and were left to die there of hunger and cold? Why, then, do you expect Georgescu to show elementary humaneness to a Jewish colleague who, after all, isn't even dying of hunger and cold?

Don't be upset, dear R. So long as there are people like you, I can go on living. What really pains me is that your eardrums, whether you keep them safe in the national patrimony or whether you entrust them to a kike's retina, can no longer be healed: my dearest hope, for a long time, has been that you may be cured so you can hear some of the lovely things God left on this earth, the earth men have poisoned and destroyed.

## February 5

Days of an eerie sensation, like floating above the ground. My whole life, it seems, belongs to someone else. I write as if in a dream. I am not absent from reality, but remote, and this tints all levels of existence with a strange hue of unreality. Life is here, close by, but there is a thin layer of blue mist between us. Present conversations seem like memories of past ones. Thoughts have no footing but hang in the air, as if coming from afar, echoes from some other existence. Everything is . . . suspense, a strange feeling that something is about to happen.

## February 11

Forty-nine: the age when you get engaged to old age.

## March 9

Last night at my house the performer L. recited several Yiddish poems before a group of friends and other interested people. I find no progress in his art over the three years since I first heard him. True, he has great sensibility, a warm, musical, sinuous voice, well matched by a gaunt face with hollows and prominent bones, as if molded by an inner fire, a face that serves him well to mime his readings. But there is no growth, no freshness, no spontaneity to add new dimensions to the recited poems. His few interesting innovations have become ossified through repetition and use in almost all the pieces. But then, the very genre of poetry recitation has inherent limitations, it becomes sterile and loses depth, particularly if heard repeatedly. One feels the lack of a great director's inspiration—as if there were directors to build up this kind of talent. Anyway, the mixture of song and recitation, most suggestive at times, eventually deadens emotional response. The ingenuity, the surprising freshness, turn to triteness. Still, it is hard to describe the joy caused by L.'s vibrant rendition of selections from a literature so rich in inspiration, so forcefully expressed, although, unfortunately, in an unmelodious language, because directly influenced by German and with too many linguistic borrowings from it. Yiddish is wonderfully suited to storytelling (hence Sholom Aleichem's succulence), but less so to prose in general and very little to theoretical discussion. In poetry, high artistic excellence has been achieved despite the limitations of the language. In everything I have read, the German language is massively, obsessively, pervasively present. The great controversy that splits Judaism between Yiddish and Hebrew has, no doubt, a political undertow. It is nonetheless true that, from an artistic point of view, the advantage lies entirely with the language of the Bible, spoken today as a living language by Palestinian Jews, for it is original, ancient, and it has personality. Of course Yiddish, like any linguistic phenomenon, was not created by a single person's whim, or fortuitously, but developed as a natural process out of the inner needs and the external circumstances of a community whose cultural aspirations could not be stifled by any means. But awareness of this fact cannot affect a negative attitude toward its lack of musicality and toward a syntax which some people may find heavy. So far as I am concerned, I can overcome any distaste and enjoy the tremendous artistic accomplishments in this language. I am beginning to consider seriously my old plan to put together an anthology of Yiddish poets. It mostly depends on the possibility of gathering materials.

## March 28

A long time since I last touched these pages, mainly because of intense work. I have been caught up in the Yiddish anthology ever since I stepped into this unfamiliar poetic universe. I have discovered many poets of great creative vigor. The problem of getting hold of materials has indeed been difficult. By sheer luck I stumbled upon young Rabinsohn,[6] a Hebrew scholar raised in the strictest religious tradition, but at the same time a great artist, in love with poetry, and himself a poet. He put at my disposal his entire, well-stocked library, his expertise and his enthusiasm. He

6. Chaim Rabinsohn (1915– ), Romanian-born poet who ultimately settled in Israel.

also read me some of his poems, which have considerable artistic value. A frail little man, with sunken cheeks, a neurotic given to flights of fancy, and full of boundless energy. The initial scope of the anthology will be substantially broadened. It will include fifty poets rather than just the original twenty-five. If three or four poems are to represent each one's contribution, the work will be much more voluminous than at first intended. It remains to be seen whether I will be able to complete it and overcome the many obstacles on the long and difficult road ahead.

## April 9

I am working steadily on the Yiddish anthology. Now I have gathered an enormous number of volumes of poetry. Very many poets, and pretty good ones, if one takes into account how recent this output is. Yet too few and of relative value if they are to represent the strong and varied local cultural makeup of several million people. The intrusion of too much Russian, Polish, or American atmosphere overshadows the specifically Jewish sensibility of this poetry. Moreover, the language does not seem to have evolved toward the zestiness, ingenuousness, or pure musicality required for real poetry. It is, however, very close to folklore. Such Soviet poets as Charik,[7] Fefer,[8] and particularly Hofstein,[9] are among the best. But their political indoctrination, however slight, mars their art. Only the American Leivick[10] rises to the height of great creation, particularly in his latest volume. Halpern,[11] so in vogue today, melodiously evokes aspects of American life, and achieves certain Heine-like effects, a mixture of sadness and humor, on specifically

7. Izzi Charik (1898–1937), a Soviet Yiddish poet born in Belorussia. He perished during the purges of the 1930s.

8. Itzik Fefer (1900–52), poet prominent in Soviet Yiddish literature. Arrested in the Stalinist anti-Jewish purges in 1948, he was put to death, together with other Yiddish writers, on August 12, 1952.

9. David Hofstein (1889–1952), a Soviet Yiddish poet. His elegies for Jewish communities devastated by counterrevolutionary pogroms appeared in 1922 with illustrations by Marc Chagall. A victim of the Stalinist purges, he too was arrested in 1948, sent to Siberia, and shot on August 12, 1952.

10. H. Leivick (pseud. Leivick Halpern, 1866–1962), Yiddish poet and dramatist, born in Belorussia. He emigrated to the United States in 1912.

11. Moshe Leib Halpern (1886–1932), Yiddish poet born in Galicia. He emigrated to the United States in 1908.

Jewish themes. Kadia Molodowsky,[12] musical and sensitive, greatly resembles Ricarda Huch.[13] Of all, the Moldavian I. Manger[14] remains the greatest poet, but his poems have universal, rather than specifically Jewish value. His verse, poor in imagery and vocabulary, nevertheless has a searing melody that enfolds the reader from the start.

## April 14

I spent last night at the bedside of an old friend. He died in my arms after I tried the impossible to save him. A two-hour contact with death—how many times now?—with that physical intimacy of death and the formalities that take place somewhere at the periphery of our being. Some poetic tradition has it that every man dies his own death. This may be true about the idea of death at the time illness is first acknowledged. Perhaps only as a kind of rebellion, as a way of meeting pain and the frightful realization that death, conceivable for everyone but not you, can touch your own self. But this state of mind is overcome very quickly, first by personal optimism, then by the hope medical care inspires, and finally, by the great, absurd, eternal belief in miracles. The descent into physical death takes place very quickly and, in this longer or shorter period, the whole thing happens in a twilight of consciousness, a kind of indifference in the absence of any life rhythm and its essential conditions. In this sense, all human beings die the same death. My dying friend was in no pain at all. The customary formalities took place simply and quietly. Not a single protest, none of his old jokes or familiar smiles in that moment of warm intimacy. Never before has death seemed so easy and never before have I envied the dying so sincerely. For a second, detached from my own self and alone with him in the rustling silence of the room, the thought of my

12. Kadia Molodowsky (1894–1975), Yiddish poet and novelist, born in Lithuania. She settled in New York in 1935.

13. Ricarda Huch (1864–1947), German poet, philosopher, and essayist.

14. Itzik Manger (1901–69), Yiddish poet, dramatist, and novelist, born in Czernowitz. In 1939, fleeing the Nazis, he escaped to London, then he moved to New York, and later to Israel.

own final departure cast a spell that brought me to the
brink of temptation.

When it was over, out in the street, the violet, distant
night held traces of the same obsessive enticement. And all
the way home in the cab I had the feeling that a friendly
shadow was riding along with me and that we were traveling
somewhere toward a dawnless night. I remembered a strange
detail: after the last breath, the dead man's face had only an
expression of total rigidity. Yet ten minutes later, a warm
smile bloomed on his face. It was like an answer sent back to
me across the border he had just crossed. Another confirmation that the smile is the emblem of eternity.


## *May 10*

After the brief Norwegian invasion, a new wave of concern and alarm shatters even the peaceful optimism of men
like myself. Immersed in poetry and dreams, harassed by
increasingly difficult material problems, I had accepted the
war as a fact against which I no longer reacted in any way.
But now, suddenly, after the lamentable session of the
British Parliament, war has really broken out. At dawn,
the German armies marched into Holland, Luxembourg,
and Belgium. Switzerland has mobilized. History has chosen the decisive area for the final settling of accounts. This
time the shock of the great drama has reached all the corners of Europe, its very marrow. The upheavals, the surprises, the general turmoil will completely transform the
world. What will happen to us? Rumors fly, amplified by
fantasy and fright. As always during intense, historic
tragedies, the wires are busy.


## *May 13*

All nationalist egotisms converge now in a focus of bestial
hatred. This frenzy must lead to a general collapse ending in a
new, a clearer, a more stable world order. Each little country
believes it can determine its destiny by increasing its nation-

alistic and militaristic fervor. Hitlerism is the explosive used to revolutionize the world. Egotism and nationalist conceit, brute force and spiritual collapse were merely medicine for a dying order. I thought of all this yesterday during an introductory lecture on warfare, part of a course on civil defense which some of us, Bucharest doctors, were asked to attend.

## May 19

The Germans' incredibly fast penetration into France has set off immense panic throughout the world. Nerve-racking suspense affects all human activities. Sleep, meals, conversations are pervaded by the obsessive dread of the greatest catastrophe in history: German hegemony over Europe. The human mind is crazed by the thought that one or two thousand tanks can decide the fate of the whole world. Pessimists see the dark image of a France and an England brought to their knees by the Germans, who, once the old, established European balance of power is gone, will rule the whole continent as they see fit. Hasty reshufflings of governments and of military high commands, fumbling reactions to the torrent of war machines, shatter even the remaining strongholds of hope. Of course this is the price the Allies now pay for their business transactions, their unconcerned, blithe usury, and their taste for leisure. For ultimately, piles of gold cannot fight machines built with incredible daring by slave labor and on the hunger of a whole nation. But steel is not the only decisive factor. In France, it seems, revolt is smoldering and it may yet send off sparks in all directions. It was there that once before a new era in history was started. There is a limit to the power of tanks, and a spiritual assault by the masses may well mark that limit.

## June 16

Paris has fallen.
Although during the last few days this immeasurably tragic moment seemed imminent, the people of the world

are shattered. Those who have lived in or visited the unforgettable center of the entire continent, cried or gnashed their teeth. Few were able to hold in check their indignation and deep sorrow long enough to look objectively at the circumstances which have dealt this blow to the very heart of France. Even the most reactionary minds begin to realize that the fault lies with a decadent capitalist society that has subsidized Hitler with two billion dollars for rearmament against Russia; a society that has offered him on a platter so many countries and territories to feast on; a society that has rejected the Soviets' earnest offers to join forces in the effort to crush Nazi Germany; a society that entered a deadly war without proper military preparation while fully aware of the adversary's power. But this realization strikes people haphazardly, without logical connections, without documentation, rather like occasional flashes streaking through their sentimental, bourgeois comfort. Still, events unfold so quickly that each day brings them further enlightenment. The occupation of France, the rumor that its soldiers, ill-trained and ill-equipped, refuse to fight and face certain death, the rising protests of masses against leaders who have pushed them into this infernal slaughterhouse—all this reveals, belatedly and with sad eloquence, the rot and corruption of Western imperialism. The situation today is such that our strategists, who swarmed at street corners, have lost their credibility. Instead, prophets have come into their own. The role of prophet is much more convenient, even when mysticism is mistaken for reason: to verify a prophecy one needs much more time and space than that granted between two battles. I have heard many prophecies. Most of them don't have the slightest basis in political reality. All prophets are, at best, sentimentalists. The occupation of France was foreseen even in the age of strategists. But having occupied France, Hitler will not be able to organize Europe along his principles. He will not be able to extend his conquests beyond a Europe whose west and center alone (not counting Russia) require forty million tons of oil a year just to maintain normal activities. Where will Hitler get oil, grain, tin, copper, and all the other raw materials imported from colonies? What navy will he send to occupy colonies? A navy it will take him several years to build? With what capital? And while France and England go on fighting? America and Russia will not supply anything to the invading Hitlerism. Where will Hitler get the capital necessary for the transition from a war economy to a peace economy? This inextricable situation will bring Hitlerism down, even though it has overrun Belgium, Holland, France, and Norway, for these countries will need reconstruction and food. Perhaps then Russia, while standing idly by, and without firing a single shot, will reap the harvest of Germany's downfall and of the prior collapse of Western imperialism. Is there going to be, for us here, a period of darkness, terror, bloodshed, and deadly shame? Very likely. But we will pay this price for a free future.

*June 18*

Three days after the Germans took over Paris, France laid down its arms and Marshal Pétain petitioned for peace. This news, broadcast yesterday afternoon, caused immense sorrow and total dejection. Everybody had foreseen France's imminent defeat, but nobody expected her to capitulate. We are all in a fever, anticipating the response to be given by Hitler and Mussolini, now meeting in Munich. Invaded by darkness and shaken by doubt, the world holds its breath. A long syncope, no insight possible. The English are determined to fight to the end. Will they, really, now that no nation is left willing to die for them? Will the French hand over their navy to the Germans? What is the Soviet Union doing? Will the occupation of Balkan countries have an impact upon Europe? What about Southeast Europe? One can't tell anything.

*June 22*

Today at 6:00 P.M. the armistice between France and Germany was signed at Compiègne, with the pomp and circumstance and rhetoric required by this historic hullabaloo. Humiliation and generosity, cruelty and noble acts chronicled on gramophone records, mark the useless death of youths from all Western countries. For the time being, all details of the accord are kept secret.

## June 25

Events roll on at such a dizzying pace that it is impossible to grasp their immediate meaning, let alone forecast their outcome. Every day something new happens. The armistice between France and the German-Italian Axis has been signed. Some of the elementary realities of war begin to surface, slowly.

For us right now, Hitlerism manifests itself in the new governmental doctrine. Germany, in the wake of its temporary military victory, exercises uncompromising pressure. A tragic political and historic intermezzo begins for our country, and one cannot yet predict how long it will last. At this critical moment, Iron Guards have been freed and welcomed by the king; they now make up the core of the new totalitarian party called the National party. The old politicians abstain from joining it, for the time being. Serious measures have been taken against the Jews, forbidding their participation in all kinds of civic activities. The momentum of this so-called revival under the lucky star of Hitlerism might achieve the total destruction of Romanian Jews along the lines of programs already carried out elsewhere. But even more terrifying is the idea that the fate of our whole country is at stake. Of course, the majority is unable to see that, as the people have never been properly informed. The tragic fact is that their reasoning is based on incomplete data, on unverified rumors, on the glitter of bright surfaces. I suspect the turmoil and confusion in Romanian political circles is such right now that even they do not know what these sudden last-minute totalitarian improvisations will lead to. A., an old politician and government adviser, has called the whole matter a *vicleim*. [15] Others

15. A Romanian folk play performed at Christmas and New Year by costumed villagers.

shrug, unable to understand a thing. Only Jews are anx-
iously anticipating new legislative viciousness. What else
can we expect in the near future? Indeed, why should *we*
escape all the bestiality that the well-known Hitlerist doctrine has unleashed elsewhere? The presence of the Iron
Guard in a totalitarian government means only a strict implementation of the program to exterminate the Jews.

*June 28*

The upheavals of history are drawing nearer. Every
week a new dramatic page is turned. Last night, the news of
the Russian ultimatum demanding that we cede Bessarabia
and Northern Bukovina fell like a thunderbolt. It seems
that the Germans and the Italians, despite our political totalitarian kinship, have refused to help us and so a Crown
Council met the Russians' twenty-four-hour deadline and
finished by accepting their demand.

Despair and turmoil in the city. The cabinet has been
revamped. Marshall Urdăreanu, chief of staff of the new
National party, has been dismissed. To compensate, at noon
two Iron Guards were named undersecretaries of state. Rumors in every corner, on everyone's lips. There is talk of
Hungary and Bulgaria making similar territorial demands
on Romania, of our possible military opposition. Official
communiqués are laconic. Tension, pressure, insomnia . . .

*June 30*

As expected—growing resentment caused by the manner
in which the Jews in Bukovina and Bessarabia welcomed
the Russians. Rome's official radio dispenses in cold blood
the most unheard-of infamies, which our newspapers print
under fat headlines. First we were informed that three
thousand Jews demonstrated against the National party in
front of the Soviet Embassy and that this is what prompted
the Russians to demand Bessarabia (?!). Now the same
sources spread the allegation that the Jews of Bukovina

have stoned the retreating Romanian soldiers. This is how one paves the way for the punishment of the scapegoat. Everyone is disgusted that the Jews native to Bukovina and Bessarabia returned there immediately after the annexation. Of course, nobody protested when the recently formed National party announced its intention to turn Jews into outcasts; yet everyone found it necessary to criticize Jews for fleeing back to their Russian-occupied hometowns, after twenty years of persecution here, topped by the recent laws and violent demonstrations in this country. Their crime is that they did not hesitate to choose Russian asylum rather than the "solicitude" of Germany, Poland, and Romania. We are in for dark times. As of tomorrow, the National party is to begin official actions. Today, Jewish medical students missed their final exams: they were stopped from entering the university building. The mistakes oligarchies make are always covered up by reactionary movements.

### July 2

A heavy, unbreathable atmosphere. Rumors of disorders, of pogroms. The chilling articles by Cezar Petrescu,[16] in which he started unearthing anti-Semitic myths—the peasants' revolt against their poisoners, the Jewish innkeepers, the loss of Bessarabia—have suddenly stopped. Instead, Pamfil Şeicaru,[17] who welcomes a German protectorate in our country, spills his venom in print, shrewdly disguising his thirst for Jewish blood. But people must come to their senses soon. Perhaps those prefects and officials who were "killed" by Jews will return from the dead; the exaggerations and lies spread by refugees from Bessarabia and Bukovina will be checked; there will be an inquest into all the disorders fatally connected with a hasty army retreat; and an account will be given of the past and present situation in the lost territories. But the findings will not alter much the face of things. Our leaders will con-

16. Cezar Petrescu (1892–1961), a Romanian journalist and writer of fiction.
17. Pamfil Şeicaru (1894–196?), a Romanian journalist.

tinue to exploit these diversions to cover up their political ineptitude and the total disorganization of our life for as long as the overflowing waters of European history are not settled in a new bed. Until then, we, the outcasts of this nation, shall pay for all its sins and suffering.

My embarrassed Gentile friends avoid me, and I am embarrassed by their embarrassment. When we do meet, all they can offer me is a compassionate look, a sigh, and a quick handshake. The painful silence forces me to talk of anything but these burning issues. Yet I, I feel the need to pour out, right there in front of them, all the tears that are choking me, my sleepless nights and the despair at this new exile—how many now?—in my own land and my own language.

### July 3

Immense tiredness, as if I were ill, caused by the crushing invasion of politics into our daily existence. An escape to the shores of poetry is no longer possible. My sluggish brain is hashing and rehashing every event, examining and rejecting every rumor, putting together facts and predictions. This exhaustion brings on an increasing feeling that I am losing the ability to appraise lucidly the fate of the Jews in this country—at times like a state of confusion before one blacks out. Everyone I meet adds his news of yet another infamy to those already known. I barely manage to free myself for a couple of hours from the iron chain of anxious anticipations, of dread rumors and commentaries— and here it is again, a freshly issued official list of new government members. (How many now, since the beginning of the war?) It is a government of German sympathizers headed by Gigurtu,[18] with Manoilescu[19] for Foreign Affairs, with Iron Guards as generals. The Minister for Minorities —Hans Otto Roth.[20] There is nothing more to add. The good Romanians who, up to this minute, hoped that our

18. Ion Gigurtu (1886–?), a Romanian pro-German politician.
19. Manoilescu was a member of the Vaida-Voievod party.
20. Hans Otto Roth (1893–1953), a Romanian politician, president of the National German party.

country would not be handed over to the Germans, are speechless and terror-stricken. Those I have talked to think that the Germans have conquered the country without a war.

## July 5

The new administration has made public its program: political cooperation with the Rome-Berlin Axis and enforcement of total nationalism, that is, out-and-out anti-Semitism. The final seal on Jewish destiny. A characteristic talk took place between two Jewish representatives with Dr. Vaida-Voievod.[21] They went to see him and offer the assistance of the Jewish community to Bessarabian refugees. Vaida told them: "I am impressed by your gesture, but you must realize that it can have no publicity because, right now, we must not only avoid anything that might make you look likeable, but we must do everything possible to obtain the opposite effect. I, as you well know, am no anti-Semite. On the contrary, I believe that ethnic elements should have proportionate representation. But today this is no longer possible. Nothing can be done for you. You had better be aware that you are in for dreadful times."

## July 8

A Gentile friend wished to offer me some solace following the official declaration by our minister of arts, Horia Sima,[22] who said: "There must be free expression in art, but only for the Romanian artist. I cannot see how a kike could make any kind of contribution to our Dacian-Roman art."[23]

"You must not pay any attention to that," said my friend, "or let your sensitivity be hurt by it."

21. See "1938," n. 6.
22. Horia Sima (1908–195?), commander of the Iron Guard. He replaced Codreanu (see "1938," n. 21) after the latter's arrest in 1938. In March 1939, Sima fled to Germany and returned in July 1940 to join Antonescu's government.
23. Romanian history stresses the Romanians' descent from both the Dacians and their Roman conquerors, minimizing or simply denying any other mixture of races.

I explained to him that my sensitivity had stopped reacting and consequently I no longer suffered. What our latest official representative of the arts has declared in such a pretentiously succinct manner has been uttered on innumerable prior occasions by many other more or less qualified pontiffs.

"Well, then? If there is nothing new, why react?" my friend concluded, happy that he had convinced me—and the streetcar, arriving after a long wait, cut our conversation short.

## July 9

Despite the urgency of so many serious problems, the new totalitarian cabinet has started to implement its policy of "integral nationalism" with some anti-Jewish measures. The newspapers *Semnalul* and *Jurnalul* have been suspended, and today it was announced that minorities will no longer be permitted to write in Romanian, but must use their own language. It seems that we, the Jews of Muntenia,[24] who speak only Romanian, will have to write in Yiddish now. We have not yet been told whether we may still use the Latin alphabet or whether we are restricted to the Hebrew one. It isn't worthwhile noting all the rumors. We await developments with calm despair.

The other day, in the Cişmigiu, seated close together on a bench, a man and a woman—she with a bunch of tiny pale roses in her lap. As I walked by, the man told her something and the woman reproached him in a velvety voice: *"Oh, ne dis pas ça, tu fais mal à mes roses!* [Oh, don't say that, you are hurting my roses!]"

## July 11

There are some humorous touches in the reports the news agencies shower upon us. Thus we learn that the Re-

24. In Southern Romania (Muntenia) Jewish culture was not as widespread as in Moldavia, where Jewish culture flourished under Galician influence.

public of Andorra has taken drastic measures: it has closed
its border and has raised the number of its policemen from
six to twelve. Prior to this, the comic-news award was held
by the report that two months ago Luxembourg, following
German aggression, had its entire army of three hundred
fifty men join the French forces to fight the common enemy.
Today we learn that our country has withdrawn from the
League of Nations. Strange, since we believed the League of
Nations had withdrawn from Europe long ago. This is indeed a daring foreign-policy action, bound to enhance our
image. . . .

Things seem to have quieted down for a while. Following
the Munich talks there is no further news of Hungarian
and Bulgarian unrest. The Axis has cynically admitted that
this is merely a lull; but at any rate, the time we will gain
may be useful. In the meantime, our main concern is with
internal problems. A strange thing is happening here: the
government's enthusiastic anti-Semitism seems to have been
checked by the Germans, who consider unrest in our country inconvenient at the moment. We therefore find ourselves in the paradoxical situation in which Hitler is de-
fending the Jews of Romania against anti-Semitic excesses.
Nor have decisions reached by our cabinet at a meeting four
days ago been made public. Satisfaction is derived from
stylistic flourishes concerning regulations about membership in the National party that seem to have bitterly disappointed baptized Jews.

## July 16

Were I ever to make notes for an autobiographical
sketch, having lived for almost half a century, some of the
signposts would be the following:
My first clear memory dates from the age of four or five
when, one afternoon, my terrified mother rushed into the
yard where I was playing with one of my sisters (who later
died of diphtheria), took us in her arms, and ran to hide in
the house. A student demonstration with cries of "Down
with the kikes!," "Death to the kikes!" was moving along

our street. I still carry in my ears the noise of hurled stones and of crashed windows along Strada Dudeşti where we had just moved from Strada Artei, behind the courthouse, my birthplace. Unable to pay the tax imposed by public schools on Jewish children, I attended the elementary Jewish school. As a Jewish student, I stood no chance for admission to the Romanian high school. I registered at the Jewish middle school, which later succeeded in getting me transferred to the Romanian school for my senior years. All through school and up to my baccalaureate examination, savage anti-Semitic outbursts of my schoolmates in the crudely picturesque language of slum children. In 1907[25]— the terror with which I expected the marching peasants to enter Bucharest and the massacre they promised, while at the same time I went on dreaming about Eleonora Duse on her Romanian tour. At the baccalaureate examination, the personal attack of my school principal, Bogdan-Duica, an openly brutal anti-Semite—directed against me and my dissertation theme, "Romanian Folk Poetry." I graduated thanks to the only Jewish teacher on the examination committee, Candrea, who knew and valued me. Anti-Semitic reactions of my colleagues and professors in medical school. During the war—threatened with a court martial. The reason: as the youngest doctor in my company, I was sent by my colonel behind enemy lines to rescue the cart with the officers' luggage. Having tried in vain to push the cart uphill on a muddy slope, I abandoned it when the German machine guns closed in on me. What the "foreigner who has sold out his country"—and the officers' luggage—"to the enemy" had to endure during the war has been told elsewhere.[26] Because I was a Jew, the Romanian Writers' Association rejected my application for membership. Later on, for the same reason, my volume of poetry,[27] nominated for the annual prize, was rejected, and the prize went to the deceased Calistrat Hogaş.[28] My citizenship was "revised"

25. The year of the Romanian peasant uprisings.
26. Emil Dorian, *Convorbiri cu bălanul meu* [Conversations with my horse], Bucharest, 1925.
27. Emil Dorian, *Cântece pentru Lelioara* [Songs for Lelioara], Bucharest, 1922.
28. Calistrat Hogaş (1847–1917), the author of poetic prose evoking the Romanian countryside.

and I was dismissed from my job. Now the nation dismisses me again. In conclusion, during this half century, my existence unfolded between the cry of "Down with the kikes" in 1800-and-something and that of "Down with the kikes" in 1940. During all this time, I gave the best of myself, over and over, loving and waiting, understanding and loving. What I saw and heard around me all this time—Jewish beards torn out, synagogues desecrated, insults and beatings, injustice done to my daughters, the whole gamut of infamies, of injuries and insanities, of refined or cruel brutalities—I suffered, in the belief that someday everything would be accounted for, paid for. Yet today the balance of this half century closes with new humiliations and new crimes. After all this time, when I loved and sang, understood and forgave, what kind of change for the better can I expect for my family, for this country, for this whole continent?

Unbelievable, the stories told about the endless number of crimes committed on trains in the last two weeks. Unfortunately, the names and dates in the cases known to me directly have been confirmed. Dr. G., the engineer Z., Dr. W., the civil servant G., the traveling salesman L., and others, all drafted, on their way to or from their military posts, witnessed the disappearance of Jewish soldiers, the butchery at Dorohoi,[29] and unexplained funerals. This pogrom organized by the army against comrades-in-arms is an incomprehensible aberration. Today we know more about what happened in Bessarabia and Bukovina when the Romanian army withdrew: acts of revenge by the Communists, who had been persecuted before, retaliation and destruction by the withdrawing soldiers, violence on the part of the population that stayed behind. All this, common occurrences under such exceptional circumstances. I can understand that the embittered soldiers behaved cruelly. What I cannot comprehend is that later, as the army passed through a peaceful little Romanian town, it shot down like dogs a group of Jews in the cemetery where they were praying at the grave of a Jewish officer. Such senseless sav-

29. Romanian town in Northern Moldavia near the Bukovina border.

agery! Let us admit that, in some frontier village, the recent frustration and anger could have led to attacks against a population of odd and dirty-looking Jews with side curls. But how can one explain the cold-blooded, organized crimes committed on trains against Jewish officers and soldiers on their way to perform their duty or returning from its performance? How can a soldier push another soldier out a train window? We are no longer dealing with the misguided zeal of some youths on their way to a rally who have fun molesting a few Jews and pulling out their beards. We are dealing with the senseless murder of innocent people at the very moment when they were showing devotion to their country, although insulted by legislation and threatened with starvation. How far can the authorities go and shamelessly continue to call Jews to military service? Is it cynicism, or an invitation to massacre?

## July 18

It was to be expected, this revolt by clerks in ministry offices, because the projected anti-Jewish legislation and the officially promoted anti-Semitic atmosphere threatened to deprive them of their livelihood. For if Jews no longer conduct business, where are the clerks, who are accustomed to substantial bribes, to get their real income? Yesterday, for instance, at one of the banks in the capital, a Jew tore up in front of a teller's window the import permit for which he had paid the goodly bribe of 35,000 lei. Another one tore up his permit for which he had paid 50,000 lei. Both had merchandise waiting at customs, one in the amount of 200,000 lei, the other—320,000 lei. The goods, unclaimed because of the uncertainty of the situation, would be sent back to Germany. Quite a few other shipments of merchandise returned from Romania, where the only customers might be a few thousand Jewish merchants, must be piling up in German warehouses. That is probably why Germany issued its famous recommendation to Romania to show moderation in its anti-Semitic measures.

Slovakia, the newspapers have announced, has decided that Gypsies and Jews are to do the forced labor required by the government.

We are being repeatedly told that the cabinet has met and has worked out solutions to the Jewish problem, but that there is hesitation to make them public. In the meantime, the city buzzes with rumors, interpretations, and "definitive" information, some ominous, others rosy. Nothing is certain so far. Except for the announcement in today's *Curentul:* one of the first measures will be to demand that Jews resume their former names. Thus it is possible that the name of Dorian will also die. I referred those who asked me why I adopted this name to a page from my first novel.[30] It was but natural for the Bulgarian Panait Stanoioff and the Pole Mihail Smolsky to change their names when they began writing in Romanian, the former to Panait Cerna, the latter to Mihail Sorbul.[31] But they, being of a "pure race," are not subject to the legislation "to fit into the framework of the new national policies," in the official style of the day. This sterile parroting of Hitlerist measures cannot even arouse sincere indignation; the German Hitlerists themselves may have a good laugh at the news. I am noting this mainly to give myself the illusion that I am actively present in these days of transition to a new period of history.

The dilettantism of the present cabinet, or perhaps its lack of homogeneity, results at times in sad absurdities. The night before last, the minister of cultural affairs, Radu Budişteanu, sneaked into the radio broadcasting studio and interrupted a music program to announce personally a decision he had just made in his capacity as head of the ministry. The bewildered listeners were at a loss as to how to interpret such a tempestuous action, and today's papers make no mention of it whatsoever. The honorable gentleman made a complete fool of himself, people think. He announced that he was cutting off the official subsidy of one

30. Emil Dorian, *Profeţi şi paiaţe* [Prophets and clowns], Bucharest, 1930.
31. Romanian poets, of Bulgarian and Polish ancestry, respectively.

million lei to the Mosaic religion (a sum which was never paid anyway) and that he forbids the Greek Orthodox priests to baptize Jews. The latter measure is futile since, as everybody knows, baptism is an act of divine grace and not even church authorities can tamper with it, the only function of the priest being to officiate over its mystery, whenever it occurs. But the minister of culture reached the peak of the ridiculous when he asked other Christian denominations, such as the Catholics, to follow his lead in the interest of our country. As if the Pope had nothing better to do than serve the interests of the Romanian people! Dilettantism falling into the absurd. . . .

## July 25

Hitler's speech has served no practical purpose. England goes on fighting. For several days Europe's radio broadcasts overflowed with waves of indignation. All in vain. The final act of the European military tragedy begins, to be followed by an epilogue of total destruction.

## August 1

Today I lost my last source of steady income. The Banca de Credit Român,[32] where I served as doctor for ten years, has fired me on the grounds of its nationalist reorganization. I was given the fifteen-day notice to which any domestic servant is entitled after one month of employment. What next?

## August 6

A colleague informs me that today, in the offices of the Legislative Council, he read the text of the new law on the position of the Jews in our totalitarian state. This is what the law states:

32. The Romanian Credit Bank, one of the largest in Bucharest.

Only those Jews are Romanian citizens who participated in the war of 1877; their descendants, if orphaned by the war; the Jews who were citizens before 1916. Of the Jews who participated in the war of 1916–18, only those are Romanian citizens who fought in the front lines and were awarded citations or decorations. The other Jews, even those who fought in the war, shall no longer be citizens, but may continue to practice their professions. Those Jews who entered the country after 1918 are devoid of any rights. The law is followed by an order to dismiss all Jews from the army and subject them instead to a new military tax.

The absurdity upon which this law is based has no limits. A physician could never have been in the first fighting lines, for he had to care for those who returned wounded from that very spot. While on duty, some of the physicians contracted typhoid fever. The ones who died were decorated. The ones who survived will not have any citizenship rights because they have not fought in the front lines. A cavalry soldier could not have been in the trenches either. He was positioned behind them and would come in after the infantry and the artillery had finished their work. And so it is with many other tragic instances where war veterans are now dismissed with shameful disregard.

Through a strange coincidence, I learned about this new law just today, August 6, the anniversary of the battle of Mărășești.[33] In that burning hell, I worked together with the courageous doctor Donescu, the former chief of service from Focșani and our regiment's physician, a sixty-year-old major who carried on despite his age and an acute gall-bladder attack. (I remember how at one point he was furious with a stray colonel who had drunk all the cognac and rum from our first-aid trunk and who kept asking everyone where his regiment had gone.) But that might not count on my record as having fought in the front lines. One must substantiate claims to bravery. Well, I also remember our stopping in a forest in the valley of Zburăciorul where the headquarters of the Twelfth Division, led by general Popescu-Sanitaru, were set up in a grove about two hundred me-

33. A Moldavian village where, during World War I, in a desperate battle that lasted over a week, the Romanian armies repelled the Austro–Hungarians.

ters away. Suddenly, while I was shaving under a tree, a squadron of German planes appeared from nowhere. I heard explosions and then cries coming from the grove. I ran there and found all the officers wounded. The doctor of the division, Colonel Constantinescu, and the chief doctor, Captain Stănescu, had fled. I set to work all alone, watched by the planes that kept circling over us. Young and naive, I refused the decoration, insisting that I simply had done my professional duty. But today all this is no longer important.

### August 9

Only one day has passed since the law on the new status of the Jews was officially promulgated, after radio commentaries hailed it as "a way to purify Romanian blood and Romanian destiny." Until this morning—while the printing presses of the *Monitorul Oficial*[34] were preparing the surprise (subtly intended to pave the way for our territorial losses)—I wondered if the new law might not indeed be a work of national hygiene. I imagined the results of a purification of the nation on such a large scale that it would also cancel the rights of all Romanians of Polish, Gypsy, Greek, or Ukrainian descent. What would then be left of the Romanian blood affected by such serious anemia! Unnecessary anxiety, though, for the law refers only to the Jews, and its author, I. Gruia, minister of justice and professor of law at the university, informs us that the Jews are irreversibly excluded from the life of the nation, even though those who belong to the first category still appear to retain certain rights.

Like most of the laws, this one is especially harmful first to the poor and then to the middle class, the professionals. The wealthy Jews, the businessmen, and the industrialists will continue to do well for a while. The white-collar workers, the physicians, and the lawyers are ruined. Very interesting is the preamble to the new law. Its embarrassed author tries to explain what cannot be explained, by

34. See "1938," n. 3.

interpreting a few paragraphs of the constitution and crowning the whole matter with an attempt to define what a Jew is. It is almost comical to watch him struggle for a basic principle that would allow a definition. He speaks of "religious criteria," more restrictive than the "biological criteria" (he does not have the courage to call it plain racism) and the "blood criteria"—which are not physical but ethical (?!). It is embarrassing to follow this impotent juggling of the pseudo-scientific hoaxes of our time which have served two maniacs' political ambitions. For this country, the outcome of the law is the immediate dismissal of Jews from the army. After all, once Russia's territorial demands are met, we will not need so many soldiers! The ten thousand Jews employed by the army, after losing the privilege to serve, will have to pay a tax proportionate to their income. A hefty sum will be collected.

Onward with history's agenda!

Many Gentiles do not understand the feeling of human degradation the Jew experiences now that he is a pariah in Romanian society. They view his reaction as parading a sensitivity entirely out of place today. What you are still permitted to do is important, not what is forbidden. Lovinescu[35] tells me that the new law is "liberal and equitable." Right from the shoulder and without a trace of embarrassment. Only a poet (whose wife is Jewish), whom I met today in the street, was quick to open the subject before I could get a chance: "My dear Dorian, what *is* it this Hitler wants to settle with you! As soon as he makes friends with a new country, he insists that you must be brought down to this miserable state!"

More interesting, though, are the comments of the Jews themselves, who have already started to produce jokes, flagellating their own fate. Today someone tells me that, in accordance with the three categories of Jews established by the new law, the Gentiles now have three ways of greeting us: "Mr. Kike," "Hey, you kike," and "Up yours, kike!"

---

35. Eugen Lovinescu (1882–1948), a foremost Romanian critic between the wars.

43? see p.288

According to the latest anti-Jewish law of August 6, military service is considered an "honor," and that is why all Jews have been dismissed from the army. But lo and behold, Jews who were left destitute because of this law are suddenly called up again. Thus a professor who was expelled from the university and was practically begging for a job, is now sent to the western front where the Hungarians are threatening to annex Transylvania. So how about honor? Should Romania agree, God forbid, to territorial concessions, won't we be surprised to see, when the army withdraws from the frontier, a new version of the atrocities perpetrated in Bessarabia! After all, there are Jews in Transylvania too.

A century ago Romania made the mistake of introducing here all the Western institutions created there by revolutions, which did not fit the character of our people nor their level of development at the time. Now, one hundred years later, a similar mistake is repeated—the introduction of a totalitarian regime whose doctrine and institutions do not fit the Romanians' psychological, economic, and political makeup. The only thing suitable here is anti-Semitism. But the totalitarian doctrine entails more than anti-Semitism.

## August 21

Am contributing to *Infrățirea*[36] a polemical article on the history of the Barașeum.[37] The paper that Maxy[38] is editing with the joy of a child who has been given a marvelous toy begins to take on a more interesting shape. *Infrățirea* lacked homogeneity until now. We still have a long way to

36. A political and literary Jewish newspaper.

37. The first Jewish theater and conference hall built in the poor Jewish quarter of Bucharest. The author took an active part in the project. During the war, after the exclusion of Jewish writers and actors from Romanian life, the Barașeum housed important artistic events providing moral support for the artists and their public.

38. M. H. Maxy (1895–1971), a Jewish-born Romanian painter. One of the significant artists between the wars and a Romanian leader of modern art, he was also active as a journalist and teacher. After the war he became director of the Bucharest Art Museum.

go: free the magazine from its ties with the politicians of the Jewish community and concentrate the Jewish writers' energies on it. We must stress a policy of constructive criticism and cultural direction and pursue it with competence and authority. The old hope for a newspaper that could solve the problem of the unemployed Jewish writers with the help of the Jewish bourgeoisie and officials definitely has to be abandoned. My last interview with the president of the Jewish community only reinforced my determination to avoid any future contact with the Jewish leaders now in office, who will continue to wallow in obscure and murky politics as long as no radical change sweeps them away. I boldly demanded a modest sum as an installment against a tentative loan for a weekly newspaper which could help bring all the Jewish journalists back to work and enable them to become independent. The counteroffer was to form a corporation with stock owned by the politicians of the Jewish community who, of course, as the newspaper's owners would also earn a small pittance and, unavoidably, control publication as well as the writers' freedom. And yet, perhaps even in the near future, *Infrățirea,* through private initiative and financial support, may still bring a group of courageous and independent journalists under its banner.

## *August 28*

The maiming of the Jews through legal and economic measures continues unabated in the midst of grave concern over our country's territorial integrity. Hundreds of Jewish lawyers have been irrevocably disbarred, teachers dismissed from high schools, and students subjected to regulations of the most authentic Hitlerist kind. As for Jewish teachers, sixty-four were dismissed. Following the new regulations, Marguerite is no longer allowed to attend her class. If Europe is taken over by Hitlerism, this state of things will become permanent. But how can one accept such a solution to the world's problems?

## September 2

Our country's friendship with the Axis and our economic despoilment by it, far from bringing us any reward, has torn away half of Transylvania from us. After we maintained a firm position and declared uncompromising resistance at Turnu-Severin,[39] after many days of well-conducted propaganda—suddenly the thunderbolt of a so-called invitation from Vienna to resume the interrupted negotiations. Manoilescu, the minister for foreign affairs, and Valer Pop, the delegate from Transylvania, went to defend the undisputably just Romanian cause. But there they were faced with arbitration. Our friends from the Axis claimed they had only two days available, so that the Romanian delegates had to submit. The explanations Manoilescu offered to Romanians over the radio, in a voice that trembled on the verge of tears, were unconvincing. They benefited the Axis most. Who had forced Manoilescu to accept? He could have resigned and avoided sitting down with the Germans, the Italians, and the Hungarians, after the great achievement of territorial amputation. But he represented, as one says nowadays, the government's "dynamism," that is, the maximum in unconditional genuflections before Hitler. Manoilescu was duped by a system the Germans patented after Hacha's performance: the Czech leader, to save the bourgeoisie's wealth, did not hesitate to sell his country, with a great show of turning pale and fainting at the signing of the agreement. It remains to be seen how Transylvania reacts and whether the peasantry and the workers will accept this agreement between the Hungarian and the Romanian bourgeoisie who gave in so easily to save their positions. Some action has been started in Transylvania, and even in Bucharest a demonstration was organized, but the government stopped it immediately. First we hear one of our own ministers call out in our own country "Long live Hitler!"; next, Radio London broadcasts a nationalistic call to arms by a native of Transylvania. In the end, consoled by German and Italian guarantees, about which we know nothing beyond Manoilescu's assur-

39. A town on the Danube in Southeastern Romania.

ance that "the German army will shoot" (whom?), our leaders will cede the lands extorted through gangster tactics and will proceed to a reconciliation with the Axis, no doubt using the axis of the Jewish question, always good in times of national distress.

*September 5*

New and startling changes following the unrest throughout the country and in Bucharest. Panic and disorganization, servility to Hitlerism, and national humiliation have brought down the Gigurtu-Manoilescu government. Yesterday morning, the king summoned General Antonescu,[40] former member of the Iron Guard and—so they say—a personal friend of Corneliu Codreanu. After long debates, the general—just out of Bistriţa prison—obtained the suspension of the February 1938 constitution, thus limiting the royal powers and installing his own dictatorship. The city is buzzing with rumors. The situation in Transylvania has grown into firm opposition to the Hungarians. Antonescu is known as a former Anglo- and Francophile. Will he now start the war? Will he abandon Transylvania to the Hungarians? Will he continue the relationship with the Axis? Actually, we don't even know who is going to govern. Perhaps this new leadership is only a transitional stage. But transition to what?

EVENING

Sudden shooting in the streets. More and more often. Panic. People flee into courtyards. I do not want to believe it, but the sound of machine guns—perhaps coming from Calea Victoriei—is growing louder. Telephone calls . . . Within seconds, the news has spread throughout the city. I am told that street demonstrations are progressing along Popa-Tatu toward Griviţa.[41] The CFR[42] workers? Unper-

40. Ion Antonescu (1882–1946), Romanian general and politician. In disgrace with the king since 1938, he was imprisoned at the Bistriţa monastery.
41. A Bucharest neighborhood housing railroad yards. Their workers were known as a stronghold against the German occupation.
42. Căile Ferate Române, the Romanian railways.

turbed, the radio keeps broadcasting the correct time and adds some insignificant information. Radio London quotes a telegram just received from Bucharest reporting that the Iron Guard has taken over the National Theater Plaza and the army has opened fire on them. And I who live right next to the theater . . .

No news during the night.

## September 6

And this is how revolutions are made: last night the Iron Guard under Horia Sima's leadership was permitted to organize a demonstration in the National Theater Plaza. It seems that "somebody" fired a gun, and the soldiers shot back. Prime Minister Antonescu rushed to the palace to explain to the king that the street demonstrations were growing dangerous and could not be stopped, short of the king's abdication. He served the king with an ultimatum and, at 8:00 A.M., Carol gave up the throne in favor of his son Mihai. This version, coming from London, may not be entirely accurate. Antonescu may have obtained the king's abdication right after he assumed power. The nuances are no longer important. One thing is certain: the general did assume power, reduced the royal prerogatives, then obtained the abdication and brought in a new king while himself remaining effectively the chief of state. Mihai's inauguration took place hastily this morning, together with Carol's abdication. My day was spent on the telephone, reading all the news in special editions and listening to the radio in an atmosphere of great tension. Iron Guards have appeared everywhere, with their choruses, their newspapers, their demonstrations. Corneliu Codreanu's portrait is in all the windows. An official proclamation accusing the former king of unimaginable crimes and infamies is pasted on all the walls: he was "a drunkard, a lecher, a deserter, and a traitor." His crimes and robberies are shamelessly listed without consideration for the minor detail that his own son currently occupies the same throne. The newspaper articles are all in the same vein: "Esther's Downfall," "Milady and Her

Dirty Clan," and so on.[43] Large crowds mill about in the streets. The Iron Guard's enthusiasm unfolds in demonstration upon demonstration all over town. The radio has just announced the recall of Elena, King Mihai's mother, and the dismissal of a staggering number of high dignitaries. In the present din and confusion, which diverts attention from the Romanians' systematic withdrawal from Transylvania, the people rejoice and unburden themselves by cursing their former master. They do not realize that all this rot was caused by an entire leading class who robbed and cheated and feasted, never caring for the people's needs. The new chief of state must solve a difficult national situation in extremely grave European circumstances, a situation which may prove too much for his strength. The pages of history fill up from one day to the next and are turned over with dizzying speed.

*September 11*

Difficult days, full of worry and anxiety. People dwell on General Antonescu's military coup, wait bemused and feverish. In the first few days anti-Carol sentiments were voiced and expressed in print in a manner which went beyond permissible limits in a surviving monarchy, if the monarchy is to continue. *Universul, Porunca Vremii,* and other newspapers owned by the Iron Guard published articles of unprecedented impudence and vulgarity. The downfall of the old regime became a tavern brawl. The leaders then began to wield carefully the drill of moderation, to reestablish a minimal illusion of sanity in the torrent of decrees, communiqués, appeals, and proclamations issued by the new dictatorship. The pressure exercised by the Iron Guard continues unabated, and no one can be sure that it will not exceed the leaders' initial intentions. So far it has been impossible to constitute a cabinet, and it is hard to tell whether one must give up counting on the cooperation of old-guard politicians. The handful of ministerial appointments to date reveals a desire to collaborate as little and as

43. The allusions are to Magda Lupescu, of Jewish origin, King Carol's long-time companion.

late as possible with the Iron Guard. At any rate, there is great evidence of hesitation. It seems that in Bucharest the Iron Guard is still being restrained, but in the provinces it has free run. Transylvania has not yet been completely evacuated. An eerie feeling—the presence of the national flags, celebrating a new king, at the very moment when we are giving up our lands. The attempts to rebuild our country are greatly hampered by the influx of immigrants, of state employees, by payroll difficulties, demobilization problems, political trials, and civil suits over property rights. Clouds are gathering.

*September 15*

The revolution goes on. Among the endless decisions and decrees, today's stands out: Romania is an Iron Guard state, with a new list of ministers. Many of them are Iron Guards, headed by Horia Sima, named vice-president of the Council. The government recognizes only one party, the Iron Guard, which is entrusted with "the moral and material rehabilitation of the Romanian people and the development of its creative forces." General Averescu is the head of the Iron Guard party, and Horia Sima—the commander of the movement. The same decree proclaims that "all fighting between brothers is at an end." This is the second report of a revolutionary force in full swing.

Am working with Călugăru[44] and Maxy on a new issue of *Infrățirea*. A diversion, to forget the heavy weight of the days. Articles, editing, petty details of Jewish questions in the importance of which I must force myself to believe. We will even have a literary page. . . .

*September 19*

Again, difficult times, perhaps crucial for Romania's future. There is a real possibility of a massive German infil-

44. Ion Călugăru (1903–56), a Romanian-born Jewish journalist and novelist.

tration. People have seen high-ranking German officers, sealed trains, troops in Galați.[45] In response to the unrest in the country, Antonescu and the patriarch again issued appeals to the nation to abstain from showing hostility against the Germans and Italians. It seems that Soviet pressure has increased enormously. Ribbentrop paid an unexpected visit to Rome. Might there be some truth to the rumors of peace between Italy and England? Perhaps it is not in Italy's interest to declare war on Russia, side by side with Germany, which, according to some, may be forced into this diversionary action following its aborted invasion of England. Is this why the Germans hasten to mass troops at strategic Russian points? In view of Russian pressure, the Balkan problem will most probably be discussed at the meeting in Rome.

This morning, in a bookstore, Victor Eftimiu[46] openly declared: "Today, tomorrow at the latest, we shall sign a military treaty with Germany." And, pulling his passport out of his pocket, he added: "Screw the Dacian-Romans, I'm clearing out."

The installation of the Iron Guard continues and gradually infiltrates all aspects of life. It does seem, however, that they have come to power belatedly, so that there is little new they can implement. At most—sanctions against old-guard politicians. The extermination of the Jews is still beyond their reach. The general's government avoids taking retaliatory actions for fear of serious consequences. That is the reason for such a flood of appeals for peace and order and forbearance. As for the Jews, earlier measures have taken care of them. The present government does not bother with us *for the time being.* Optimists actually foresee better times, which is no doubt naive, for the Iron Guard regime is evolving toward unrestrained excesses. It is very doubtful that Germany will occupy Romania.

45. Romanian Danube port, important for navigation and trade.
46. Victor Eftimiu (1889–1972), a Romanian playwright, poet, and fiction writer.

## September 22

A few final touches are still needed before the Jewish situation is solved. And it seems that they are forthcoming. Today the question of Jewish physicians was opened. Lacking a quorum, the Medical Association postponed its meeting for a week. However, an open letter to the ministry was read, a letter requesting a solution to the problem. The Iron Guard demands the dismissal of all Jewish physicians. Possibly, once the Jews' rights are juridically established, our situation will become clearer. The majority of Jewish doctors is very pessimistic, and concern has grown in the last few days. The Gentile Doctor Gomoiu (considered a spokesman for the Jews), instead of resigning, is doing everything in his power to hold on to his position as president of the association. But he no longer can do anything to help his supporters. Next week we shall know whether and under what conditions we will be able to practice medicine. In the meantime, young Jewish medical school graduates may no longer register with the association.

The war is starting up in Africa, which—now that England is not to be invaded—has become Germany's and Italy's target. I am almost positive, for today massive anti-Semitic demonstrations were reported from North Africa. Prelude to a new bloodletting.

## September 27

The accord among Germany, Italy, and Japan, spreading the war to all continents, was concluded today. Here, we go through an Iron Guard revolution into which local prophets read long-lasting meaning. In other words, schoolchildren, students, lawyers, actors, and other unfortunate Jewish victims fight the decisions, proclamations, and decrees issued by the new exponents of national happiness. As to Romanian interests—nothing constructive. The sad part is that so many Jews are concerned only with the paragraph that affects them, for better or worse. Very few understand that the real problem is beyond immediate events and that at least some of their energy would be better spent in other areas.

## September 30

What I expected happened yesterday: in its general assembly, the Medical Association asked for the expulsion of all Jewish physicians. We are now allowed to treat only Jewish patients, not Gentiles. The Gentile physicians, however, may treat both Jews and Gentiles for, said Dr. Popovici-Lupa, who made the motion, "the Iron Guard's principle is: you may take money from the kikes, but you may not give them money."

Then an official protest was read against "the kikes who had the impertinence to come here today and contaminate this organization of physicians with their presence"—and all the Jewish doctors were promptly evacuated. I stayed at my own risk and watched.

The Iron Guards dominated the meeting. Dr. Gomoiu tried feebly to oppose them but finally fell into their arms. To no avail, probably, for the present executive committee will be dissolved. In the passionate words of the speakers— lies, slander, and aberrations riding on a black wave of hate —no Jewish doctors served in the wars, all were quacks with false diplomas who destroyed the prestige of the medical profession in Romania. I can no longer understand how I managed to stay on, congested, my brain on fire and my jaws clenched. I with my hopes that the meeting would take place in a decent atmosphere which would allow me, who am familiar with matters of medical practice, to read a speech I had prepared in the belief I could set the record straight.

## October 3

Following the decrees which eliminate new categories of Jews from productive life, I have been very busy with Jewish concerns. Meetings on the project of a new Jewish theater where the decision seems to rest with enterprising capitalists and unscrupulous competitors. Attempts to bolster the influence of writers and artists, especially from the reasonable group of *Înfrățirea,* aren't very likely to succeed. In the meantime, we are discussing another project, a Jewish daily, whose sponsor is O.M. I myself feel that a Jewish daily is neither possible nor necessary. Impossible, because I can't figure out where one could get the astronomical sums of money swallowed up by a daily, which must rely on a small number of people and limited funds for enormous expenditures on printing and paper. Even the optimistic estimate of one million lei for a beginning merely covers the costs for one month. And then what? Rich Jews are as inaccessible as always, while political cooperation with the Jewish community is not only hard to achieve but also unlikely to bring in money, since it itself is in financial trouble. But above all I do not see what purpose a Jewish daily would serve when the Jews no longer have freedom of the press. Comments about measures taken by the government may not be printed; polemics with the Romanian press?—certainly not; Jewish conditions in other European countries? —impossible! (Information is hard to come by, and we are not allowed to draw comparisons between their misfortunes and ours.) Hardly any news from across the ocean reaches us, and as to news about Jews in Romania, that would barely fill a bimonthly paper. Everything speaks in favor of a weekly: political and social restrictions, the defeatism of Jewish financiers, and the lack of newsworthy material. Also, a weekly could feed a dozen journalists who are unemployed at present. For the main problem does seem to be the livelihood of these people. Nevertheless, an attempt will be made to put out a daily. Will we get permission for it? We must study means of distribution and, certainly, of financial support, means to withstand the attacks and the hatred of the Iron Guard press when faced with the famous pens of the Jewish journalists.

Heavy work on the new issue of *Înfrățirea,* in which I am deeply involved. I do hope it will turn out well and comparable to Western publications. I would like this magazine to become a weekly for all Jewish writers.

*October 8*

Awful, half-baked, stale bread. Definitive victory of the Iron Guard after the massive demonstrations on Sunday, October 6, and the presence of German troops in our country. These are the important events of the last few days. Antonescu's grave and unforgivable mistake: he put on the Iron Guard green shirt over his general's uniform.

Marguerite's debut in print. Two charming poems in a fresh style and with original imagery appeared in *Infrăţirea,* commended in a short preface by Ion Călugăru.

*October 12*

The German armies have entered Bucharest. The government and Romanian military officials greeted the German officers at the North Station and housed them at the Athénée-Palace Hotel. Trucks carrying German troops, German planes . . . most people consider this a kind of protectorate. The British legation is leaving. The war is just beginning, and we don't know whether this time it will bypass us.

In the meantime, the destruction of the Jews is being carried out according to a definite plan, coldly calculated and executed with the most valiant thoroughness by the Iron Guard. If this pace is kept up for one year, our disaster will be complete. But this is not the worst misfortune. What will happen to this country? I fear that our leaders' lack of experience, the mystic fanaticism with which they hurl themselves into situations they try to master, will create a wave of destructive excesses that will thwart the attempt at an orderly transition from the leadership of General Antonescu to the Iron Guard and will plunge the country into chaos. That is when we Jews will live our darkest tragedy. For General Antonescu, through his bourgeois leanings, still stands for ideals different from those of the Iron Guard, which has always been a subversive organization, both in its battle tactics and in its methods of organization and propaganda. The workers and the peasantry rallied around it in the belief that their complaints would be redressed when capitalism disappeared, unaware that when the Iron Guard spoke of "exploiters" they merely meant . . . the Jews. It remains to be seen whether the Iron Guard leaders can channel this mood of the masses their way or whether their administrative ineptitude, together with the pull in an opposite direction represented by Antonescu, may not lead to their total destruction.

## *October 22*

Today, a decision by the Ministry of Education forbids the printing of any kind of Jewish writing, including translations into Romanian. Systematically, everything is being brought to the bitter end. If they could forbid Jews to think in Romanian or even to write on a slip of paper in the privacy of their home, they would not hesitate to do it. Fortunately, language is a native country from which no one can ever evict you. I constructed scores of verses in my head today, I played with words and images, practiced virtuosity of speech, as if to underscore a presence I love beyond anything else.

I have just read a report by Dr. Filderman,[47] a memorandum to the government on the new legislation regarding Jewish physicians. Disastrously conceived. It is most unfortunate that the present regime allows no contact between Jews except through the Jewish community (that is, Filderman), whatever the problem. While preparing the memorandum, he consulted no physician, although those belonging to the Cercul Medical had jotted down a few important points. Filderman simply asks that Gentile physicians extend their services to Jewish patients whose condition is critical because we have no Jewish surgeons, and requests kind consideration for Jewish physicians established in Romania prior to July 1919. (He does not understand that the

47. Wilhelm Filderman (1882–1963), a member of the executive committee of the Union of Romanian Jews, a member of the Romanian parliament, president of the Jewish Community of Bucharest, later president of the Federation of the Jewish Communities, and author of several works on the Jewish situation in Romania.

Iron Guard's draft legislation refers to *residents* established in this country before this date.) Moreover, he makes a sentimental plea for justice in this matter for the sake of the country's welfare. He fails to voice any complaint against the possible dismissal of Jewish physicians from the Medical Association. No protest against the segregated organization of Jewish physicians which can be administered but not supervised by Gentile physicians. The draft legislation allows no independence whatsoever to the Jewish Medical Association which, under the new professional conditions of Jewish physicians, without officially sanctioned functions and practice, will still have to handle some medical cases. This association is not even allowed to elect its own president or hold a free meeting. I won't bother to mention the insulting interdiction to conduct any scientific research or to publish a single Jewish medical journal, etc., etc. Not a word on any of these points in the memorandum. Can we salvage anything? I doubt it.

What empty, useless activity! The fatigue I've gathered year after year and stored inside now heaves a muted cry of helplessness. Nothing but fatigue, rounding my shoulders, heavier than ever on this late autumn day with a useless sun, a world of unforgiving disasters. So many struggles and tragedies, so much sorrow and egotism in this dark, in this rotting century of hate. I shall not be surprised when the first signs of surrender appear. So long as I still have some change in my pocket to chase every day after butter, sugar, soap, and other needs of the protoplasm, I shall wait and, as they say, do my duty. Afterward, I could put an end to it. In truth, I am no longer interested in the future. I am too weary.

## October 30

I have a new occupation: instructor in anatomy and hygiene in a Jewish high school where I am employed as doctor, a position which also requires teaching these subjects. Today—an introductory lecture for seniors. Grown-up boys, attractively self-assured, though ostentatious. I prepared the lecture well, but I cannot gauge the impression it made. A strange world that I cannot yet fathom. The syllabus is rigid, the objectives narrow. Right now, I find it less interesting than I imagined in my former dreams of being a teacher. Perhaps the contact with adolescents is too limited or comes too late. We will see how things develop. I will bide my time. In the meantime, I am looking forward to meeting another class in which, I am told, the students are better.

### November 12

On top of all the daily misfortunes and despair, we were struck by last Sunday's disaster, a catastrophic earthquake on a scale never before experienced in our country. We were fast asleep when, toward dawn, at a quarter to four, infernal shaking and noises woke us up. The walls and the floors creaked wildly and wouldn't stop rocking. The lights went out. In the dark, the windows blacked out, I ran to the children's room, screaming warnings over the hellish noise, and dragged them out of bed to guide them to Paula, who was moaning, petrified, on the threshold of the room. The fear of death gripped us. The catastrophe lasted forty endless seconds. When, later, the lights came on, our home was unrecognizable. Books all over the floor, furniture shifted, shards of broken objects everywhere, large cracks in the ceiling and the walls, and wrenched pieces of mortar scattered all over the place. We could not go back to bed. We got dressed and went out in the cold, drizzling rain. Disaster everywhere. The bricks and the debris fallen in the street obstructed traffic, which was as busy as on a holiday. Women in furs thrown over their pajamas; speeding taxis with passengers rushing to check on their relatives and friends; people clustering to tell their tales at lit-up street corners. The worst disaster, as everyone soon found out, was at the Carlton. The twelve stories of the apartment building collapsed like a cardboard toy, burying hundreds of people under the debris. It was impossible for us to get close to the corner of Brătianu Boulevard and Strada Regală, cordoned off by soldiers. We could only glimpse, in the night, firemen and workers' silhouettes against a mountain of debris higher than the top of the first-floor shops, lit up by enormous spotlights, like a surrealist movie. We returned home, teeth chattering, dumb and frozen, and proceeded to call our friends on the phone to find out how they had fared.

In the midst of general prostration, four hours after the catastrophe, the Iron Guard did not hesitate to announce new measures against the Jews, although the population seemed penitent and ready to join brotherly hands to face this misfortune that disregards racial criteria.

## December 20

For five weeks I haven't touched this notebook, despite the intimacy between us that had become habit. A psychological paralysis when faced with events; fear of misinterpretation, or at least of misconstruction of my notes; the feeling that any kind of writing is useless; the moral and intellectual hibernation into which I have sunk—all this kept me away from these pages. I was dizzy with everything that happened and so terrified that I felt close to madness at the thought of what is yet to come. I went through my drawers and library shelves, and mutilated them.

During this time, the Jews have suffered enormous and decisive blows. Clerks in private enterprises have been fired, mistreated, and robbed at police stations and Iron Guard centers, left at the mercy of hirelings and punks, cruel and illiterate youths. The Jews have been deprived of schooling and of recourse to legal action. Gentile patients have been forbidden to seek the help of Jewish physicians. During the week of mystical exaltation honoring Captain Codreanu[48] as if he were a saint, on the occasion of the exhumation of his corpse, the following people were executed: Professor Nico-

48. See "1938," n. 21.

lae Iorga,[49] Virgil Madgearu,[50] Victor Iamandi,[51] General
Argeşeanu,[52] and Gavrilă Marinescu.[53] Other political prisoners, about sixty-five in all, were detained pending trial.
This news created a terror which is still spreading. Although the Iron Guard special police has been abolished,
the Jews cannot relax, feeling—quite naturally—that the
terror will continue. There hasn't even been a search for the
assassins. Despite the horrors and the lawlessness that were
unleashed, the reinterment of the holy bones of the Iron
Guard's first commander took place with full majesty. On
top of it all, the aftermath of the earthquake and the economic difficulties have created insoluble problems. The exodus of Jews to Palestine and Bessarabia has reached incredible proportions. All Jewish newspapers and magazines
have been shut down, except for *Infrăţirea* (!), which is
forced to appear weekly. My doctor's shield has been
removed, my practice is nonexistent.

## December 25

Christmas. Stale. Wilted. Not a book. Impossible to
write a line. Huge snow. Roads snowed-in. I am too numb
and bored even to jot down these few lines.

## December 30

Everybody is in a hurry to be done with this matchless
year. The upheavals it has brought are still in full swing.
Everybody, everywhere, is hopelessly waiting. The feeling
that all decisions, solutions, truths are provisional lends life
a hallucinatory air. Those who passionately discuss and in-

49. Nicolae Iorga (1871–1940), a prominent Romanian historian of international stature. An active politician, he was the leader of a nationalist anti-Semitic
movement. He became prime minister in 1931.
50. Virgil Madgearu (1887–1940), a Romanian economist and politician. He
served in several cabinets.
51. Victor Iamandi (?–1940), a Romanian politician.
52. General Argeşeanu (?–1940), a Romanian general and politician. He became prime minister in 1939.
53. Gavrilă Marinescu (?–1940), the police prefect of Bucharest.

terpret the political and military situation are inspired by wishful thinking, their respective mentality and economic situation; but many feel tired. I am indifferent to everything said on the radio or written in newspapers. I eat and sleep and endure misery and worry. This is how things stand now, at the beginning of the new year: Germany has occupied France, Belgium, Holland, Norway, Luxembourg, and half of Poland. With England it conducts air warfare. The Italians are conducting a campaign in Greece, where they are being defeated. In Africa, the English continue their offensive and are besieged at Bardia. Official speeches, documentaries, and commentaries announce the continuation of the war. No one can foretell how it will develop. The Germans have massed troops here, especially in the last few days. Hotels have been requisitioned, many schools have been evacuated—particularly Jewish ones. There are rumors that they will cross the Danube. But Bulgaria has not *yet* added its signature to the tripartite pact among Hungary, Slovakia, and Romania. In the meantime, Roosevelt's speech, promising England total support, made a great impression on the antagonists. England, which rules all the strategic maritime points and dominates the seas, is still powerful, particularly since it has succeeded in its attack on Libya and, together with Greece, on Albania. According to *Pravda,* Stalin has declared that war with the greatest enemy approaches. Who is the enemy is not quite clear. What will happen?

It seems that the war is steadily turning southeast. That is our New Year's gift. As for the Jews, the set policy continues unswervingly. It is difficult to foresee what 1941 will bring. There are new grounds for hope that we will emerge unscathed. But speculations don't matter any longer, since things are progressing the way they do, since people are worn out, since most are drained, nerves shattered. Even these few lines in which, be it out of emotional exhaustion or for some other reason, I can no longer tell all, are of no importance any more, neither for me, nor for anybody else. A corpse holding a pen in his hand.

# 1941

*January 10*

The same dreadful atmosphere, day in, day out. The weight of political developments becomes increasingly unbearable, and we continue to be in the dark as to a possible Balkan war.

The Soviet Union has flatly denied any connection with the presence of German troops in Bulgaria, claiming that the action there was taken without its knowledge and consent. Germany has issued comments on this denial. Bulgaria stands firm and so . . . the show is postponed. Who knows what the alternative to this change in program will be? One of my patients, a Greek, assures me that the Germans will not force their way into Bulgarian territory and certainly not into Greece, where they cannot afford fighting on as massive a scale as in Poland or France. For the time being it is we who suffer because of the influx of foreign troops. The struggle to get our daily food becomes an obsession. Butter, very hard to find, sells at an exorbitant price. Eggs have disappeared from the market. Meat is scarce and available only occasionally. What will happen in another two months when the reserve supplies are depleted? Activities are almost at a standstill. The Jewish merchants are being systematically eliminated. Jewish stores are arbitrarily expropriated. Very many Jews are led to Iron Guard police stations where they are beaten up, hundreds of thousands of lei taken from them, then they are forced to hand over their stores . . . "Romanianization." In the last few days, a widespread and furious anti-Masonic campaign—I can't figure out why. It may have sinister motives. Or might it just be a political diversion? Doubtful.

## January 20

Flu with high fever and maddening muscular aches. I just learned that yesterday at a meeting of the Law School faculty, as Minister Iasinsky talked about "The Politics of the Axis and the New European Order," the audience suddenly began to shout, "We want Horia Sima!"[1] Now, in the evening, student demonstrations in the streets. The Iron Guard against whom? Rumors about a German officer killed in front of the Ambassador Hotel. What is going on? Shaking with the flu, I let go and—with a certain voluptuousness—sink into a pool of indifference.

## January 22

I cannot go on like this. Despite my illness, I get out of bed. For the last two days nobody has dropped in to bring me news. Yesterday two members of the Iron Guard were killed right in front of police headquarters. Today we heard cannons and machine guns all day long. The street demonstrations are turning into a rebellion. Iron Guard newspapers print inflammatory articles against the leaders of the state. Quickly and unconvincingly, General Antonescu has broadcast an appeal. The cannons are growing louder. Radio Bucharest, occupied by the Iron Guard, has an-

1. See "1940," n. 22.

nounced their victory. We do not know yet who is in power, General Antonescu or the Guard. What about the Germans? What role do they play in this unexpected collapse? We are completely in the dark.

Now, at two o'clock in the afternoon, the telephone lines are suddenly cut, we are isolated from the world. Radio Braşov has also been taken over by the Iron Guard and continues to broadcast their victory every hour. The sound of machine guns and cannons goes on ceaselessly. At dusk, armed soldiers, ready to shoot, lined up right under our windows, in the backyard. They are watching the building of the Defense Ministry across the street. Repeatedly, we hear in the dark: "Back off, or we'll shoot!" Soldiers crouch behind fences. We get away from the windows when officers threaten us with raised guns. My daughters huddle together in the waiting room, in the middle of the apartment. A wounded member of the Iron Guard shook the main door of our building, threatening to shoot if we didn't let him in. He was treated by the doctor who lives on the first floor. The night moves slowly, full of deafening noises—now the shooting seems to come from our neighborhood. Radio Bod broadcasts the progress of the Iron Guard: the Fourth Army Division from Iaşi and a division from Craiova and Braşov have joined forces with them, General Dragalina is marching on Bucharest. Special editions of *Cuvântul, Buna Vestire, Biruinţa.* No other newspapers appear. Nothing is known about General Antonescu. Machine guns and cannons. We go to sleep in our clothes, the girls on the couch in my waiting room; feeling entitled to my rest as a patient running a fever, I go to bed, puzzled by the events, with the detachment of illness. . . . A last phone call from K. through a sudden, inexplicable connection: ". . . here . . . looting . . ." Then nothing. And tomorrow?

## January 24

We had a civil war. General Antonescu himself made the announcement: the Iron Guard tried to murder him and assume power. He spoke bluntly of his wayward children, the Iron Guard, inexperienced and inhumane people whose mistakes and shortcomings he had tried to cover up for these last four and a half months, and who had joined in a plot with the secretary of the interior, General Petroviceanu. They hid arms in the barracks of the national guard from where they were to attack the prime minister's offices across the street. So here we have the Iron Guard leaders officially described as highwaymen and Horia Sima called a murderer. Felonies and crimes are disclosed and perpetrators named. This complete change of direction in only three days. Gradually we learn about the fight at police headquarters, inside the Telephone Company building, on Strada Roma,[2] and—something I could never have imagined—the pogrom that for two nights and two days swept through the Jewish quarter.

What happened in Văcărești, Dudești, and the surrounding neighborhoods is indescribable. And there is no need to describe it. Suffice it to list the destruction, the looting, and the bestial crimes. But even that is impossible, as new details come to light every day. The extent of the tragedy is not yet known. Germans and other foreigners with cameras are still there taking pictures. The exact number of the dead and missing cannot be established. We will never know the maddening details of their end, of their fear before the end. The fury of the looters has not spared anybody or anything. Shop after shop with shutters wrenched off their hinges, windows smashed, walls burned, rooms emptied—it is impossible to tell what had been there before. The mind cannot grasp how looting bands were able to wreak such utter destruction in so short a time: drugstores without a trace left of bottle or glass, barber shops with smashed mirrors in layers on the floor—a barber's chair left in the middle, alone and puzzled like someone alive. . . . On the broken window of a German shop, a note: "Broken by mistake. Damages will be paid. Signed: Commander Bocşa." Here—a store littered with watches ground to powder. Next to it, an old woman crying in the middle of a dry-goods store black with soot, empty. A gutted movie house, a photo studio, a restaurant, a lamp shop, a shoe store—all empty, walls charred. In the middle of the street a car and on its seat an abandoned prayer shawl. An empty can of gasoline,

2. A street in downtown Bucharest.

which the looters had dragged through the ghetto, exploded, setting the street on fire while people awaited their death behind locked doors. The madness of destruction and crime descended on the homes in the ghetto as well. Everything that could be carried out of the houses was stolen, the owners beaten, some murdered. Here is a three-story house set on fire in retaliation after a Romanian officer shot three Iron Guards who were dragging a wounded, naked girl through the street. A synagogue burned down. Another one. The majestic Sephardic synagogue has been completely destroyed. They set it on fire with cans of gasoline placed in its four corners, and the looters danced by the flames. Countless Jews were taken from their homes by Iron Guard bands and led to several spots in the city where they were slaughtered. On the road to Jilava[3] dozens of corpses have been found, their identification papers scattered about. Before the victims were killed, their noses were smashed, their limbs broken, their tongues cut out, their eyes gouged. The two sons of an old rabbi were shot in his arms. Jewish corpses were hung from hooks in the city slaughterhouse or simply dumped in the street. One of my patients who lives in that neighborhood saw them. Some were chewed up by dogs. More corpses at Băneasa.[4] They are still lined up like slaughtered lambs lying under the falling snow in the yard of the morgue. The sidewalk in front of the morgue is black with waiting relatives. The list of beaten and tortured people is endless, and the crimes cover the complete range of a demented imagination—Jews forced to drink gasoline with Epsom salts—crosses cut on the skin of their back—torture and killing—on and on. All this has not prevented Ilie Rădulescu[5] from stating authoritatively, in the first issue of *Porunca Vremii* to appear after the bloodbath of these three days, that "the kikes have fired on the army!" Despite General Antonescu's categoric statements. . . . Little by little an explanation is being concocted for acts that cannot be explained. But the press will find one. And *Porunca Vremii,* which has always incited its readers to pogroms, merely rushed to be in the forefront.

3. See "1938," n. 22.
4. A suburb of Bucharest.
5. Ilie Rădulescu was the editor of the anti-Semitic *Porunca Vremii.*

## February 2

On the radio, official data on the crimes and robberies committed by the Iron Guard. The information issued by the authorities and the Chief of Staff is completely at odds with the press, particularly with the official anti-Semitic organ *Porunca Vremii,* which has not been too squeamish to mention the victims hung from cattle hooks. When arrested, the looters and criminals confessed freely that they had acted on orders or suggestions from Iron Guard leaders, though sometimes on their own initiative as well. Today's broadcast on the murder of ninety-two Jews in Jilava, and of those pursued after escaping from there, contains details of cruelties unequaled in human history. Here too, as elsewhere among criminal monsters, there have been women. Ilie Rădulescu candidly protests against the poor reputation the pogrom has given our country. And all this time we learn more and more horrible details. Still dazed, as if coming out of anesthesia, the Jews speak of nothing but this tragedy. I haven't talked much to Gentiles. Poor S. is ashamed, keeps apologizing for being Romanian, and rails against the Romanian people, her own people, whom she does not recognize; she questions their right to have a country if they are capable of such behavior. Her reaction upsets me. She is infinitely kind—if only she had a better grasp of politics . . .

In the meantime, German troops keep streaming in. The figure mentioned to date is already one million. Some think it is even higher. Downtown, German workers are installing wooden telephone poles and wiring them for their private use. According to some newspaper articles, in the light of Hitler's speech (of no interest whatsoever) and of the teeming troops here, it seems the Germans are establishing in our country a base for their forthcoming attack on Southeast Europe. Next month or later? In the meantime food is growing scarcer. Bread tastes of nothing but cornmeal and leaves you hungry. There is no more cheese, onions are forty-five lei a kilo and hard to get. The people's traditional fare—bread with cheese and onions—has become an ideal out of their reach. Medical work is almost at a standstill: the new minister of health, Professor Tomescu, sees to it that everything conforms to the latest Iron Guard legislation.

## February 5

New official disclosures on the events of January 21–24. A document broadcast on the radio and published in newspapers refers to "the real pogrom in Dudeşti and Văcăreşti" and places the number of victims at 490 dead and wounded. It underscores that, of the 144 Jews, 118 were murdered. Among Romanians, there are also 118 dead. But the actual figures are much higher. Every day one discovers new corpses of Jews who disappeared the night when the bells rang, signaling the beginning of the pogrom. Obviously, the prosecution of criminals and robbers, even when the victims were Jewish, is being staged as propaganda against the Iron Guard; otherwise one would not dwell at such length on so many horrible details. Sympathetic comments, however, are absent, while, characteristically, great publicity is given to the relentless pursuit of Romanianization of Jewish enterprises. Jewish employees are being replaced by the hundreds. In a department store, I saw a specialist in fountain pens replaced, after twenty years of service, by a young postal clerk; at an exclusive ladies' fashion store, an experienced manager was replaced by a waiter. Given the general atmosphere in the country, it is hard to understand the rapid changes. Nor do the Jews understand anything any longer. Some have grown optimistic merely because of the suppression of the Iron Guard and the relief from terror. Others, on the contrary, are just beginning to panic only now and await new pogroms. Few realize that a pogrom is a diversionary incident and takes place during a process of social change that occurs, at one time or another, in every corner of the world. Throughout the centuries, at all important turning points in history, almost everywhere —in England, France, Spain, Germany, Russia—the massacre of Jews has heralded crucial economic changes. It is hard to believe that in revolutionary Russia, during the White terror, when the armies of Wrangel, Dansikin, Petlura, encouraged by the West, roamed the country, there were twenty-five hundred pogroms in nine hundred places, with two hundred thousand Jews murdered! In those days, Europe still exhibited a hypocritical morality that protested against anti-Semitic persecution. But in the last few years, Jews have been expelled, tortured, massacred—while people, or rather countries, looked on with total indifference. We still don't know the whole truth about the latest pogrom in Germany following vom Rath's assassination.[6] There, too, synagogues were set on fire, stores destroyed, and people killed. One thing we do know: no one from abroad voiced a protest against these savage acts. Today, such a protest is less likely than ever. Memory is short, and many Jews thought they could count on the generosity of the German troops stationed here. Some German soldiers may have intervened when Jews were about to be murdered by the Iron Guard, particularly in houses where they were billeted. But in many known cases, they remained aloof. Nor did their presence hinder the unscrupulous robbers and criminals. German soldiers are quartered in the school and yard behind the Spanish Synagogue on Strada Sf. Vineri. The schoolmistress, who occupied the remaining living quarters, did not return on the night of January 22, and the only people present were two German refugees—a Jewish woman and her son. The robbers did not hesitate to make their way between the German trucks, loot the synagogue, and carry off the two refugees. The son was found a few days later in the morgue. Elsewhere, when some desperate Jews screamed and begged the German soldiers for their "humane" help, the soldiers replied coldly, "We have no orders in this respect!" On the other hand, there is the case of the headmaster of a school, also occupied by Germans. He was accused of throwing a German soldier down from the second floor, but when the Iron Guard tried to get him, he was saved by a German who threatened them with his gun.

Last night Dr. Lev, the German minister of labor, a guest in our country, was invited to give a talk on the radio, in the course of which he declared categorically: "Ro-

6. See "1938," n. 17.

mania is a land of milk and honey and oil. . . . We Germans are Romania's friends, not because of her charms but—I want to make this perfectly clear—because of our self-interest.''

Official disclosures about the former Iron Guard's movement increase daily. Now at last there is talk of "hundreds of Jewish corpses" found in the forests around the capital, while previously the official count stood at 118 Jews and as many Gentiles. People mention the 1903 pogrom in Kishinev, as if to minimize the horror of the one in Bucharest, forgetting that in Kishinev there were sixty dead. The black deeds of the czarist hooligans do not begin to compare with the sadism and the deranged imagination of these bands here. It seems that the effects of Iron Guard leadership in other areas of Romanian life have also been disastrous. The ill-fated activities of the commissars in charge of Romanianization—totally unprepared children—have destroyed business and industry. Education has been disrupted under the leadership of Traian Brăileanu, the university professor and translator of Kant who during his school inspections would declare that the teachers must learn from their students, and not the other way around. As a result, the students (Brothers under the Cross)[7] took weapons to their classes and destroyed labs and libraries during the rebellion. And many other aspects of national life, disclosed in print and on the radio, are eloquent examples of the general disaster.

. . . and the kikes, well aware that everything that happened to them in the last few months happened because they're kikes—which has nothing to do with anti-Semitism—haven't complained to the government, haven't asked for compensations, haven't published a newspaper voicing their grudges. They haven't even lodged a protest with the League of Nations! But what can you do? Kikes will be kikes: they like to pose as victims even after they've been murdered.

I asked a Jew who lives in the area where the pogrom took place: "How are you? How did you manage to es-

7. The "Brothers under the Cross" formations were a preparatory stage for future members of the Iron Guard.

cape?"—"Thank God," he replied, "they went to my neighbors!"

## February 8

Sperber,[8] the Jewish-Romanian poet from Bukovina who writes in German, visited me yesterday. Tall as a poplar—large, bottomless eyes, a warm, kind, baritone voice. He brought me his volume of poems, *Geheimnis und Verzicht,* which I had read. His favorite themes are rural; he lived a long time in the country, or at least in a little border village where he was in close touch with peasant life. He has translated Ion Pillat[9] remarkably well, I am told. Steeped in nature, his own poems are idylls that neither develop the great themes of poetry nor touch, even in passing, upon social themes. While they are not major poems, their style has real qualities. He liked Marguerite's poems and asked most insistently for a copy. What a strange evening we had around the table, listening to him, in the midst of newspaper dispatches, news broadcasts, and all our everyday worries!

For two days now the town has been in a fever. Churchill's speech, the shelling of Genoa by the British navy, the British army's rapid advances in Africa after the capture of Benghazi, persistent rumors that the Germans are crossing into Bulgaria. Constant broadcasts on foreign radio stations, discomforting measures suddenly taken to black out the whole town, the British envoy and his entourage recalled from Romania.

*Porunca Vremii* persists in maintaining that there is no connection between "genuine" nationalism and recent events, and that the kikes were murdered merely for profit. Actually, men and youngsters who didn't have a penny on them were picked up in the street and at their homes; the Iron Guard snared passersby into synagogues transformed into torture chambers, then took them outside the city and

8. Alfred Margul-Sperber (1898–1967).
9. Ion Pillat (1891–1945), a Romanian poet of the traditionalist school.

shot them. With astounding hypocrisy and glaring bad faith the newspaper concludes: "That is the truth. Romanian anti-Semitism has nothing to do with these reprehensible occurrences. Romanian anti-Semitism has always been a worthy struggle for the national weal, and has nothing in common with the practices of petty burglars. Let us then be perfectly clear about it and let the kikes stop playing the role of victims of Romanian 'hooligans'—an insult they keep throwing at our clean struggle for national liberation from Jewish enslavement."

### February 16

Fifty years old. Who can afford, today, to linger over this moment, a borderline between two phases of existence, though the actual one may have been crossed earlier or is yet to be crossed? Balance of accounts, plans for the future, personal reassessment—nothing has any meaning in the tornado of madness sweeping through the world. In the past, it was a year that marked a resting spot, where one could gauge the value, more or less, of the drift of one's former efforts. Today, everything is wind-tossed, the past bloodied, the future—terror and emptiness. I know many young people who have physically aged in recent times.

I keep thinking that my mother died at fifty-seven, and that I am now fifty. Only seven years left?

I am glad that I have never been preoccupied by the question of immortality, in any of its forms. I can grow old peacefully and without wondering whether or not I leave anything behind. The other day a fellow writer, sixty years old, asked me with infinite sadness: "Do you think we will be remembered someday?"

I have reread some pages from my notes over the years. Perhaps in order to check if I have lived. I find them mediocre, lacking the interest which intense and real experience generates. Daily triteness, tepid thoughts, no depth, the horizon shrunk to a line, a lack of preoccupation with great issues and real problems, perhaps a dearth of intellectual courage. Days stitched together by bland notes. Here, too, I have accomplished nothing worthwhile. Not to mention my twenty-two books and the readers' opinions formed over the twenty-five years I have been writing.

The press carries today a complete report on the implementation of the August anti-Jewish legislation. The data reveal that, over a period of seven months, all the goals set for Romanianization have been reached: Jewish doctors, lawyers, clerks, professors, skilled workers, etc., have been fired. One can't help but wonder: whom did this benefit? What advantage did the country gain? What moral strength? What material good? And I don't understand how, in the midst of all our disasters, so much blind determination can be devoted to so sterile, so negative an undertaking.

## February 24

A colleague I met the other day in the street introduced me to Mr. Alexandru Saint-Georges, director of a museum of the Fundațiile Regale[10] and a passionate collector. He looked like a shopkeeper in his Sunday best. Dispensing with all amenities, he requested my assistance to approach Jews who might own objects of interest for the museum and ask that they donate them to him. So far the museum has no special Jewish section, but there is a collection of religious objects, Jewish flags, Torah scrolls, plaques of various Jewish societies, Jewish books from the libraries confiscated in Bessarabia, and so on, which have been catalogued and shelved in special closets. "It is a grave error," he pointed out, "for the Jewish museum and archives to be located so close to the Sephardic Synagogue, because it wouldn't have taken much for all the collections to have been destroyed." So he wanted them for himself. And to convince me of the importance of the problem, he added serenely: "You saw what happened in Strada Atena." He had

10. See "1940," n. 1.

just visited the synagogue there, and had seen the destruction wreaked by the rebellion. "If the same things recur, not a single object will be left, and that would be a great pity."

I asked him: "And next time, do you think that only Jewish *objects* will be destroyed?"

The passionate collector did not understand. All he could see were objects. As my colleague and I walked on along Calea Victoriei, he pointed out a store with doors and windows boarded. The sign bore in yellow letters the name *Strulovici*. The owner was killed—they cut out his tongue and gouged out his eyes. My colleague knew him quite well. Mr. Saint-Georges is looking for objects for the Jewish section of a museum.


*March 2*

Yesterday Bulgaria joined the tripartite pact. But a few days earlier the German army stationed here began marching toward the Danube. Streetcar and bus service to the city limits was stopped and the city traffic rerouted. For a while, many Bucharest residents caught outside certain peripheral points could not reenter the city. General Antonescu's plebiscite has slipped into a position of secondary importance. People are shaken by the prelude of a new campaign in the Balkans. The continuous presence of German planes over the city, probably in preparation for reconnaissance flights to the south, causes general nervousness. New waves of political discussions, most of them conducted without any real knowledge of what is going on in the world. The majority of people, of course, see only the immediate problems, men eyeing big and small countries, moved by more or less justifiable motives. Some people see a broader historic process unfolding in capitalist societies, and the war as working against them like an adamant doom machine; all events—fatal moments leading to the imminent destruction of capitalism. Others tremble for the fate of England, which is expected to organize a future Europe in accordance with its ideal of warmed-up democracy. And there are those who see salvation in the continent's submission to Germany's virile and innovative genius. The other day, the sister of a colonel, a country prefect, blessed the Lord for the German presence here, for "Romanians are not and never were capable of self-rule. Proof: even a century ago, they had to call upon a king of foreign origin to organize the state."

## March 9

Doctors, even Jewish ones, have been called up for civil-defense duty one night a week, at various firehouse stations in the city. So far, there has been no need at all for medical assistance. But should there be, God forbid, an air raid some night, how are Jewish doctors to care for Gentile victims when the law forbids it? The other day the authorities shut down the office of a Jewish physician because, rumor has it, he took care of Gentile patients. The law draws no distinction between Gentile soldiers, Gentile civilians, and Gentile victims. A Gentile physician replied very courageously (today, courage is indeed an almost exclusively Gentile virtue) that he knows only one law, the law that entitles him to the free practice of medicine. But what can a Jewish physician answer?

The German anger at America for having passed an act to assist England is turning to fury. The official German press immediately found out who the culprits were . . . the American Jews! Morgenthau, Baruch, Lehman, and several other Jewish political figures. They are the ones who committed the crime of inciting Americans against Germany. And that, the German press stresses with unblinking cynicism, will not help the Jews in Europe. They will pay with new suffering for the American Jewry's hateful gesture.

There are, of course, leaders who know the truth, just as there are minor ones who take seriously the gobbledygook in the German press. Might this tempestuousness and threat of revenge against the Jews be a sign of German weakness? And how can new suffering be inflicted on Jews when they have already endured the worst everywhere?

What else can befall them? Confiscation of property, deportation to camps, mass murder. And then? The old Romanian saying, "the Turk will pay" must be changed to "the Jew will pay." And when he pays, he pays on a global scale.

In the era of nationalistic exaltation, the Iron Guard created an unbearably bombastic style. Words were coupled in a manner that distorted the beautiful and eloquent simplicity of the Romanian tongue. You will often find new words formed in an arbitrary way, adjectives used so inappropriately that phrases became amusing absurdities. Particularly when Jews are the topic, writers seem drunk on misused words. Anything can be "ritualistic": food, thought, a kiss, a business. Similarly, "talmudic" is applied to anything concrete: a talmudic cloth, a talmudic gesture. Today I found a new adjectival phrase, sprung from frustrated hatred: "mosaidic [*sic*] mentality!" I wonder what its author had in mind, that gentleman who, not long ago, wrote of "the Romanian people who's [*sic*] wounds are deep."

### March 18

The law on rents, impatiently awaited, has come out. All leases, except for those of Jewish tenants, will be renewed. Gentile landlords can ask Jews for any rent increase, not on the basis of property value, inflation, or unexpected expenditures, but merely because they are Jewish. Had realistic considerations been taken into account, rent increases would have applied to Gentile tenants of Gentile landlords as well. The latter are cheated. And since Jewish landlords of apartments leased to Jewish tenants must also be penalized, they are not allowed to require rent increases. A radical law at the present sociopolitical juncture would, of course, have stipulated that no Jew may rent an apartment from a Gentile landlord. But such a measure would have dealt a deadly blow to Gentile landlords who, under the law now passed, will be able to lease their properties to wealthier Jews. The legislators' preoccupation is revolting.

Where are we to live now? Housing is scarce, and as for

Jewish landlords, it has never been easy to deal with them. But now, should they have an apartment available occasionally, they will be inaccessible. Actually, whether Jewish or Gentile, all landlords are the same. But we must be optimistic, so I am told. Here's why, according to a nephew of mine: Slovakia has barred Jews from steambaths, public swimming pools, certain shopping centers, theaters, etc.— while we still have the right to offer ourselves to be skinned by any Gentile landlord who can use a lease to demonstrate his nationalism.

No way to escape the oppressive obsessions of the people around you. You want to forget, for a moment, and, in the street glistening with sun, to think of spring. A colleague stops you to ask:
"People keep mentioning April fifteenth. What do you think will happen then?"
Still dazed by the light, you answer:
"The lilac will bloom."
"Come on, seriously," the colleague insists.
"Why do you ask?"
"They are working on dreadful laws against . . ."
"Against the Jews! That's an old story."
You look around: the sun is gone. And you walk away, gloomy again.

As of next month, my economic problems become insoluble. I can only look with horror at the six months ahead. The money for everyday needs, besides fixed expenses, is in tragic disproportion to productivity. The population is crushed to the ground, and I am alone in its midst. There are still plenty of optimists: some have money, others houses. The water has not yet come up to their ankles. They still tell jokes and wait . . .

*March 25*

In the midst of political upheavals, of heightened tensions, of all kinds of rumors and ominous forebodings, I am forced to move. My landlord, a naturalized Greek, felt it appropriate to exceed all limits of inhumanity and take advantage of my special situation as a Jewish tenant. I had to look for an apartment at a time when impossible conditions prevail: an extreme shortage of housing created by the new system of leases. At several apartments for rent, prospective tenants were shown around in groups, as if they were tourists in a foreign museum awaiting their turn outside locked gates. Faced with the landlords' stubbornness and unreasonable demands, I decided to rent a house on Cuza-Vodă, by the Mărăşeşti boulevard. An isolated area, but quiet and perhaps more secure from possible anti-Jewish legislation. The difficulties posed by wood-stove heating are compensated for by a garden full of trees, which also consoles me for the burden of the exorbitant rent. To soothe my embittered heart, I keep telling myself we will be better off there. And I keep finding myself making floor plans and housekeeping arrangements, weighing the possibility of a partial sublet to lighten the economic disaster of these times. Lelia dreams of keeping a dog in the yard, friends offer their help to fix the garden, while I make drafts and take measurements. But it is such a long time until moving day, we don't know what will happen.

*March 27*

Revolution in Yugoslavia. The regent, Prince Paul, has been deposed. Peter acceded to the throne and appointed a militarist government that arrested the former cabinet as well as the two ministers returning triumphant from Vienna where they had signed adherence to the tripartite pact. According to reliable sources and this afternoon's broadcast from London, deliriously happy crowds demonstrated in front of the Soviet and British embassies. In our city—bewilderment and sadness, joy and relief, an overflow of comments. For the first time, it is possible to speak of a turning point in the course of the war. The Russo-Yugoslav friendship, the new configuration in the Balkans, may lead to a turnabout in Bulgaria too, where, rumors have it, the

Germans meet resentment and sabotage. Hence, unexpected changes must necessarily follow. The news of the Yugoslav revolution has made an extraordinary impression on Romanian circles, harassed as they have been for some time by Iron Guard arrogance and by our neighbors' irredentism. People express publicly and without hesitation feelings of embarrassment, regret, doubt, but also admiration. Somebody said that the Yugoslav revolution is the first nail in Hitler's coffin.

*March 28*

Last night, the communiqué regarding the expropriation of urban properties held by Jews threw a wet blanket over the excitement created by the events in Yugoslavia. The news, which was meant to be released Saturday, was announced at midnight, to dampen the spirit of a blindingly bright day and to bring about a diversion as quickly as possible. The effect was, indeed, unambiguous. Foreign events receded and took a back seat. Even poor people who don't own a hut shared the emotion caused by this mass confiscation of all Jewish urban holdings. There are people who have toiled painfully all their lives to buy a modest home of their own. There are some Jews in provincial towns whose property amounts to a hovel or a miserable shop. They, too, will be thrown out into the street. True, quite a few Jewish landlords are indeed exploiters, particularly in Bucharest. Yet the law singles out not *exploiters* but *Jews.* Besides, the specifics as to how the real estate will be distributed among Gentile lawyers, clerks, doctors, and military personnel, and in particular the rationale for this legislation—which invokes not economic and social need, but Christianity and nationalism—are hopelessly sad and unbelievably absurd. Take, for instance, my new landlord: a very pleasant and industrious man who owns a tobacco factory, a luxurious apartment on Strada Luterană, houses with large gardens close to his factory and in various other neighborhoods, an estate of over one hundred million lei. His only family is a daughter married to a diplomat. How has the situation of his countless miserable tenants changed if the exorbitant rents go into the pocket of a Gentile rather than a Jewish exploiter?

## *April 6*

Sudden spring, a powerful heat wave which makes you dizzy and tires body and thoughts. As if overnight, gardens have broken out into impetuous greens. I spent all of yesterday afternoon at our new home taking care of the garden, a marvelous, all-absorbing occupation. I took a spade and started digging the earth. Naturally, lacking practice, I got tired very quickly. Still, it is not hard work, and the satisfaction is full, round, immediate. As the spade penetrates the earth, a feeling of contentment runs through you, the voluptuous pleasure of being in direct and total contact with the source of life.

After fifty years, most of which were spent in the midst of Bucharest's buildings, the contact with a garden is filled with pain and regret. You feel you took the wrong turn: the peacefulness of flower beds and the sunny green of the foliage tell you that you have been cheated of certain experiences in which truth touches different chords. But it is too late for everything, too late even for regrets. . . .

Torn away from the preoccupation with the garden, you are overwhelmed by the tumult of events, rumors, expectations. Bulgaria is on the brink of war. The Hungarian prime minister, Count Pàl Teleki, committed suicide because "his country's honor" was at stake, as newspapers put it, and this has again caused a few moments of depression. But it seems that the Germans are still masters of the situation in Hungary. Yugoslavia is mobilized to the teeth, awaiting the attack. Any day now, the whole area around us will burst into flames. But in the end the Germans will be unable to overcome all the mounting difficulties. Many of the best sources claim that the people in Germany consider the war lost.

This very day, at dawn, the German armies marched into Yugoslavia. Radio London announced that the Soviet Union had concluded a nonaggression and friendship pact with Yugoslavia, effective immediately. A clarification of Turkey's position is also expected shortly. So then, the conflagration has started. Will it engulf us too, or will we be merely singed?

## April 9

The uproar over the expropriation of Jewish urban property has subsided somewhat, overshadowed by the acute drama of military action in the Balkans. Besides, according to many people, this legislation will not be too strictly enforced. The Romanian bourgeoisie did not welcome it wholeheartedly, aware no doubt that the changes it implies will be harmful to its own interests as well. There is persistent talk of a letter to General Antonescu written by Dinu Brătianu, head of the Liberal party, who voices very serious opposition to the Jewish expropriation and points out that this action means the beginning of communism; he asks our leader how and with what funds will he be able to pay compensations at the peace conference. To date, the Center for Romanianization, which is supposed to implement the expropriation, has still not published the details. So those who did not waste a tear over the fate of the big Jewish property owners, were right. For the time being, all these wealthy Jews are doing very well, cashing their rents and buying large quantities of foodstuffs, no matter what the price. Between now and the end of the war, those with money or with properties will manage, while the rest, the unfortunate ones, have entered a period of desperate attempts to make ends meet. The struggle for food supplies becomes tragic. Meat is available once a week only. But who can afford it? We haven't had any beef in two months. Bakers have stopped making white bread, rolls, French rolls, croissants, many pastries. There will be no more lemons; instead, one hundred thousand kilos of citric acid have been ordered. It may be prudent for us to stock vitamin C, as we may not be able to avoid an epidemic of scurvy. It is even impossible to find cornmeal for *mămăligă*.[11] People scoff at

11. Corn mush, a Romanian national dish and the peasants' staple food.

the government's useless attempts to persuade them that the Germans bring their own food supplies, and indignantly watch endless columns of German trucks carting off all kinds of foodstuffs. As of today, there is no more soap. Other things will follow. And we don't know whether this is the only war we will have.

German troops have made a wedge between the Greek and the Yugoslav armies, advanced toward Albania, and occupied Salonika. The news caused some panic, although according to certain information it is only a matter of withdrawal to a more secure defense line, the military plan having always included the possibility of giving up some positions. For the time being, the Germans still have offensive supremacy, although they suffered diplomatic defeat. So long as they are victorious, they will have no domestic trouble, perhaps for quite a while. But with the first defeat, there will be unexpected reactions among the civilian population and even within the army.

For the time being, the German armies are still victorious on the European continent. They will conquer countries, will win all the battles, but they will lose the war. The Soviet Union has the raw materials, the grain, and the oil. Europe cannot be won with military or racist victories when, of the forty-five million quintals of grain produced by the whole continent, forty million belong to the Soviet Union, while of the forty million tons of oil, Russia produces thirty million.

We shall watch the Balkan military chronicle.

## April 14

A new attempt by B. and W. to produce an anthology of a few Jewish writers. The idea is to provide a small income for this handful of writers as well as to make our presence felt. The plan: to gather material at random from any writer, with the only qualification that he be Jewish. C. and I opposed this selection criterion, feeling as we do that nowadays Jews cannot indulge in ivory-tower literature but their writings must be a form of action. This point was well received by everybody except young W., who had a different plan in mind. The consensus, after consultation, was to set up a committee of four or five people to gather and organize the material. We will face difficulties, primarily with the censorship, but also with the raising of funds. However, the determination to shape carefully the image of the contributing writers and to maintain the chosen cachet for the literary material, immediately began to weaken. P., who is in a hurry to earn some money so that he can resume his "cultural offensive" on the few wealthy Jews who still contribute moneys, has already approached me today, expressing bewilderment and impatience with our plans. He has in mind something entirely different: a slim volume of about one hundred pages, which could be printed quickly and possibly on credit. Jewish enterprises, miserable flowers nipped in the bud!

Only now have I gotten around to reading the second volume of the *Notebooks* of Dr. Adolf Stern,[12] although I have had the book for some time. It was highly praised, and I had hoped to find it of literary value. I don't know who edited it—there are many errors, and the rhetorical style mars the scenes, characters, and events described.

On the whole, only the pages dealing with politics are interesting. The rest—a string of repetitious descriptions of conferences, banquets given by the Jewish lodge, his vacation trips, scenes from his family life, too personal to be of interest. The book as a whole mirrors perfectly the oratorical gift of the former Jewish representative in parliament. His speeches, his baritone voice, even his leonine appearance exuded grandiloquence. He led the life of a wealthy member of the upper bourgeoisie, sentimentally—though not insincerely—concerned with Jewish suffering in his era.

The general observations in the notes referring to the Jewish problem are both interesting and saddening: the problem has remained unchanged in fifty years. Although the political and socioeconomic circumstances were different then, the tragedy of Romanian Jewry then and now is the

12. Adolf Stern (1848–1931), a Romanian-born Jewish politician. Among his many offices were secretary to the first American consul in Romania, leader of the Union of Romanian Jews, member of the Romanian parliament, and president of the B'nai B'rith lodge of Romania.

same. Which goes to show that anti-Semitism has deeper roots than we suspect and that it can be eradicated only through a fundamental social change.

I knew Dr. Adolf Stern during the last years of his life. I visited him often, and at tea time, when we were alone, he would reveal to me many intimate things, memories, and insights into people. As he developed hearing problems, I became his physician. But he also asked for my help as a writer to rework his translations from Shakespeare. His manuscripts lay on my desk for many weeks, but I made no progress except for a scene from *Romeo and Juliet.* I suspect that many other writers with whom he associated were invited to assist him with this task. The heavy and rigid language of his verse translations required more than occasional polishing. The whole thing would have had to be redone from scratch, a huge undertaking.

Our friendship led to the development of a program to organize Jewish Romanian writers and artists. A most useful project, since by now it would have developed a cohesive policy, giving the Jewish masses cultural leadership. I repeatedly tried to persuade Dr. Stern to will his mansion to the Jewish writers and artists of Romania. At times I felt I had succeeded, at other times, I lost hope. He kept postponing his decision most adroitly, under one pretext or another until, one day, he was dead.

## *May 1*

A two weeks' digression over the minor tragedy of moving. Absorbed by brutal, physical work, I withdrew from life and people.

I am still alienated and at a loss while trying to adapt to the climate of our new abode, with its greening garden which I have not yet enjoyed because of the work needed on the rooms inside. I feel as if I were living in a village, while Bucharest is over there, far away, and I left it long ago. In this feverishness of settling down, I keep searching for—without finding—myself. I keep stumbling over fears of what is yet to come. Recently, radios have been confiscated from Jews, and there is talk of confiscating other objects.

The atmosphere in this apartment is most pleasant and marvelously conducive to daydreaming and intellectual activities. But there is so much sadness wherever you turn, in the daily waiting, in the wastefulness of living provisionally —I cannot escape reality. The rain keeps falling over spring's tired daylight and on exhausted human resilience.

## May 5

Cool days gliding by, unnoticed and unexperienced, while the labor to settle down in our new apartment and the efforts to adapt to the neighborhood go on. I put my books and manuscripts on shelves, without looking at them, without sorting them out. It was as if some writer who had left the country or died had entrusted me with his papers. Life seems dried up, without sap, like hardened earth furrowed by deep cracks. I don't know where this road we all follow in the dark will lead us. We live on mouth-to-mouth rumors and German communiqués. The season has lost its meaning. These pages, too, are senseless.

## May 10

One year now since the war began in earnest. At dawn on Friday, May 10, 1940, the Germans invaded Belgium and Holland, unleashing the offensive which, in five weeks, led to the destruction of France. Within a single year Europe underwent changes nobody could have foreseen. Since then and to this day, everybody awaits the outbreak of a conflict between Germany and Russia. Now that the Germans have occupied the Balkans, this seems more likely than ever.

## May 23

I haven't touched this notebook in quite a while, perhaps because it is taking so long to settle down in our new apartment. I did try a couple of times, but a hand accustomed to hammer, drill, saw, and paintbrush could not hold the pen. Little did I know that painting a closet, building a clothes rack or bookshelves or the other things needed in a household, could equal in importance European events. Passionately absorbed in these minor tasks, I turned my back upon the whole world, with all its sorrows and clamor. Now and then, some anti-Jewish decree, among many other indignities, managed to draw me out of my burrow. Thus, I went to surrender my radio at the local police precinct. All its personnel was mobilized in view of this "national task." Offices became storerooms, stocked to the ceiling. Jews were waiting in line. Packages everywhere, on the floor, in corners, even on thresholds, packages, packages with labels as large as tombstones, the funereal lettering declaring the make, the date, the owner's name. An obliging policeman relieved me of the radio sooner than I had hoped and shortened my humiliating wait. Now we expect new decrees. There are persistent rumors that Jewish households will be forbidden to employ domestics. The time is ripe: the pattern has been for rumors to be circulated for several weeks before any measure is put into effect, so that the Jews may grow accustomed to the idea of yet another indignity.

## June 5

Having a garden changes entirely your perspective on life. The sudden budding of flowers you planted from seedlings is now the most meaningful event. Clearing footpaths, weeding, cutting the grass, watering, can fill the days with satisfaction. There is not even time left for communicating with your diary, that arid garden where the days grow bitter and scorched. Verses travel smoothly through your soul like clouds gliding without strong temptations, and you let them float away without regret, toward some hedge of memory where you pile all the unfinished stanzas and anemic good intentions. Then evening comes and it is even harder to tear yourself away from the shady, aromatic spot; you wait for that invisible god to fly over flower beds and paths, dusting sadness on the nodding flowers and the loneliness of trees. You never see him, but you feel his breath and flight, and before you know it, you wake up in a sylvan darkness swarming with dreams.

## June 10

The war rumors are now maddening. The city throbs with the most farfetched interpretations of the tension between Germans and Russians. Everyone holds on to a different certainty, each unquestionably right and each equally absurd. Even the sanest people, with clear and more or less rational ideas, become the victims of the measures currently taken. There is mass mobilization, although the agricultural season is now at its peak. Innumerable German contingents, in military formation, headed toward Moldavia. Countless provincials seek refuge in the capital. House and personal searches by the score. In the last few days there have been predictions about the very day, even the hour when war between Germany and Russia is to break out. Radio London is feverishly at work. Still, nothing will come of it. That is, there will be no war, because something is brewing on the diplomatic level. But—will that be all?

Miss Beate Fredanov, who wants to build up a repertory of poetry, asked me to help her make a selection. She was somewhat disconcerted by the tone of the Jewish poets I read to her. During the two hours' reading, I rediscovered some old, almost forgotten works. The young actress has a lively face, deep, expressive eyes, a slightly affected voice, and a tiny, slim frame, lit up by an inner fire, all the stronger now that she has been ostracized from the official Romanian stage.

## June 15

After a tense, emotional waiting period, while the official theatrical season was in progress, Filderman[13] (our *"Füh-*

13. See "1940," n. 47.

*rer,"* as the intelligent and witty neurologist Dr. K. dubbed him) obtained a permit for two Jewish performances: *The Sanger Brothers,* a play selected by A. for the Baraşeum Theater repertory, and a recital of music and literature. Those spectators previously unacquainted with Miss Fredanov had the opportunity to see the whole range of her talent. Great sensitivity, a warm voice, expressive features, her acting sustained by a well-controlled passion. The play itself was weak and inappropriate for the occasion, but the stage design by Maxy[14] was harmonious and displayed to advantage his mature art.

Despite the pettiness and dirty politics prevailing in the Jewish hornets' nest, there was a small profit. It went to some of the writers and artists who have been starving for several months while nobody gave a hoot. As to publishing funds, they will remain a dream, since several additional performances would be needed to raise sufficient money.

## *June 19*

In the last few days the panic over the war has reached unknown heights. Restrictions on movement, gas rationing, evacuation of children, setting up of hospitals—all these and other measures of the kind taken on the eve of war. There are also frightening rumors. London contributes news intended to discount the possibility of a misunderstanding between Germany and the Soviet Union, or even of mere tension while negotiations are in progress. Rather, it broadcasts confirmations that Germany has issued an ultimatum asking Russia to supply grain and oil, and to relinquish not only occupied territories but national ones as well. Hardly anyone believes the official Soviet denials, carried by Tass, that there is such an ultimatum. People are fleeing to the country. My plans to work have gone down the drain. I cannot stay aloof while this circle of catastrophes tightens around me. My garden is my true consolation. But in the last three days it drowned in the rain and I can only watch it from my window. An autumn rain, falling

14. See "1940," n. 38.

day and night, a dark downpour in which people sag and grow gloomier.

### June 21

Today I was ordered by cable to report for military duty to Tîrgovişte, although a couple of days ago another cable instructed me to stay in Bucharest. The rumors and alarm in the city seem to indicate that we will go to war any day now. I still find it impossible to believe. The idea of going to war when I am fifty years old, leaving my family behind, deprived of my material and moral support, makes me unbelievably bitter. Out of my past rises the choking fog of those two years of moral misery, of sickness and emptiness and death, which I faced with determination while the shadow of my waning adolescence looked on, in sad wonder. How will I manage, now that I have been morally crippled and materially brought to my knees? This time around I have been stripped of everything even before the war. All that is left for me is actual death, the physical surrender of a body tired out by sickness and struggle. All my dear ones are dismayed and terrified by what can happen today to a mobilized Jew. I stare at them, not knowing what to say to give them strength. To the very last I cannot believe that we will really be plunged into a bloodbath.

Violent rain. The soul of the garden, to which I have become deeply attached, rises toward me, up here. Today I planted the last seedlings. Will I see them flowering in the fall?

### August 8

After six weeks of total silence, I halfheartedly return to these pages which used to be my daily solace. I found it impossible to write a single line. The thought of death paralyzed my hand, yet today death brings it back to life: the poet Rabindranath Tagore died, far from the native country of his ardent visions. The news carried me back to my youth and I glimpsed the Hindu seer's barge, full of dreams, floating out of my adolescence. His passionate wisdom, his reveries, the richness and poetic grace of his philosophy suddenly came to me like a fragrance and I lost myself in them with the thirst of a creature maimed by a dark and bloody history. The thrilling moments of my adolescence reached their peak, later, when we celebrated the prophet's visit to Europe and to our country. It was a time when poetry was regarded as an event.

It surprised me that, among the news of bloodshed and editorial columns full of hate, someone remembered the white-bearded wizard, in his toga and sandals, who looked upon people from the height of a star-studded garden.


## August 10

A month ago I returned from Găieşti, where I was attached to the hospital set up in the agricultural training school. With the help of young ladies from the local Red Cross, we readied beds and gathered all the required supplies. Two weeks later, General Headquarters issued special orders, whereupon I was sent back home together with all the other mobilized Jewish doctors. That is how long the military episode in the present war lasted for us Jews.

This brief diversion into so-called military service nevertheless gave me the opportunity to learn about quite a few aspects of contemporary life. I spoke to many people—peasants, villagers, soldiers, and officers I met at train stations and on trains. I was horrified by the pervasive hatred toward Jews, whom everybody considers traitors, commandos, Communists, vipers—an uncontrollable hatred spreading like a contagious disease: people don't know when the epidemic has touched them—suddenly the sickness is in their blood. Any slanderous remark about Jews, whether printed in a newspaper or uttered by someone, no matter how nonsensical, is immediately believed. A third-class car, full of Russian sailors, prisoners of war, was attached to my train to Tîrgovişte. The news spread with lightning speed to every station we reached. In a second, civilians emptied the platforms and soldiers left their cars, rushing to see the prisoners. An understandable curiosity—except that the majority clamored for knives, axes, picks, anything to gouge the eyes and chop off the noses of the "kikes," protesting their being transported in passengers' cars. A poor Gentile who dared to object that "after all, they are people, and they fought because they were ordered to," was almost lynched. Then I understood that, in our country, the "kike" is a kind of Soviet citizen, in the absence of any real one. Who knows what tragic confirmation this insight will have as the war goes on! A colleague of mine, a colonel, shared a compartment with a young priest who, noticing at one station some Jews being transported from their village to a concentration camp, remarked: "Why do they bother? Why put them on a train? I would shoot them outright!"

Life in Găieşti was like any other draftee's wartime life. An endless village, stretching out on the road between Tîrgoviște and Pitești. The sad rural look of all Romanian villages, dusty, with gloomy, poverty-stricken little houses. The distance between the hospital, the train station, and the agricultural training school was about four kilometers, and I had to cover it at least twice a day on foot. No one had bothered to provide us with rooms or make arrangements for meals. I was forced to stay at the Hotel Trocadero, the only one in the village, where in a room with an iron bed, a tin washbasin covered with stinking newspapers, a shard of a mirror, and a chair, I had to fight legions of bedbugs all night long. The village has no running water, no electricity. The so-called toilet was a shed outdoors, with a hole in the ground to crouch over. Its stink, mingling with the smell of the linden trees in bloom, reached all the way to my room, where it was impossible to keep the window closed. The only important institution in town, where not even a movie house could be improvised, was the coffeehouse. With time on my hands, that was the place where I had to sit and brood over my loneliness. Actually, there was a park across the street, a rather charming garden with a little stream running through it. But it belonged to a wealthy man, because Town Hall had missed the opportunity to acquire it. Now it was overrun by weeds, sad and dirty, with no benches and no paths—so my repeated explorations soon ended and I was forced to sink again in a chair at the coffeehouse table across the way, engulfed by gusts of dust.

The Găiești residents were resigned to these gusts, but I still tried to find refuge indoors. The decor inside was tasteful, and they served a variety of pastries comparable to the best of Bucharest creations. However, once inside, I had to hold conversations with the proprietor—a nice man, actually: he had a huge head, protruding lips, a voluminous nose and large eyes, an unkempt mane, and spread over his face, a warm, naive smile, as good as one of his confections. Passionately involved in politics, he commented on every event and searched the faces of all the local dignitaries in an attempt to draw from their expression conclusions about the state of affairs.

Our hospital was set up in the agricultural school, located in a very picturesque spot. It looked like an old monastery, with buildings lined up along the three sides of a large inner court. Behind the principal's residence, acres and acres of land were used for gardening, agriculture, and beekeeping. While the students worked the sizable area of land, the produce was sold by the principal, as I was given to understand by locals assigned to the hospital. He came from Bessarabia (a "Russian," it was whispered) and spoke only Russian with his wife and maid. The military personnel attached to the hospital, the Red Cross ladies, and particularly the administrative officer had quite a job persuading him to hand over all the buildings for hospital use. It took us several days to accomplish this transformation. Young girls and ladies of the "Găiești elite" assisted with their conversation the soldiers who scrubbed windows and floors. They made their appearance dressed in the proper Red Cross uniform, expressing their regret that there were no wounded. A baroness and a boyar's wife from the area worked there diligently, with particular attention to the smallest details. Then, a series of lectures in hygiene was offered, and I was harnessed to the job. My teaching proved most effective, naturally, and mutual liking was sparked right away. I asked the captain pharmacist—a very pleasant and decent fellow, who took to me from the start—to tell everybody that I was Jewish, but it seemed he never did. The matter was soon settled by order of General Headquarters. The high society of Găiești learned that it had harbored "a beast, a traitor, a commando, etc., etc."

One rainy morning, wading through billows of mud, I

took leave of my local medical commanding officer, who, ill at ease, mumbled some vague explanation for my dismissal. I already knew the truth. Again, in Tîrgovişte, the major in charge of mobilization was equally embarrassed and overly polite. On the train, Jewish doctors from all over, on their way home, the war behind them.

## August 11

Anti-Jewish measures, unexpectedly harsh, have spread throughout the country. Jew-hatred has become hysterical. All the versions and explanations of the executions in Iaşi, and all we know through official channels, fall short of what really happened. After the Iaşi executions, Jews were rounded up in villages throughout Moldavia and evacuated in sealed cars, where many died a horrible death of thirst and asphyxiation. The tragic details are endless. The most sadistic imagination could not equal what happened at those train stations where the sealed cars with their load of doomed people stopped. Hundreds of women, children, men, herded into freight cars, licked the sweat off one another, drank their own urine to quench their thirst, screaming in agony until they perished. Crazy stories: a man paid twenty thousand lei for a glass of water; others offered priceless jewelry for a sip. A Romanian officer, crazed by the unearthly screams of the dying, jumped onto the platform carrying a bucket of water. When a sergeant stopped him with the butt of his rifle, he cried: "I am a major in the Romanian army! Shoot me, but first let me give them some water!" For those who survived, the road ended in a concentration camp.

## August 12

Having drawn the balance of all the rights I have been deprived of and those remaining, I reached the conclusion that I am still left with the right to my sadness. But if the state cannot contest it, my personal relations can.

## August 13

For the last few days I have been in a state of mental
and physical collapse. I am trying to overcome it, but I am
frightened. Circumstances have overwhelmed me, daily
upheavals have exhausted me. But most of all, I am ap-
palled at my inability to cope with economic problems. All
roads are blocked, my obsession with death grows stronger
and stronger, on streets where I wander without purpose,
in the garden invaded by autumn, in bed when I try to
sleep. An immense weariness rises from all the corners of
my soul, from my very childhood, from muscles tired by the
manual labor I am forced to do, from all the thoughts and
the determination to meet life with vitality and optimism,
when life seems wilted, senseless, and without purpose. This
may be the moment to put an end to it all. I am no longer
curious nor do I understand curiosity about news; I am neither optimistic nor pessimistic about the future, in light
of so many political calamities that have brought me down.
My right to despair may be contested or even criticized by
narrow-minded people. It can certainly be misinterpreted.
This, too, leaves me cold—which may be an indication of
how serious my state is. I am tired, tired, and I no longer
have the moral courage nor the strength to meet material
problems with some heroic gesture. Sooner or later, the
question of economic survival will come up. Who will ask
it? Will it be me, again? Home, people, friends—everything
turns to a thick fog, choking my thoughts and draining my
willpower. I would like to fight, I try to tear myself out of
the vortex that is pulling me down. I did manage to complete a translation, it sits ready on my desk, but everything
has a taste of ashes and sticks in my throat like a foretaste
of death.

## August 15

Getting worse: I'm plunged in silence and cannot stand
company. I'm supposed to explain what the matter is with
me, and I cannot. Impossible to explain depression to a normal, lucid person, who hasn't lost hope or the ability to

enjoy life, however long he may have to wait. While someone near and dear, personally involved, is likely to misinter-
pret my silence because he imagines there is a specific reason for it. Since the behavior of the depressed is very much
like that of an angry man, a person close to him will want to
know the reason or the object of his anger. An asthenic
finds normal life very difficult, because he cannot withdraw,
he can neither keep quiet, nor rest, nor struggle in privacy
to overcome the ashen taste of uselessness, the feeling that
he is powerlessly watching his life disintegrate. Only after
his death do people begin to understand, because death can
shatter even a fool's serenity.

Lately, I have lost some eleven kilos. This, too, may have
contributed to the deterioration of my state, or perhaps the
other way around. But I must fight, I must struggle to cut a
path toward life, even though it may not hold out the promise
of material stability, or of joys. A life where I will have to
chew news and rumors over and over, do household chores,
yawn in the face of empty days that bring nothing but the
despair of yesterdays and tomorrows, unable to read, to
write, on a treadmill grinding out vapid comments on the
universal tragedy whose outcome no longer interests me

## August 16

Huge efforts to work, with no tangible results. No progress with the translations from Yiddish. I leafed through
old, unfinished manuscripts, and wondered how I was ever
able to undertake such work. The claws of misery are still
tight around me. I am perfectly aware of my illness, which
I keep analyzing and hoping to overcome. But what if I
don't succeed? I want to gather all my strength, whatever is
left of it, for the difficult days that lie ahead.

## October 15

Again I stopped writing, unable to touch this notebook.
In this short time, it seems to me, I have lived twenty

years. From the young man returned from forced labor, his hand hemorrhaging, whom Gentile doctors refused to treat —worse, they even undid his bandage, only to send him away, wound exposed, spurting blood—to the Jewish family drowned in the Bistriţa River just the other day, horrifying things have happened during this war, illustrating the tragic Jewish condition. To be sure, Jews are neither better nor worse human beings than the French, the Russians, the Serbs, or any other victims of this war, but it is obvious that they live and die under much more tragic and shameful conditions. We have been without a radio, without a phone, without work, the men taken to forced labor, with the threat of concentration camps, putting up with all the measures to impoverish and humiliate us, culminating in the decree to wear the Jewish insignia on our chest. The latter measure has been the most cruel and the most dangerous one. Thanks to successful pressure, the decree was canceled, apparently throughout the country. But then the order came for the deportation of all Jews from Bukovina and Bessarabia to Transnistria. The small towns were emptied in a few days: old people, women, children, left not knowing why and where to, with bundles containing a handful of their belongings and with the small amount of money the authorities allowed them. How long before our turn comes, here in Bucharest? Rumor has it that this matter is under cabinet discussion. So many rumors have turned out to be true, nothing is impossible.

## October 20

My decision to make a mental note of current events and important dates isn't working. So many things are noteworthy that, as the weeks go by, memory cannot sort out their meaning and connections. Yet someone must go on jotting down all he sees and hears, the daily comments, all the military and political events, for as long as he can hold a pen in his hand. In the street and on the streetcars, history keeps weaving, minutely but most vividly, colorful commentaries. One could keep a street-and-streetcar diary. We are cut off from radio and telephone communications, and yet, when we leave the house, we sense a European situation quite different from what our newspapers tell us. The war has taken an unexpected turn. After four months of relentless German efforts, the Russians have not been defeated. Having failed to conquer Leningrad, the Germans massed in the center for a deadly attack on Moscow and closed in on the fortifications around the Soviet capital. In the south, they crossed the Dnieper and occupied the coast along the Azov Sea. The situation is not favorable to Russia for, according to some officers I overheard on the streetcar today, she won't be ready for an offensive before next spring. In the meantime, as winter is closing in, comparative losses are the subject of heated polemics. The Germans maintain they suffered the modest loss of eighty thousand dead, while inflicting millions of losses on the Russians. The Russians, however, claim they lost only one million two hundred thousand to the Germans' three million.

Romania has occupied Odessa, which has now become the capital of Transnistria.[15] "We gave Cluj[16] away, and got Odessa in return," a man said to an officer on the sidewalk in front of the Bavaria Café. Headlines clamored that Romanian troops "were enthusiastically welcomed by the citizens of Odessa." The second page reported fighting in the streets.

In the last two months I managed to do something I would not have thought possible: I worked on, and almost completed, the anthology of Yiddish poets. This may be the main reason why I completely neglected this notebook. I reached a point where I no longer read the newspapers, knew nothing of what went on in the world, and had no other interest than Yiddish poetry. The harder the blows rained on Jews, the more passionately I plunged into work reaffirming the permanence of Jewish contributions to art. The list of poets translated has extended to forty, and the number of poems to one hundred and twenty. I no longer need Rabinsohn's[17] help. I can read and understand every-

15. Ukrainian territory between the Dniester and Bug rivers, bordering on Bessarabia.
16. Capital of Transylvania.
17. See "1940," n. 6.

thing. Translations I could not hope to do two years ago, present no difficulty now. I feel that most of them are good, in the sense that they are artistic and not merely craftsmanlike. There are very many poets and their poems are varied and excellent indeed. Living with them intimately day by day has been a revelation. No voyage could equal my travels to so many different lyrical climates, my stay among so many outstanding personalities, with their highly individual views and their visions of life. Only now do I realize how little I knew of this world until two or three months ago, when I really delved into it. Who will write a critical and historical introduction to my anthology of Jewish poetry? All the Yiddish poets have left Romania and are scattered, who knows where. Manger[18] is in Tunisia. I cannot reach Leivick[19] in the U.S. And even less the poets in Russia. Still, for the time being, I have plenty to do. I only hope I can find enough Jewish poets to last me till the end of the war.

## October 23

A new decree against Jews: all Jews, men and women, are ordered to contribute personal clothing to the state. Even the poorest ones who own just a torn shirt. Contributions are based on the 1940 income-tax returns, even though we don't have the same income today. A clerk who used to make eight or nine thousand lei must furnish: two coats, three suits, four shirts, four handkerchiefs, four towels, four pairs of socks, two pairs of boots, two hats, two woolen blankets, two mattress covers, two pillow covers, two sheets, two pillowcases. Those who paid income tax on over five hundred thousand lei must hand in a storeful of clothes and linen. At first, people laughed, since the law demands the impossible. There is no sole leather, there are no more boots, and even if there were, Jews are not allowed to buy them. The sale of woolen goods and blankets is forbidden by law.

18. See "1940," n. 14.
19. See "1940," n. 10.

Nevertheless, those who fail to comply with the decree are subject to penalties of from five to ten years in prison and to fines of one hundred to five hundred thousand lei. Some 75 percent of all Jews in Bucharest would have to go to prison. A Gentile remarked that the kind of clothing needed was probably Romanian national costumes, since the peasant soldiers released from hospital will be unable to wear city clothes. A Gentile woman friend of ours said that it would be immoral to dress them in clothes taken from Jews, who are held in deep contempt. The scoffing goes on, but the thirty-day deadline is drawing near. Yesterday, Strada Lazăr, the center for secondhand clothes, was teeming with people, ready to pay fantastic prices for used suits and footwear, since the law specifies "pure wool" and "leather soles." All this after last September's requisition, when Jews gave for the wounded in hospitals countless supplies of pillows, mattresses, beds, bed linen, underwear. Gentiles were not asked to contribute even a spool of thread. Requisition clerks went from street to street, demanding whatever pleased them from rich or poor, and not just once, but over and over. Now the new law does not take into account these earlier contributions.

A teacher of geography, a Gentile, told me that he showed a Gentile friend the newspaper in which the law appeared. He had folded the paper so that the headline could not be seen. When his friend read the article, he cursed the government: he was under the misapprehension that the demands for contributions applied to Gentiles. But upon unfolding the newspaper and seeing the heading, his friend's indignation miraculously subsided: "Well, that's a horse of a different color. But then, we should send our clothes in to be given to the peasants, and in exchange we could ask for the good ones donated by the Jews."

## October 27

The letter General Antonescu sent Filderman has been given front-page coverage in all newspapers, creating a sensation. It mentions how the Jews harassed our troops when we evacuated Bessarabia a year ago.

Today, on the streetcar, a peppy and sprightly little old man with a basket in his hand got on at the Şerban-Vodă stop, and immediately started a harangue:

"Imagine that! The kike's general, this Filderman, dares to call General Antonescu to account for killing kikes! Doesn't he know that the kikes spat on our soldiers? They're only getting what's coming to them. It's either them or us!"

The conductor went over to get him his ticket.

"Where to?"

"To Bellu."

"Then you'd better get the streetcar in the opposite direction. Instead of running off at the mouth, why don't you pay attention to what streetcar you're taking?"

"So you're a kike, too?" the irate citizen replied.

They almost came to blows. A policeman who happened to get on settled the matter.

I enjoy sweeping the dead leaves in the garden. That particular sound, the dry sonority as they roll under the broom, pleases me. A kind of sadistic pleasure perhaps, but not too wicked. I envy professional sweepers their big machines and the large, leaf-covered areas they have to clean up! Voluptuousness . . . Somebody warned me not to talk too much about it, lest I be sent to forced labor as a streetsweeper. My age protects me for the time being. But who can tell, maybe someday . . . Many students and intellectuals have been sent to sweep the streets. A pub owner in Colentina,[20] they say, joined the ranks of Jewish students assigned to this task. He was in pain at the thought that his son, too, was a student.

*October 29*

A huge wave of new persecutions against European Jews. And America hasn't even entered the war yet! What further measures of massive extermination will be taken then? In the meantime, according to the Swiss press, Germany empties its cities of Jews and transports them to Po-

20. A suburb of Bucharest.

land. Some twenty thousand were deported from Berlin and Vienna. It is unlikely that we will escape a similar fate. Jews in all walks of life, throughout the country, are in the grips of panic. In the Romanian part of Bukovina staggering numbers of Jews have been evacuated, under tragic circumstances. Four thousand were deported from Rădăuți[21] alone. Just before the roundup, two doctors committed suicide. The wife of one of them, a German Gentile, told the horrifying details. The head of the hospital where his two dying colleages were brought, laughed, wondering that more people weren't taking their own lives, since the same end awaited them wherever they would be sent. No exceptions were made—pregnant women, paralytics, people over seventy-five years old, all were deported. The vengeful atmosphere created by General Antonescu's letter keeps our fears alive. Might there also be some domestic problems which caused such very harsh sanctions? We don't know anything. As usual, unfounded rumors are circulated, but in the general despondency they are soon taken seriously. There is persistent though totally unfounded talk of a possible pogrom. By whom? How? Fear will believe anything.

## November 8

Waiting, waiting . . . grinding worries and terror from day to day. We live on rumors, anticipating new anti-Jewish measures to be taken and old ones to be more strictly enforced. It seems that the forced-labor brigades will be placed in concentration camps for the winter. In this case, there will be no escape for the Jews until the end of the war. Actually, one could truthfully say that life for these brigades is even now a concentration-camp life. Is it conceivable that the commanders of these brigades and their underlings will give up their profits during the winter? At a certain location not far from Bucharest there are twenty-five hundred Jews. For the slightest favor any of them receives, any easing of their burden, or whenever one of the supervisors gets angry, he demands one hundred lei per Jew, that is, a quarter million lei a week. And the supervi-

---

21. A town in Bukovina.

sors get angry very often, at least once a week! The situation is no better elsewhere: a construction supervisor was assigned seventy-five Jews to do some work on a railroad. All were city people, mature heads of families, professionals or businessmen. The supervisor, a young boy, welcomed them thus: "Hey, we have work to do, and we gotta do it! If you don't want me to get angry, you will give me . . . let's say, a pol²² a day!"

The mentality of a whole era is reflected in countless incidents such as these. Will anyone record them? Meanwhile, the war goes on.

*November 11*

Our garden died, perhaps last night. This morning brought snow and sleet. A carpet of wet leaves, the trees half naked, the hedges wretched. Just a few shrubs with some fight left in them. The last tobacco flowers give up their ghost, and a few white dahlias beg to be sheltered indoors. No one looks at them anymore. This autumn is more terrible than any other: like leaves in the garden, people lie in the fields. The increasing physical and spiritual miseries that overwhelm us chase metaphors away. You turn to stone. No room left for poetry, sensitivity, any of the old ways of life. To reflect seems empty and ridiculous, memories are in ashes, poetry—an embarrassment. Dead leaves and rain. People move like mechanical ghosts. You stop in the street to chat for ten minutes with a Jew, and you return home sick to your heart. This morning a newspaper declares in large headlines: JEWS MAY NO LONGER SHOP EXCEPT AT SPECIFIED HOURS. One of the latest decrees. Why right now, when there is nothing to buy in the market? Who can tell? Wealthy Jews will go on shopping at expensive grocery stores. No one has stopped them *yet*. The poor haven't bought anything for a long while. . . . We expect still other decrees. It is rumored that, although all Jewish employees will keep their jobs, they will be paid forty-five lei a day, the same amount as those doing forced labor, and required to deposit the rest of their salary with the Recruit-

---

22. A colloquial term for twenty lei.

ing Center. That's equalization: why should some have everything, and others nothing?

## *November 14*

One could write a diary of rumors: a notebook would be filled in no time. It might be interesting to keep track of all rumors and see what the proportion is between those that prove false and those that materialize. There is again panic among Jews. Again? The fear of deportation to the Ukraine has not stopped for a minute. It is every Jew's obsession, each waking hour. Nothing is absurd any longer. News from the Jews in Transnistria drives you insane: traveling on foot in the rain, through mud, women and girls raped, starvation, one bread a day for ten people, suicides, other agonizing tragedies. Today I recoiled when I saw B., his face ravaged, as if emerging from a pile of ashes. Tortured by the rumor of Jewish deportation from Bucharest, he grew indignant at the sight of two Jews chatting and laughing. How can Jews laugh?

A professor who read Hitler's speech in a German newspaper found the following passage, which had not appeared in the Romanian newspapers: "Should we lose the war—which is an impossibility—this much is certain: *one* people will have ceased to exist and will not witness our defeat. We have taken all the necessary measures [*Wir haben dafür gesorgt*]." Hitler spoke of many other things, but it seems that the only European problem he can still solve is the extermination of the Jews. All the other subjugated nations he can drain, he can humiliate through armed force. The Jews—he annihilates. Is this indeed possible on as radical a scale as he envisions? However, his preoccupation with the idea that Jews should not enjoy Germany's downfall indicates weakness, a beginning exhaustion of moral and economic resistance.

The law requiring Jews to give the state clothing, underpants, and other belongings, is being definitely and most

thoroughly implemented. Requests to relax some of the absurd requirements have been denied at the last moment. The
government was petitioned to exempt at least the needy appearing on Jewish welfare associations' rolls: request denied. Beggars for bread and a shirt, the disinherited who
freeze and starve, are supposed to submit stamped petitions
to tax collectors' offices, bribe clerks in order to get official
certification that they are paupers, and thus be allowed to
contribute no more than a shirt, some handkerchiefs, socks,
underpants, and a towel. The Jews are hysterical. The
wealthy ones, who as soon as the decree was issued bought
up dozens of coats, suits, boots, etc., now have them available. The others are running around in a daze from street
to street, unable to figure out a way to collect goods equal to
a dowry. A lawyer sent a summons to the Mociorniţa shoe
factory, demanding delivery of a pair of boots according to
government specifications. The factory owner replied, also
through a bailiff, that the very same authorities forbade
him to sell boots, the purchase of leather and soles being
blocked. So the lawyer included in his package of clothing
the manufacturer's reply. Somebody suggested that the
Jews ought to steal the required goods from stores. Tried
for theft, the maximum penalty a Jew can get is six months
in prison, while failure to hand over the required belongings means imprisonment for from five to ten years! The
penalty for a major crime is also five years.

*November 18*

Today on Strada Batiştei I saw for the first time an example of compliance with the law: a coach filled to overflowing with pillows in new green cases, a stack of blankets, bas-
kets with overcoats, shoes, etc. It looked as if someone were
moving, or like a delivery to a large store in the market.
People, amused, laughed as they looked on.

I met the novelist C.A. today: an unchanged bohemian
with salt-and-pepper hair disheveled by the wind, kind,
piercing eyes made sharper by high cheekbones, his tie awry
and his shirt a dubious color, his suit threadbare. I hadn't

seen him in a long time. He was in mourning. I did not know he had lost his twenty-seven-year-old son, the youngest judge in the country. I expressed my sympathy, but he cut me short:

"Your tragedy hurts me more than my loss! Why don't they poison you all, all at once, rather than torture you like this, bit by bit?"

The streetcar echoed with his loud, defiant apostrophe, and all the passengers turned to look at both of us. We went on talking and it struck me that this Transylvanian was very knowledgeable. Apparently it takes someone really well informed to react the way he did.

*November 30*

The collecting of Jewish belongings has created a complicated bureaucracy: centers, subsidiaries, various services. The main synagogue swarms with people come to pay all kinds of taxes. The Comunitatea[23] is taking advantage of this unique opportunity to get hold of all Jews and force them to register as members. There are almost as many clerks behind desks as petitioners in the waiting room. To one side, there is the "solicitors' office"—an imposing name, hiding an office where the poor Jewish lawyers, reduced to the legal function of certifying incomes, stamp the letters *A.B.C.D.* on documents. A motley crowd waiting. In one corner, a young lady who may have been flirting with the temptation to convert, stubbornly refuses to join the Comunitatea. A tall, hefty gentleman, very well dressed, looking like someone who never stepped near a ghetto, waits, dignified and resigned, by a table, to make contact with the Jewish law-enforcers. People rebel against the pressure to extort large contributions and begin to reject any compromise. A man shouts: "Let the millionaires who are leaving on their private yachts pay, not us, the penniless, left behind to bear the burden!"

In the building next door, where the Jewish belongings

23. A body representative of the Jewish population in every city, charged with the administration of its schools, religious life, and welfare.

are collected, you are struck by the smell of old cloth and linen penetrated by the stale, smoke-filled air. Mountains of clothes, underwear, footwear, blankets. The goods are checked, receipts issued. All of them, according to the best informed sources, go to Germany. We are the only allied country in which the Germans behave as if we were a vanquished one.

The other day a man said:
"You know, the Jewish situation has improved!"
"How so?"
"Now they may include darned underpants among the personal belongings they must hand over."

The meeting with George Brătianu[24] was more productive than expected. He listened and admitted that there was justice in the cause submitted to him. He recalled that he had previously interceded with the government in behalf of the Jews and promised to intercede again. In his view, it is not fair to deal with the Jewish population in the current manner. Some errors and abuses are understandable in the context of events in Bessarabia, during a war, but here, where the population is peaceful and hardworking, how can one condone a system of organized persecution? He implied that it would be too much to ask that action be taken against "elements who have emigrated" (the Iron Guard). Unchanged—a liberal, a Germanophile, and even an anti-Semite, yet willing to help the Jews. . . .

Someone who read my anthology of Yiddish poets remarked that there aren't many love poems in it. The observation is quite correct, and I myself often noticed this lack in the course of my work. Indeed, vibrant eroticism, flights of passion, or amorous reverie are generally poorly represented in Yiddish poetry—at least among the thousands of poems I have read for my selection. And this is not because Jewish poetry is incapable of expressing them. The love the Yiddish poets sing is full of sadness, and more often than

---

24. George Brătianu (1898–1955), a Romanian historian and head of the dissident faction of the Liberal party.

not, it is used as a secondary element framed by the broader themes of death, remembrance, or social revolt. That is why I was truly moved when I came across the "Pastoral" of Aaron Zeitlin[25]—its classic, luminous, and idyllic harmony raise it to great art. I shall have to search again, and specifically, through the dozens of books and magazines that have taken my room over. When I look at so many volumes of poetry, I am overwhelmed by despair, and sometimes I feel how vain is my attempt to rescue a thought, a bit of dream, overlooked or forgotten, out of the works of over one hundred poets. My despair grows worse when I add to them the countless hundreds of poems in other literatures. Literary waste, a cry in the wilderness, an ocean of nothingness in which any anthology must drown. And so will this one.

## December 8

The war has broken out in the Pacific, a war announced and expected long ago. The city reacted frantically, with passionate casuistry, to Japan's involvement and to this final act. At the same time, we received England's declaration of war on Romania. Again the feeling that a whole new series of actions is taking place, accelerating the rhythm of war. Everybody is highly impressed by the Russian offensive. In some Romanian circles it has even created a kind of minor panic, and although there are a thousand kilometers to Odessa, still, some people have begun to wonder.

## December 10

The other day I attended a tea party at S.'s home, where I met the former Minister Mihail Ralea.[26] To all appearances, we were among friends, or at least among people openly hostile to the aggression going on in the world. More

25. Aaron Zeitlin (1898–1973), a Polish-born Hebrew and Yiddish writer who later lived in the United States.
26. Mihail Ralea (1896–1964), a politician and prominent Romanian critic and philosopher.

than that: the people there, I had been told, had leftist leanings. But in our country, such statements must be taken
with a pinch of salt.

Mihail Ralea is someone who, in our country, passes for a
democrat, that is, more often than not, an open-minded man,
ready to adapt his views to the platform of any party which
holds out a promise of rapid promotion. Intelligent, a good
speaker, with slight demagogical overtones, quick-witted,
caustic, he was eager to stress his position as being a prag-
matic one, that is, with a strong leaning to the left. We spoke
to him about the Romanian people and of a variety of questions that might find a favorable solution, a happier outcome,
but he replied: "There is nothing we can do. We are a nation
that murdered two hundred thousand women and children!"

Then he gave us details on the murders in Bessarabia
and Bukovina. My flesh crawled on hearing them. Groups
of women drenched in gasoline and set on fire. A hundred
children buried up to the neck, so that only their heads
stuck out, then machine-gunned. S. saw a photograph one
officer carried of a group of Jews who were made to stand
on a table in a dining room, their heads covered with nap-
kins, with ropes tied around their necks, the other ends tied
to ceiling beams. Then the table was removed from under
them.

We also discussed the Jewish problem, of course. Ralea
said he was aware of everything that was going on and
asked for our suggestions and proposals. But during the
ensuing discussion, when we mentioned the atrocities
brought on by so many anti-Jewish laws and known to everybody, it turned out that he was not quite as well informed
as he thought. Harassed, plagued by lawsuits brought
against him in his capacity as former minister, his fear of
the Iron Guard still unhealed, he could not see his way to
intercede in behalf of the Jews with the present government, even on humanitarian grounds. Dr. L. had assured
him, following a conversation with General Antonescu held
a few days earlier, that the general was determined not to
take any further measures against the Jews. But nobody
was inclined to believe this news. Ralea may try to influence
some political figures, convinced as he is that what is done
to the Jews causes great damage to the Romanian people.

What impressed me throughout our long discussion was his obsession with saving his own skin, should there be a radical political change in days to come. We parted without establishing any grounds for a more promising future.

### December 14

In a new speech, perhaps the weakest of all his speeches to date, Hitler made history by claiming that not England but Germany had brought civilization to Europe, insulting Roosevelt, whom he labeled mentally unbalanced, and declaring war on the United States, with Italy and Japan at his side. The war has thus become indeed a world war, stretching over all the continents on the globe. Now future developments are anyone's guess. Will war end in Europe but continue in the Pacific? Will it end everywhere all at once? In Europe, it seems, the outcome depends on the battles in Russia. A few days ago the Germans announced withdrawals, front-line rectifications, some necessary retrenchments. The Russians, however, speak of a counteroffensive along the whole battle front, of disengaging Leningrad, of massive thrusts toward the center, and of pursuit in the south. In Africa, too, England has taken the offensive. The world is still waiting for Turkey to make its position clear. It seems to be the only country left out of the war. Because of the oil supplied by Russia and of the aid received from America, it is likely that Turkey may take a stand very soon. Important things will happen then. . . . The usual comment.

### December 16

Another wave of unrest among Jews. Everybody is talking about a total solution to the Jewish question in Romania, that is, the deportation of all Jews to Transnistria.

I have come upon a real treasure: a large number of issues of the *Literarishe Bleter,* a magazine which used to appear weekly in Warsaw, in Yiddish, and which became the focal point of all movements in literature, the arts, and the

performing arts that flourished in Jewish centers throughout the world. All the poets whose works I have searched
out over the last two years have been published in its pages.
It is invaluable for the completion of my anthology. Num-
berless portraits, biographical and critical data, and a
wealth of poetic material are scattered in its pages over the
years when the magazine appeared regularly and equaled in
quality the best Western publications.

### December 20

The Germans have managed to popularize in a very
short time certain concepts that have reached all strata of
the Romanian population. The other day, a little girl ran
into a yard in the Lucaci neighborhood. At the gate, two
little boys who must have been chasing her, stood shouting
at her. One of them, barely six years old, screamed: "Fuck
you, kike! I'll have you sent to a concentration camp!"

### December 23

I am struck by the great influence Heine exercised on
Yiddish poetry. Jewish poets must have read him out of
empathy with his roots, and not because of their familiarity
with the German language. To be sure, very few Yiddish
poets have had the advantage of a culture broad enough to
become acquainted with many European poets. Still, there
are few signs of contact even with German poets, except for
Heine. The influence of Rilke, of Stefan Georg, of many
others would have been evident, were access to a language
sufficient reason to explain influences.

Perhaps, eventually, I myself will have to write the
preface, a brief essay on the history and characteristics of
the Jewish poetry represented in the anthology. But there
is no rush just now. There is even time to work on the anthology itself. Nevertheless, I have already prepared the
negatives of the photographs that have been supplied by the
generous Moscovici.[27]

27. Heinrich Moscovici (1892–1979), one of the author's intimate friends.

*December 29*

Christmas—the first one we haven't spent at home. We visited friends, mostly out of a need for mutual support during this waiting period whose end seems at times near at hand, at times out of reach. The food was still abundant, considering how bitterly difficult it is to get supplies. Good wine, but very expensive. The relaxing hours spent at Maxy's, with laughter and memories, the actors Finţi and Beate Fredanov, then Călugăru[28] and Benador[29] dropping in, were bracing. I have not relived, this time around, the usual sadness brought on by the Christmas atmosphere, a sadness that drags itself unwillingly all the way from my childhood. In general, I seemed not to notice the holiday. I didn't see the city, was not stopped by shop windows, didn't meet people, didn't exchange gifts. The official solemnity of the occasion dissolved in an inner stirring of memories and of this year's remembered suffering. I have hardly ever spent a Christmas without writing poetry, so this year is exceptional even insofar as my poetic activity goes, since I worked instead on the translations from Yiddish. For me, a new world, a new perception of a different kind of creativity which adds further depth to the suffering of the past year. And yet another novelty: my daughters are grown up, they have become independent people and no longer want to accompany their parents, no matter where we go. They have joined the circle of their generation, with its unrelenting youth. A kind of loneliness I never knew before, a new opportunity to render accounts, to experience sadness and worthlessness, and the skipping of a heartbeat at the sudden awareness of time slipping by.

*December 31*

We have grown used to stopping for a moment at this borderline of wonder and sorrow that we call the end of a year. A classic exercise—to reflect and draw up the balance

28. See "1940," n. 44.
29. Ury Benador (1895–1972), a Romanian-born Jewish novelist.

sheet. There is enough motivation to do so when you look at the past year from the perspective of its end. Perhaps no other year has been so overburdened as the one ending today. It is no exaggeration to say that I feel as if I have lived through ten years. Some occurrences seem to be distantly projected into history. Between the crimes and plunder of the Iron Guard regime, culminating in the massacre during the rebellion early this year, and now, when the war should have been over (according to Hitler's solemn promises)—the road is covered with blood, pillage, terror, and breakdowns caused by justifiable despair. This is a difficult time for someone who looks objectively at what goes on around him in order to record everything he sees and to make peace between what he sees and what he thinks. Perhaps this attempt is less useful and less interesting than one might think: the gift of foresight and the confirmation of predictions matter only to one's personal vanity. But it is important that during this year, which seems to have reached new peaks of injustice, hatred, and crime, some people have come to realize what is really going on in the world. Even here, many a conscience has been shaken, awakened from its torpor and its satisfaction with living in the present, and prompted to seek precise information and be honest. The effects of war, abroad and at home, have compelled people to look beyond the narrow realm of their egotism and discard their habits of lazy political thinking. Until recently, they allowed themselves to be impressed by Germany's brute force, not questioning what fostered it or to what use it was put, disregarding even the pain they themselves felt at the maiming of their own country. Today, many have come to understand that the German élan is not patriotism but vandalism, thirst for murder and plunder, and that this kind of motivation takes its toll. A very disturbing question arises when one tries to understand why not one country overrun by the Nazis refuses to submit and learns how to defend itself.

According to information a reporter gave me today, it appears that the war on the eastern front continues unabated. Yesterday, Russian troops landed in Crimea, occupying the Kerch peninsula and Feodosiya. The German attack on Sebastopol has suddenly stopped. German troops, it seems, are beginning to withdraw from Crimea. What will the new year bring us? In the meantime, the Germans scramble desperately for any woolen goods, undressing even their own citizens, who, at last, are given explanations about the military situation: the freezing cold, misinformation as to the strength of the Soviet army, which is sometimes superior to the German one, etc. It will take a while, however long or brief, still—we have to wait, although there are tiny cracks, vague signs of disintegration, now whispered about in Germany. In the meantime, for me—a productive shelter on poetry's blue shores, and patience. There are holes in the devil's boots.

*Emil Dorian with his mother and two sisters, 1910.*

*Emil Dorian*
*as a student, 1914.*

*(Right) with friends, 1914.*

On the Moldavian front
at the start of World War I.

Serving as an army physician, World War I.

*Medical staff, Saint-Louis Hospital, Paris, 1927.*
*Dorian is in the second row, seventh from the right.*

*Emil Dorian in his medical office, Bucharest, late 1920s.*

*In his study.*

*Paula Fränkel Dorian
in the 1930s.*

*Paula Fränkel
as a young girl.*

*Family portrait, late 1920s, with children, Marguerite (right) and Lelia (left).*

*Emil Dorian, mid-1930s.*

*With Heinrich Moscovici in Cişmigiu Park, late 1930s.*

*Dorian's translation*
*from the Yiddish*
*of an Aaron Zeitlin poem,*
*"Pastorală" ("Pastoral").*

*Translation from the Yiddish*
*of a love poem by Itzik Manger,*
*"Creşul Nostru"*
*("Our Cherry Tree").*

Front page of Infrăţirea, *October 1, 1940, with articles by*
*M. H. Maxy and Emil Dorian. (Liana Maxy)*

*Notice distributed to all booksellers in Romania in 1940,*
*listing the names of Jewish authors whose books were not allowed to be sold.*
*(Yad Vashem, Jerusalem)*

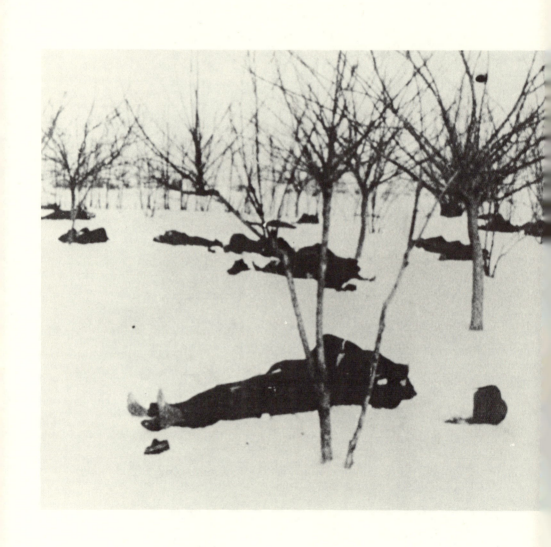

*The Bucharest pogrom, January 21–23, 1941. (The Jewish Museum, Bucharest)*

*The Bucharest pogrom, January 21–23, 1941.*
*(The Jewish Museum, Bucharest)*

# 1942

*January 4*

Under their calm surface the days are feverish with preparations for events which will inevitably take us one step closer to dreaded outcomes.

The overall tone of official proclamations indicates that the war will go on, whatever the reversals and the probable casualties. On the eastern front the Germans keep being repelled and, although the winter is frighteningly harsh, the battles are as fierce as ever. According to our local German sources, all the German men in the neighboring countries have been drafted and sent to the front, the older ones serving as military police. A German who was a captain in World War I told me: "That's a bad sign. Then too, in the last year of the war, a police force was created on the front line."

In our country too, there are preparations for massive

concentration of military forces, while the Jews are rounded up for forced labor. Some Romanians are annoyed by this measure, but it seems that there is no way out any longer. The wave of hatred against Jews will no doubt rise when Romanian soldiers join again the German troops, which need large-scale reinforcements. That is what happened last summer. Hostages have already been taken a few days ago from among the prominent Jews of Braşov,[1] "just in case," as they say. Should the difficulties of the new military campaign increase, so will the persecutions.

It is rumored that three weeks ago General Antonescu[2] refused to sign a decree issued by Mihail Antonescu[3] for the deportation of all Jews from the Old Kingdom to Ialomiţa.[4] Perhaps, next time around, different circumstances will dictate a different stand. What then?

## *January 7*

Long discussion with N.G., former representative of the National Peasant party. Four friends of mine and I met with him to exchange views on the Jewish question, but these good intentions soon petered out. G. is still passionately interested in politics, full of verve, courageous and resilient, even after a recent treatment in a mental hospital for a schizophrenic episode. He indicates great interest because of the extreme left position he had in Maniu's party,[5] but still it comes as a surprise to hear him express, with such eloquence and enthusiasm, communist sympathies and his political and military visions of a near future in step with Soviet views. He was always a democrat, but he started out as a defender of Corneliu Codreanu.[6] In our country, democracy was the most daring political posture, hiding all sorts of blunders, hesitations, and even small deviations which were in fact antidemocratic, in short—a

1. A city in Transylvania.
2. See "1940," n. 40.
3. Mihail Antonescu (1907–46), a Romanian politician who filled several political posts during the fascist regime in Romania.
4. A province in southern Romania.
5. See "1937," n. 3.
6. See "1938," n. 21.

springboard for opportunism. Strange things are happening today. Here he is, this G., a native Romanian, a Romanian patriot and politician, maintaining that Bessarabia belongs to the Russians by right and in accordance with international law, and advocating a plebiscite, while we Jews argue against him in favor of a Romanian Bessarabia, on grounds of political freedom and social justice. Soviet victory is his leitmotif in discussing all problems. It would appear, from what he said, that he propagandized his views actively, explaining matters to innumerable ignoramuses. Is it sincerity, opportunism, or insight into the role political parties will play in the near future? He was fully informed on the Jewish question. He agreed with us entirely and expressed indignation, so perhaps, generous and ready to rush to the rescue as he is, he may lend a helping hand and speak to his former political associates in behalf of the Jews.

## January 12

The anthology has grown impressively: two hundred poems. Still, I have to translate the work of several other poets and add a few more pieces by those already included. I am rather glad that personal and external circumstances have prompted this work, which, I feel, is leading to most interesting results. However, I could not have achieved very much without Rabinsohn's[7] assistance: it is he who, with the enthusiasm of a poet, his love of Jewish poetry, embarked on a real bibliographical campaign to secure the necessary sources. Although by now I have learned to read the material easily and can muddle through even without his help, he remains the guardian angel of my labor, its staunchest proselytizer, and a tireless ransacker of collections of Jewish lore and Yiddish libraries. At the same time, my dear and enthusiastic friend Moscovici[8] watches with great concern the progress of my work and offers material aid to make sure that it does not suffer because of

7. See "1940," n. 6.
8. See "1941," n. 27.

today's difficult living conditions; so he showers me with paper, with offers to cover the cost of retyping or of copying.

This work, I might say, is being completed under an auspicious star, notwithstanding the harshness of our times. My family's warmth and support, talks, reading, discussions—all is grist to my mill, for this work needs time, intellectual steadfastness, and serenity. It would be a pity if anything broke up the line of a life in which poetry remains the only luminous reality.

Zeitlin,[9] one of the juiciest poets for inspiration as well as technique, concludes an epigrammatic poem on Jews with the following stanza:

> *Guarded stands our God between the knife*
> *of Muhammad and the blade of Christ.*
> *But when a prophet's born in our midst,*
> *like the rest of us,*
> *he will grow up to be a journalist.*

The poet F., among others, remarked that real life has turned things upside down: Herzl was a journalist turned prophet.

## January 19

Endless snow for many days now. A mean winter is setting in, a winter not unlike that of 1917, which I spent in Moldavia, during the war.

Huge snowdrifts, numbing frost, and icy winds. The shortages have become a serious problem. On every street you meet people toting empty kerosene cans. We are short of kerosene, of wood. Food prices are skyrocketing. The bread rationing now enforced allows for three hundred grams of bread a day per person, but only for five days, which amounts to a daily allotment of two hundred grams. Harder times loom ahead, for when spring comes war will start up again with greater intensity.

9. See "1941," n. 25.

Time goes by slowly, all the slower because the eagerness to know what the future holds keeps growing sharper and corrodes even the deepest layers of optimism. For such a long time now we have been adding up tallies of dead people, frozen corpses, sunken ships, downed airplanes. But most painful of all is the fact that people are still unaware, have still not realized what is happening to mankind, and see only what their blinkers allow them to see, the shrunken horizon of petty, personal concerns. There are almost no exceptions, even among the young. And so this waiting becomes all the more maddening. While the snow keeps falling . . .

*January 25*

A week of terrible frost. The city, under the heavy layer of snow—which kept falling, ceaselessly, for days and days —now looks like a field of trenches. Trains cannot move any longer. Cars lie buried in snow on streets and roads, and people are struggling to find a path through the snowdrifts. It was only natural that the Jews, who must be readily available to the state for any emergency, should be summoned to clean up the mess. So teams of young people, and not so young ones, went out with shovels in a freezing 31° C. Within a few hours, many suffered frostbite. I myself took care of numerous cases of frostbitten ears.

Today, in a bookstore downtown, I overheard a conversation between a priest and a German officer. They were talking about the latest events on the eastern front: the Russian army had broken through the German lines and advanced 130 kilometers toward Chelm. (At the time, this was news to me, so I didn't believe it, but later, on the streetcar going home, I heard people talking about it as if it were a certainty.)

"Might this be the result of Hitler's assuming command on the eastern front?" the priest asked ironically. The officer forced a smile in an attempt to hide his bewilderment and gloom.

Still, the winter is long and cruel, and there will be a lot to endure. There is no way of telling what is in store for us. I, for one, am fighting hard against the increasing personal difficulties. The lack of household help forces me to undertake arduous tasks. I am so exhausted physically that I stumble through the day, drained by lack of sleep, as if I were a quarry worker unloading stones. But we Jews have reached such depths of degradation that we are grateful merely to be alive here, whatever the conditions, and not in Transnistria, where hunger, sickness, freezing cold mow down hundreds of lives every day. The news we get from there is shattering. Whatever I do, wherever I am—at the table, at my writing desk—the thought of what is happening to these human beings poisons every moment of my life with its silent scream, its barren hopelessness, its mute rage.

No one knows what will become of the rest of us. The prospect of more deportations is again in the air, but no action has been taken so far. Has it merely been postponed?

## *February 3*

The Jewish labor on snow removal is progressing fairly well. From the start, young people appeared spontaneously at work points, offering hot tea and cigarettes to the workers. In some places, next to wealthier homes, both Jews and Gentiles served food and hot beverages. Some Gentiles protested against the decree and refused to have the sidewalk swept in front of their homes. A lady with a well-known aristocratic name stopped the UCB[10] leader of a team just as it was about to start shoveling snow. The leader demanded an explanation and threatened to denounce her.

"This kind of work is done by servants, not by intellectuals," she said, and gave her name to report.

The UCB man was much impressed with the famous name and gave up. But other UCB employees—garbage collectors and petty clerks—have often behaved brutally toward the improvised snow shovelers, pushing them around, cursing them, refusing them a break, and so on. On the

10. The Bucharest Sanitation Department.

other hand, some men showed real understanding. The Jews' return home on the streetcar is a hard moment. The other riders resent these young people who crowd in, shovels in hand, frozen and exhausted: "kikes," that is, second-rate beings—and street-sweepers to boot! How dare they take up the space of decent citizens!

It seems that even physicians (Jewish ones, of course) will not be exempt from forced labor.

## February 7

The law regulating Jewish life has finally been published. Actually, it has appeared only in the *Monitorul Oficial* and the *Bukarester Tageblatt,* so I have no way of knowing its details at first hand. But according to what I hear, it seems that the newly established Centrala Evreilor din România[11] will have eight branches, each with a leader appointed by the government, which now has a special officer in charge of Jewish affairs. Henceforth, one of his representatives is to be present at all meetings of the Centrala. Now, should a Jew need to contact any government office, he will first have to approach this officially recognized body. And from now on, all Jewish activities, all institutions, will come under the supervision of this Centrala, whose first official act was to close down the Jewish newspaper *Renaşterea Noastră.*

## February 11

The other day my friend Moscovici and I called on Barbu Lăzăreanu,[12] with whom we spent a most pleasant afternoon. I did not imagine that he could be so friendly and even charming in his own surroundings. Whenever I

11. On December 16, 1941, the Romanian government dissolved the Federation of Unions of Jewish Communities and replaced it with the Centrala Evreilor din România (Central Organization of Romanian Jews), hereafter referred to as Centrala.

12. Barbu Lăzăreanu (1881–1957), Romanian-born Jewish author and journalist who contributed to the study of Romanian folklore and classical Romanian literature.

had met him previously, he seemed ready to leave after a few formal words, even before the handshake was over. I thought he was incapable of a prolonged chat. But I was wrong. This behavior with people and his general attitude toward life must be due to his shyness. His modest appearance, the soft voice, the way he quickly slips by people—all these are external manifestations of the same total shyness, when a smile is an act of courage. His wife, quiet and self-effacing in company, displays at home a cordial and lively personality which affects the atmosphere of her surroundings. I read to them from my Jewish anthology, which they received enthusiastically, and I searched through his shelves, where I found a supply of new materials. How much longer will I work? Until spring or through summer? An enormous effort is under way for the coming months on the eastern front. The Germans have no way out of their situation there. They mobilize everybody everywhere, they pull out their workers from factories, replacing them with foreign labor, and ask for troops from the Italians, the Hungarians, and from us. That is what everybody says. As for the Jews, labor battalions to be sent to Transnistria are beginning to take shape.

*February 16*

Working on the anthology every day, I am often grateful there is no time left for this notebook. My daily thoughts, the rare dreams and reflections which still cross my mind, go unrecorded. It is strange how restraints and oppression affect all aspects of inner life. Suddenly, you begin to fear that any intimate thought may suddenly become dangerous and cause new catastrophes. Your mere awareness throws a shadow over your insignificant existence, even though you know very well that, from your angle, you are free to see life and people as you please. Yet you don't. Your daily revolt treads mud, cries out to a steadily leaden sky, and still you don't speak out. Most people, everywhere, are silent. The accumulation of their silence, if it turned to dynamite, could blow up the Himalayas. Some sort of weariness, a sinking into a seemingly incurable anesthesia of the spirit, hampers any attempt to say what you think. Most of the time you can find some support in a historical explanation of events. You can tell yourself that, within the framework of socioeconomic and historic developments, and when the whole world is collapsing, individual tragedies are part of the natural course of events. The overall picture may differ somewhat from era to era, but the same causes have the same effects. You know, for instance, that Jews have been persecuted before, have been despoiled, maimed, deported, murdered, under different pretexts but with the same results. Nevertheless, insight into politics is not always enough to help you bear daily tragedy. The actuality of cruelty lies heavier in the balance than a rational understanding of historical factors. Suddenly, thought is completely paralyzed, and in that moment revolt hurts like a burning wound. Then, writing a commentary becomes useless and absurd, just as suffering usually is: useless and absurd. But what can we do? We have learned that a German industrial plant has developed a particularly powerful poison gas. Its efficacy was tested on four hundred Jewish youths picked up from a concentration camp. All of them died, of course. Soon afterward, Thomas Mann spoke on the American radio, denouncing this shameful crime and placing responsibility on the entire German nation, for the people could have prevented their leaders from committing this atrocity, had they wanted to. And that's that.

But after all, you are simply ridiculous if you become selective about the shades of brutality that are to arouse your indignation. Is the gas-poisoning of four hundred people, this scientific experiment committed in cold blood in a peaceful country (Holland), any worse than what happened in another country—the machine-gunning of innocent children, or the murder of adults, old people, babies, through thirst, in sealed cars, or by soaking them in gasoline and setting them on fire during a rampage of revenge?

So you keep quiet, keep treading your daily mud, until you hear that a frightening number of people died of starvation in Greece. And it goes on, every week of this long, this endless season, with all its days alike, ashen, cold, and stained with blood.

*February 20*

Five more days of snow. Every Jew must work for ten days, shoveling. Professional people are exempt, provided they pay a thousand lei a day. That is the going rate for a Jewish intellectual's manual labor. At this price, come summer, when each Jew will owe at least ninety working days, fortunes will have to be paid into the state's treasury. Many intellectuals, they say, have chosen to pick up a spade. People have grown resigned and it all seems quite simple and natural now. Indeed, there are those who declare they are delighted to enjoy fresh air and the healthy sleep that follows. A physician I know has propounded a new hygiene theory on this kind of manual labor, coming close to praising the government for its wonderful idea: imposing manual labor on its Jews.

It has taken me two weeks to rewrite the anthology in its entirety—over four hundred pages. A good opportunity for extensive revisions. But I am afraid of being bogged down now, although I feel I have covered everything of importance. Some works by great poets must still be added, as must several poems scattered in various magazines, and all need polishing. I feel tired facing the coming spring, not so much because of my work as because of outside events and the general mood they create. The war goes on, spreads out. And in our country, too, massive preparations for a renewal of hostilities are under way. That something of the sort is brewing is confirmed by General Antonescu's recent visit to Hitler, as well as by the unmistakable tone of the press.

The city is buzzing with rumors about misunderstandings and difficulties between us and Hungary. What will this amount to?

*February 26*

A new decree: some one hundred twenty Jews were selected from the various districts in the city and instructed by the Centrala to attend a meeting at a synagogue where they were informed that they would be responsible, under penalty of death, for any subversive act committed by Jews or Communists against the state. The lawyer L.S., horrified at being one of the "elect," asked why he had been chosen and how come none of the Centrala's leaders was on the list. No reply was forthcoming.

## March 4

Lelia had a very serious attack of appendicitis. I rushed her to the hospital, where she underwent emergency surgery. The operation was successful and I hope she will soon be completely recovered. Emotional upheaval, which has put a stop to all other preoccupations.

The ship *Struma* about which there was so much talk has met a tragic end. According to official and categorical news, the vessel was torpedoed and the seven hundred fifty Romanian Jews aboard all died. For two months these unfortunate people who had yearned to escape the terrible persecutions we endure here, having paid astronomical sums for a berth on that rotting crate, waited in Istanbul for a gesture of Anglo-Turkish generosity. But in the end they were sent back to Romania, and that is when the catastrophe occurred. Henceforth, Jews will probably give up such adventures and will realize that resistance on the spot is their only chance.

## March 10

A new anti-Semitic law: by the end of this month all Jews, regardless of age or sex, must go to the Labor Recruitment Office to be screened for their labor contribution. Those who can prove that they are doing work essential to the war effort may be given extensions of from six to twelve months. Those who cannot show such proof, and all those who do not get an extension, will be sent to labor camps. This means, in effect, that the Jews have been deprived of the right to gainful employment, except for those few who, no one knows by what criteria of selection, will be allowed to continue for just a few more months. The details are by no means clear. There seem to be two conflicting laws: one, according to which Jews between the ages of twenty and fifty-seven are subject to forced labor, while another one, based on military statutes, applies to those aged eighteen to fifty.

Now we will have to submit documents regarding our means of support, show bills, receipts, contracts, answer all sorts of questions. Then we will find out whether we still have the right to starve.

Groper[13] and Feller[14] maintain that the best of Jewish lyrical poetry, and consequently the poems that ought to be translated, necessarily reflect what is specifically Jewish. I repeatedly explained that I do not object to specifically Jewish poems, provided they have artistic merit. There is no other rationale for an anthology, which by definition is a selection of the best artistic works. We know from experience that patriotic sentiment or political views have rarely inspired works of real literary merit. I tried to translate the poem "By the River Vistula" by Melech Ravitch,[15] a very gifted poet, but I had to give up, because it lacked the minimum artistic quality needed for inclusion in an anthology.

## March 21

The only real victory is that of time. Time has slipped by me and today, swifter than ever, keeps rushing over stormy peaks. Strange that even now, a few days ago, I dreamt again of my friend Enric Algazi, buried for the last thirteen years in a Paris cemetery. He looked at me with his steel-cold eyes and kept asking, as he always does in my dreams: "Why are you still in this world? What more did

13. Iacob Ashel Groper (1881–1957), Romanian-born Yiddish poet.
14. Abraham Feller (1893– ), Romanian-born Jewish journalist, now living in Israel.
15. Melech Ravitch (1893–1976), Yiddish poet and essayist, born in East Galicia. In 1941 he settled in Montreal.

you get than I did? I, at least, have solved the riddle of time."

## March 25

A day of shy spring light, an annunciation of changes; on days such as this I used to pay my first visits to the Cişmigiu[16] for a date with the heralds of the new season.

A pleasant afternoon at home, with a mild fire in the fireplace, talking for a few hours with Arghezi.[17] Thanks to several cups of half-decent coffee (he complained that most of the time he drinks a kind of barley and chick-pea mixture) and some poems, our good mood lasted late into the evening. I read a selection from my anthology, and he was impressed, particularly by a very delicate poem by Sutzkever,[18] and praised the freshness of my translations, their originality, and the full-bodied flavor of my Romanian. He believes that the publication of this work will not only create a sensation in literary circles, but will have a significant influence.

We talked about many different current problems, about politics, about anti-Semitism, about his youth, about some of my own recollections. We shared feelings and found common targets of indignation, until the evening enveloped us and darkness brought a restful silence.

Perhaps my suspicions of his position on the Jewish question, aroused by a poem he published several months ago, are groundless. It seems to me he is pure of heart, a heart that opens reluctantly, although a certain speech affectation and his excessive courtesy clouded for me the coziness of the evening.

The battles on the eastern front continue without any indication of any clear-cut outcome likely to bring

16. See "1938," n. 13.
17. Tudor Arghezi (1880–1967), the most prominent Romanian poet between the wars.
18. Abraham Sutzkever (1913– ) a Yiddish poet, educated in Vilna. During World War II, he escaped from the Vilna ghetto to join the partisans. He settled in Israel in 1947, where he later founded the important Yiddish quarterly, *Di Goldene Keyt.*

about peace soon. The Russians keep harassing the Germans all along their front, and the belated spring has postponed Hitler's offensive to summer, when the roads will be clear for motorized units. The Germans' military capability is still good, but we don't know how the civilian population is bearing up. According to some people recently returned from Germany, the country is held together by a thin thread.

Right now, we don't know anything—neither what the military plans are nor what programs will be implemented. Romanian troops are being trained for war. The concern over Transylvania has subsided. More Romanian blood will be shed in Russia. Meanwhile, there are new laws and regulations concerning the Jews. The latest applies to rents: the Jews, being no longer protected by rent control, will have their rents raised by 30 percent.

## March 30

This second winter we are having on the threshold of April deserves to be recorded. A steady snowfall began last night, after a day of icy December winds. The snow is now ankle-deep and keeps falling, to the despair of those who used up all their wood long ago, and of the Jews, who will again be rounded up to clean the streets. Since they were made to sweep when the snow had practically disappeared, what will happen now that there really is snow!

Yesterday, a Sunday afternoon, in front of our house, at the corner of Mărăşeşti Boulevard, a Jew was diligently shoveling snow into the canal. The bearded, hatless man, his hands swollen and bleeding, is a violinist, formerly soloist with the Romanian Philharmonic Orchestra.

## April 6

A chilly Easter under a sullen sky. Fire in the stove, not a single blade of grass, not a flower. A dark mood, no feeling of spring, no hope. People still gather around relatively prosperous tables, but they are poisoned by stale talk and oppressed by fears. The Jews have again been called up for the new season's forced labor.

A headline in some newspaper announces: IT IS NOT AN INSULT TO BE CALLED A JEW. The story concerns Paul Sterian, journalist and man of letters, who started a law-suit against the literary critic George Călinescu, author of a history of Romanian literature, in which he claimed that Sterian was Jewish. The verdict was "not guilty" on the grounds summed up in the above headline. The point seems to be that only the epithet "kike" might be construed as offensive. The words "kike" or "Polack" are an insult, but "Jewish" or "Polish," especially in writing, are merely ethnic data!

The spirit must be kept alive if you are to write, and you must write if the spirit is to stay alive.

## April 20

It is noteworthy that almost all Jewish-American poets who have written in Yiddish have devoted at least one poem to the Sacco-Vanzetti case. Their death in the electric chair shook the conscience of millions, regardless of social class. I remember that, at the time, I was in Paris, where everybody was up all night in the streets to hear the decision of the judges from across the Atlantic. Huge crowds of people, shaking with indignation and trembling with impatience, stood on sidewalks, in squares, in bistros, discussing the tragedy of the two revolutionaries.

True, the majority of the Sacco-Vanzetti poems are politically inspired and therefore somewhat artificial, because of the circumstantial and transitory elements. Nevertheless, the impassioned sincerity that inspires them lends them a certain aura and draw you to that unforgettable moment when the conscience of the whole world was aroused.

For my anthology I have translated an "Elegy" by

Eliezer Greenberg,[19] a New York poet, but there are others, H. Leivick[20] among them, and Aaron Kurtz.[21]

The so-called theater group (three actors, a director, and a painter) met at Maxy's[22] for talks with six writers who were asked for their support to develop an authentic Jewish theater. The depressing daily atmosphere with its tragic overtones is certainly not conducive to such preoccupations. On the other hand, this group is continuously fighting the artistic vulgarity of the present programs at the Baraşeum theater.[23] The new projects would start in the fall, when we don't know what will happen. As heat will chase the public away from the Baraşeum auditorium, which becomes a steam bath, we are talking about only one or two literary recitals. These famous recitals amount to readings of prose and poetry, of little appeal to the public at large, and at any rate do not constitute "pure theater" in the sense understood by this much neglected theater group. Thus, efforts inspired by a worthy ideal will dwindle into banality. As usual when several writers get together for concerted action, frictions develop, as well as so-called disagreements on principle—which merely shows how difficult it is for people with different mentalities and uncertain social views to attempt working together on an artistic project. Besides, the sharp wind of censorship blows over all good intentions, destroying what is left of enthusiasm and honest endeavors.

A few days ago I went with my family to visit Arghezi, whose white villa rises on the Văcăreşti hill, on the two acres of land he owns. A family atmosphere with overtones of patriarchal simplicity, the poet dominating the life of the household. Four cats, one for each member of the family, aroused Lelia's and Marguerite's enthusiasm, in particular Alba, Arghezi's cat, white and graceful, like a china figurine. Also six dogs. The daughter, Miţura, a tall, graceful

19. Eliezer Greenberg (1896–1917), Bessarabian-born Yiddish poet and critic. He emigrated to the United States in 1913.
20. See "1940," n. 10.
21. Aaron Kurtz (1891–1964), Yiddish poet and editor, born in Vitebsk. He emigrated to the United States in 1911.
22. See "1940," n. 38.
23. See "1940," n. 37.

young lady, her hair parted in the middle, wearing a long gown. The son, Baruţu, dark, stocky, with fiery eyes, silent, shy, introspective. Both children intentionally raised to preserve their candor—and Mrs. Arghezi, sociable, talkative, hospitable, a bountiful hostess. Arghezi's white beret clashed with the earnestness of his conversation. Interesting stories, wise remarks, and a very sympathetic attitude toward our inferior situation as Jews.

On our way out they all accompanied us down the long and elegant path leading to the street, the same path ex-King Carol took a few years back. The king had been the poet's guest, Arghezi told us, after generously paying all the debts on the property. Actually, Arghezi settled there by chance, for he had been determined to leave the country. He openly told me again: "I like Romania, but I don't like the Romanians!" It is a pity—and surprising in a person of his stature—that all his indignation is diffuse and lacks the sound information expected of a thinker and a man of culture.

*May 7*

Someday somebody ought to write about the small printing office of Slova, which has become a historic place through force of circumstance. For many years it has been the meeting ground of many different people, Zionist and non-Zionist Jews, but especially Jewish writers of all kinds. It is a sort of literary salon created by the peculiarities of Jewish cultural life—an uncomfortable salon, with people sitting on desks, on windowsills, or standing around, or in the courtyard in front of the open window. Through the years, at historically and politically important moments, it was visited by many celebrities, especially Yiddish writers. The owner of the printing house, Feller,[24] a fine man, kind and obliging, intelligent and tactful, wise and learned, is no doubt the most interesting personage in this group. His discretion, his equanimity and boundless hospitality, his welcoming kindliness are what made it possible for so many

24. See n. 14.

people with incompatible interests, preoccupations, and temperaments to get together. This is the place where services are rendered, cultural and business meetings arranged, messages passed between writers and newspapermen, between them and their friends; the place where people make their phone calls and wait around to settle social, political, and literary business. Only now and then does the presence of an "unwelcome" visitor (one of the printer's clients) remind you that Feller is involved in something other than receiving visitors, taking messages, and discussing them. The visitors during the prewar era were Sternberg,[25] Altman,[26] Bickel,[27] and all the leftist Yiddishists, who argued over the theater, literature, and popularized culture. The Zionist newspapermen and a few Romanian-language writers present there established contacts which might never have been made otherwise, unleashed stormy debates and epic fights, and forged utopias, while magazine articles were being written and literary works edited. Sometimes the meetings would turn into full-fledged battles. This is the place where Altman slapped the journalist Oscar Lemnaru for an article in which he was allegedly slandered, only to apologize when matters were cleared up.

It is a pity that Feller, who is something of a writer, made no notes about his visitors and the events that took place in his small office, which is reached through a picturesque gate and after crossing a yard with four entrances, a relic of old Bucharest. Of late, the office is less crowded and the celebrities are fewer. Some have left the country, others have isolated themselves or go out rarely, dropping in only for a few moments. Jacob Groper, the poet—tall, plump, and pink—makes his appearance carrying a cane and delivers one of his Jewish moralist's perorations sandwiched in between his business preoccupations. Former newspaper-

25. Jacob Sternberg (1890–1973), Bessarabian-born Yiddish poet and dramatist, director of the Vilna Troupe in Bucharest in the 1920s, and a central figure in the Yiddish literary world in Romania until his flight to the Soviet Union in 1941.

26. Moishe Altman (1890–1981), Bessarabian-born Yiddish poet and novelist who lived in Romania and the Soviet Union.

27. Shlomo Bickel (1896–1969), Romanian-born Yiddish essayist and critic. He emigrated to the United States in 1939 and became the literary critic of the New York Yiddish daily, *Der Tog*.

men, discharged from *Renaşterea Noastră,* appear and disappear, with their nostalgia for highly nationalistic reporting. The poet Snabel, his powerful jaws clenched over his silence, a blue smile in his eyes, waiting for his books to be printed. The novelist Ury Benador, who appears several times a day to collect his phone messages and conduct some business, spending himself in jokes and offers of services, often comes in through a window and jumps over a desk, like in an old play performed by the Vilna troupe. The unemployed newspaperman Albu, a warm and kindly man with a vibrant, baritone voice, wise and likable. Then Marian, a businessman with a fine and intelligent face, who speaks shyly but says much, as knowledgeable as ten Jewish writers, well-read, in love with literature and sociology, full of common sense, humane, friendly. The sharp wit of the lawyer Leibu—snub-nosed and stormy-eyed. The writer Hervian, with his head like a prudish young lady's, a budding writer speaking in a mature and succulent style. The former lawyer Schachter, tall and husky, with a ruddy face, who could pass for an innkeeper but is a lover and connoisseur of Jewish poetry. The extreme modesty of voice and the lively, sharp intelligence in the eyes of the journalist Liman, who only listens and takes the talk in. The poet Sperber, with his silhouette, like a majestic pine rising into the white clouds of his hair, with languorous eyes, a smile like a ripe fruit, and, like a fiddler, fiddling his latest poem into someone's ear; perhaps in Moscovici's ear, who, shy and moved, takes in the atmosphere, becoming one of the writers who value him like a true friend. Then the lawyer Lascăr Şaraga, passionate organizer of cultural events, a self-appointed representative of the masses, arguing in his juicy Moldavian dialect. And a whole string of small errand-boys and big failures, swarming on the outskirts of Jewish life, today as always.


## May 9

It seems that spring has decided to settle in for good. About time, too. We have repossessed the green living room in the garden, on which I have worked in earnest this time. The seedlings have taken root in their flower beds, the grass is coming up, leaves are filling out the trees, and in the last couple of days the lilacs have bloomed. I built a bench and painted it, I have repaired another one, and I am as proud of my handiwork as if I had written two great poems. Manual work has done me a great deal of good in the state of mind I have been and while waiting for the fog of absurdity to lift. The sadness you feel in the midst of a garden is quite different from sadness between four walls. The garden seems like a filter for all sorts of dark moods.

## May 26

A battle between the Russians and the Germans at Kharkov. No precise details as yet. The losses, it seems, were devastating, particularly among the Germans. Newspapers use the same bombastic style as last year. Everybody is waiting with bated breath.

## June 2

My growing anthology is almost completed. It will be some eight hundred to one thousand pages long, including biographical and bibliographical notes for each poet. But the work keeps getting harder, not so much because the material is drying up as because the general atmosphere is getting more and more unbearable. Sometimes I feel that what a translator and anthologist needs most is the strength to give up his own creative work. So many poems asking to be written, ideas for novels, for articles, old projects to be revived—constant temptations that must be overcome if you are to sustain the mood needed for the completion of such a broad undertaking. My only consolation is that nothing of literary value could be written during these grim times. Nevertheless, the yearning for who knows what unaccomplished works lingers on.


## June 7

The biographies of the Jewish poets included in my anthology reveal that most of them led very similar lives. Almost all were born in some Russian or Polish village or small town, attended first a *cheder* and *bet midrash,* then secondary and high school. They started writing in Russian, Polish, or German, and ended up with Yiddish. Most of them were born around 1890–94. Toward the turn of the century they emigrated to America, where a great center of Yiddish culture developed, similar to the one in Eastern Europe. These facts, as well as the evolution of Jewish culture from that time to the present, pose a very interesting question: what will the future of this Yiddish literature be?—a question which, no doubt, has occurred to others too.

The present picture of Yiddish culture is as follows: In Soviet Russia, Yiddish, being the language of the Jewish masses, was from the start a propaganda tool and it is so used to this day in the press, in schools, in theaters, and on the radio. But it seems that the children born to the poets' generation have moved to industrial and university centers where the culture and language are predominantly Russian. As they integrate into the new Soviet culture, they forget their parents' language. In turn, their children will certainly know no Yiddish at all. In America, the Russian and Polish immigrants of thirty or forty years ago have created a strong current of Yiddish culture. A distinguished daily press, literary and artistic magazines, and outstanding publishing houses, all have achieved recognition. No doubt this phenomenon is due not only to the freedom in America but also to the arrival, at the same time with many European writers, of a larger working class brought up in Yiddish culture. The settling of a majority of Jewish immigrants in New York, in a closely knit group, was yet another factor that furthered the development of a Yiddish cultural life equal to that in Poland. H. Leivick,[28] Moshe Leib Halpern,[29] Moshe Nadir,[30] Abraham Reisen,[31] Zishe Landau,[32] and so on, led all the brilliant literary and artistic achievements. In London too, the Jewish community formed at Whitechapel cultivates the Yiddish language and publishes the well-known *Di Tsayt*. In the last few years, however, a characteristic phenomenon is taking place. Many Yiddish dailies and magazines have begun to include a column or even a whole page in English. What happened was that the children of Leivick, Moshe Leib Halpern, Moshe Nadir, and so on, went to English schools. Perhaps they still know Yiddish, or understand it, and some may still speak it with their parents. But *their* children don't know it at all. In order not to lose the entire readership, the newspapers start adding a page for the English-speaking generation, as they did in Russia for the generation assimilated into Russian culture. True, the war has created a Jewish awareness, yet not because of some nationalist revival, nor because of an overwhelming spiritual need, but rather and mostly because of political circumstances. The ghettos of today are a conglomeration of Jews who maintain a painful tie with the culture of their respective countries. The ghetto is an artificial creation that goes against their desire, against the natural evolution toward economic integration and acculturation. As to Palestine, although its official language is Hebrew, the battle between Hebrew and Yiddish continues because of the influx of immigrants from many different countries whose only common language is Yiddish. The problems arise only in centers heavily populated by Jews, such as in Russia, Poland, and America.

Objectively speaking then, the future of Yiddish culture does not look promising. When you consider the outstanding achievements in this language—poetry, drama, prose,

28. See "1940," n. 10.

29. See "1940," n. 11.

30. Moshe Nadir (1885–1943), Yiddish poet and humorist, born in eastern Galicia. He emigrated to New York in 1898.

31. Abraham Reisen (1876–1953), Yiddish poet and short-story writer, born in Minsk province. In 1914 he made his permanent home in New York.

32. Zishe Landau (1889–1937), Yiddish poet born in Poland. He came to New York in 1906.

and journalism of the highest order—it is hard to envision the possibility of such an adverse fate. We will have to wait till the end of the war before we can examine, in the light of the world's new political and historical development, what the chances are for the survival of a culture which, through the eminence it has achieved, has justifiably earned for itself a place in the life of mankind.

The Jews are alarmed again. New rumors of new anti-Jewish measures. There is talk of deportation to Transnistria, or at least of a new classification into categories, one of which would be deported. Then again, talk of herding Jews into ghettos, curfew after nine o'clock, enforced wearing of the Star of David. These worries started a few days ago when the Romanian authorities asked the Centrala to advise Jews not to frequent downtown stores and cafés, so as not to provoke unpleasant incidents. A few Jewish ladies find it hard to give up their daily gossip sessions at the Cafés Bucharest, Nestor, and Zamfirescu . . . and this is what causes great social problems! At any rate, it becomes a pretext for new concern. Of course, these rumors may be groundless, but all too often in the past the Jews' panic has proven to be a very sensitive indicator of events. Sooner or later, the rumor becomes reality. Besides, the Jews in Bucharest are right always to fear what happens in the provinces. There is indeed no sound reason for them to believe that they will be spared. Jews have again been deported from Cernăuți,[33] from all over Bukovina, from Dorohoi.[34] The rumors that reach us from Transnistria are horrifying. A graveyard from which an agonized voice rises, through some letter that no one can answer. Hunger, cold, sickness have felled most of the deported people. No help can be sent, and what is nevertheless sent doesn't reach them. People have grown so used to cruelty that they no longer react when they hear of it. Some talk about Poland when you mention Transnistria, which by comparison appears idyllic, and when you talk about Poland, they point to Czechoslovakia, and so forth. France, Norway, Holland, Greece are

33. Industrial and commercial city, former capital of Bukovina.
34. See "1940," n. 29.

of course also cited as examples. So then you must make the painful attempt to establish through comparisons in what corner of Europe has murder taken the most inhuman form. The Jews cannot be consoled, however, as, terrified, they await new crimes. Today's tragedies are unique because the persecutions are carried out in cold blood.

We were told that a man was asked to shoot some children found wandering in a truck on Bessarabian roads. He refused, explaining:

"No, they're children, I can't do it. If they were kikes, gladly . . ."

The children, who actually were "kikes," escaped, having chanced on such a humane person.

## June 17

The turmoil that reigned among Jews for several days has subsided. It seems that the implementation of measures against us has again been postponed. A few days' respite.

Life is so wilted, so hopeless, that at times you feel like sitting down on the sidewalk and howling until you die. People come and go aimlessly, asking one another: what do you think, how much longer? Useless to anybody, unspent energies rot. Everyone needs a drop of optimism against the new echoes of tragedies reaching him from afar, echoes of hunger and death, of life petering out without even a chance at self-sacrifice. And yet, in their general appearance, in their behavior, the majority are still well preserved. But when they stop and sit down for a moment and open up, their mask of calm slips and the naked tension, a frozen, sterile sorrow, a heartrending despair take over.

A new tragedy preoccupies the Jews: five hundred orphaned children have been gathered in Transnistria and must be fed through public Jewish contributions. Since the Centrala first learned of this problem, the number of orphans has risen to eight hundred; and while the original es-

timate of the sum needed for the maintenance of one child
was three thousand lei a month, now it appears to be five
thousand lei. All the children can get daily for this money is
half a loaf of bread (bread costs three hundred lei there)
and barley water. The simplest solution, of course, would be
to place these children with Jewish families, or even in
camps in Moldavia, where they would be easier to reach and
less expensive to maintain. But apparently they must expi-
ate the crimes for which their parents died, so they cannot
be removed from the circle of expiation in which they have
been placed. How are we going to get the enormous sum of
four million a month? Naturally, if it were possible to use
coercion, a few wealthy Jews could supply all the money
needed. For a start, a certain well-known gentleman, if he
were to sell his race horses alone, could maintain for at least
a couple of months those unfortunate children who, however generous the Jewish community, are still condemned to
hunger. The first steps have been taken, parents have been
called to attend meetings in their neighborhood schools. I
was present at one of them. Wealthy ladies appealed to the
feelings of the mothers present. One of them made the blun-
der of assuring them that the orphans in question were accustomed to comfort and plenty and that these children, unlike those already used to poverty, could not long endure
the situation in Transnistria and must be rescued quickly.
They read aloud letters from the children that tear at your
heart. I returned home sick, thinking of the children of the
needy, who must die because they are used to disasters and
know how to die, silent and anonymous, so that those destined for a life of ease can be saved. How much longer will
we hear this sort of talk?

## June 21

Someone told me he had heard an official account of
what happened in Poland, according to which seven hundred thousand Jews have been massacred so far. This is the
largest number in the history of Jewish massacres. After
the Russian revolution broke out, White Russian gangs

massacred two hundred thousand Jews in eight hundred communities over a period of two years.

## June 29

The Jews continue to be deported from Cernăuți. The details are horrible. On Sundays, Jews are not allowed to leave their homes. That is when the authorities, moving from street to street, descend upon them like dogcatchers and round them up. To muffle the victims' screams of despair, sirens are sounded. At the train station they are loaded into freight cars, fifty to a car, where they are thrown a few loaves of bread and given a bucket of water. Furniture, pillows, clothes and other belongings lie in heaps throughout the city. People, even those who are opposed to the barbaric acts committed, stop to buy these objects cheap. But since they are so cheap . . .

## July 2

Sebastopol has fallen after twenty-five days of fierce battle.

## July 6

Streitman,[35] who came to see me the other day, is rapidly failing. There is a great change in his appearance, in his uncertain walk, his memory, the general tiredness to which he succumbs more and more often. Intellectually, however, he is still quite all right. His position as president of the Centrala hasn't changed him at all. He has remained a socialite, though nowadays he socializes in a different café on Calea Victoriei. He is still a master of metaphysics, he cultivates books, people, and paradoxes, and adheres to that position "between black and white" which reflects so well his extreme flexibility. Yesterday he spoke at length of the

35. See "1938," n. 1.

need for the Jewish people to change their attitude toward
death, which is so deeply telluric with the Romanian people.
He cannot understand the Jews' immense love of life, of life
under any circumstances and at any price. There were cases
in Germany, he said, in which a Jewish child was asked to
slap his father. And he slapped him. Then he was asked to
tear out his beard. And he tore it out. What value has the
life of a man who did this to his father? If the Jews would
take a more heroic attitude toward life, they wouldn't do
certain things, and perhaps the government's attitude toward them would also change somewhat. Streitman is very
good at developing an idea. But all too often his thoughts
hang in the air, without a sound foundation. The living-
room moralist, the juggler of pretty words betrays his lack
of political knowledge and his cynical conformism, elegantly
dressed up. All of mankind is busy killing, in Europe the
Jews are murdered with glee, and he is set on reeducating
them as to the proper attitude toward death!

## July 14

A clear feeling of early fall, with all the associations it
arouses. But peace of mind is lacking, as are the wisdom to
flow with time, the preparations for dreaming, the joy of
planning a future toward which you steer with ineffable
satisfaction. At times the days are heavy and withered with
worry, at others they seem a syncope of despair. All roads
appear closed, the optimistic calculations you made sink in
a melancholy bog, and you chew news and comments with
boredom and disbelief. For it takes too long, and the last
remaining moral and material resistance begins to crack.
Still, this summer decisive events must take place in the
East and the West, and put a quick end to the suffocating
situation that grips the world. At the end of this year? Next
spring? We keep giving ourselves deadlines . . . I would like
to catch the beginnings of a better life while my mind is
still whole and my soul still clear. To be able to work as
much as my age allows, and not to live again through the
humiliation of struggling to find financial solutions just to

keep my head above water, to be neither obligated to anyone nor materially dependent, to breathe freely, deeply, fully, my own oxygen, to think as I please, to dream as much as possible, to be able to smile or rebel when I want, knowing that I can cultivate truth at all times.

An acquaintance heard Thomas Mann speak, referring again to the talk he gave a few months back on the four hundred Jewish youths used by the Germans in Holland as guinea pigs for poison gas. Mann said there were actually eight hundred victims; he holds the whole German nation responsible for this crime, which exceeds all the other bestialities committed during this war.

## *August 2*

As of tomorrow, cornmeal will also be rationed: one and a half kilos a week. But none for the Jews. This is the first time that the Jews are totally deprived of a basic food. They get half or one-third the sugar ration. Apparently, *mămăligă* is considered a national food, in which case this restriction is purely ethical. Again the poor, needy Jews will be the ones to suffer. For the rich, should they feel like it, will pay any sum for the cornmeal stashed away by merchants. But the government has forfeited the only explanation it can give for the lack of cornmeal, namely that the Jews consume it.

## *August 4*

Days of illness, when life is not experienced at many levels and the whole being is drowsy, somewhat resemble death. Crumpled in some dark corner on the couch, between two windows, I floated on a kind of dross, breathing fog and thinking black clouds. When I woke up today, I went over to the window and had the feeling I had returned from death. I looked at the neglected garden, at the trees in front of the windows, then at the room, at the typewriter. I felt clearly how it would be if I came back to life after fifty years: I would stare for a long time, I would want to sweep the garden, type on my little Remington, while everything around me stayed the same—the trees a little older, but in the same spot, people hurrying past the gate, a car, a horse, a cat, a dog, a baby crying and . . . the sun, a totally unconcerned sun spilling its heat on life and death.

A gang of Jewish lawyers who lost their jobs have descended like a swarm of locusts on the Jewish community. They are all crowded in the leadership of the Centrala, or have camouflaged themselves in various bureaucratic organizations which bear down on the Jews' work, purse, and morale. To avoid forced labor, they have infiltrated all the combines where decisions are made about the future of Jews, they have resumed their ways as racketeers, bribe-takers, denouncers. This is a plague we will not be rid of until the end of the war. In the meantime, we must resign ourselves to meeting them everywhere, fat, well fed, elegant, in silk shirts and expensive ties, maintained by their in-laws or the small fortunes amassed through more or less clean means.

I don't think any steps have been taken to write the history of the Romanian Jews' forced labor during this war. Who would be writing it? The Centrala? Is anybody making daily notes on its innumerable facets? Has anyone sketched the infinite variety of moments composing a vast and sensational fresco? Does anyone recall the sadistic militarism of the Jewish engineer C. who, in a martinet's speech at the Sebastopol cemetery, asked the men doing forced labor to work ten instead of eight hours, threatening to report to the Recruiting Center those who did not comply? Will anyone remember that day of torrential rain, when Mr. C. did report one of the Jews, suffering from a kidney disease, who stopped working after seven hours, pleading that he was ill and unable to drag himself through the mud? Did anyone note that, when the Center sent the sick man to a doctor, the doctor confirmed the diagnosis and wrote a recommendation for 120 days' leave? Among many other chapters, there should also be one on the tribulations of Jews who, instead of doing forced labor, which would have taken them to the provinces, leased land to garden. A special service sprang up immediately, with its network of intermediaries (including a doorman who would not let you in without a 500-lei tip), and large sums paid out to appropriate individuals to get the enviable position of Jewish gardener. Then a whole series of money-making measures was introduced. For instance, all the Jews leasing a piece of land were required to be there between 6:00 and 10:00 A.M.; then they were asked to pay 2,000 lei for a piece of paper exempting them from this obligation. And so on. A tidy sum was made even off the required little plate bearing the name of the gardener.

## August 8

The newspapers carry a new ordinance on the organization of "forced labor" (that is the name given to work performed by Jews, as distinct from that performed by Gentiles, who are assigned to "public works"), containing instructions on the drafting of women as well. There is also an order to search the homes of Jews because they are storing food, footwear, cloth, etc., for speculation. On these occasions, there will also be searches for shirkers, refugees from Transnistria, saboteurs, etc. What is the reason for this suddenly renewed interest in Jews? Popular discontent with shortages?

The article appearing today in the *Bukarester Tageblatt* aroused great anxiety among Jews. Of course, the statements there do not reflect the government's wishes and decisions, nor even Germany's official position, but merely Killinger's[36] consistent views, who is eager to see the speediest possible solution of the Jewish question. Yet it is enough to cause, if not actual panic, certainly increased gloom. We now learn quite unequivocally what was and what is going to be the function of the Centrala. The article was obviously

36. Manfred von Killinger (1886–19??), German Nazi politician and administrator, who in 1940 was appointed ambassador to Romania.

written on the occasion of the six-month anniversary (June 17) of the establishment of this new Jewish organization for the whole country. For a short while only some Jews were unsure as to the purpose of the Centrala and welcomed, conditionally, those who agreed to be its leaders. Now they learn from an official source what it accomplished:

"It accomplished for the first time the solution of the Jewish question (which had been approached from different angles) from a racist standpoint and on the basis of the Nuremberg laws, under the leadership of the government's representative, Radu Leca."

Elsewhere, in another article, it is clearly stated that "the Centrala's function has been from the beginning to coordinate the numerous anti-Jewish laws, to bring up to date the census of Jews, to direct them into activities useful to the Romanian state and nation, and finally, to pave the way for all the measures needed to clear Romania completely of Jews."

The census was taken and we find that in Romania there are now 272,409 Jews, not counting either those in Bukovina and Bessarabia, or the five or six thousand converted ones. The German newspaper accounts for the difference between the previously recorded number of seven to eight hundred thousand and the present count as follows: 185,000 were deported to Transnistria in the course of one year; 200,000 went with the territory annexed by Hungary; and those in Bessarabia and Bukovina were taken along by the Russians as they retreated. (No mention of the massacres by Germans and Romanians. If the Jews have disappeared entirely, it is because the Russians took them.) In these two provinces, the newspaper continues, it can be said that there is no trace of Jews left. But in Cernăuți, there are 16,000 (recently, deportations have begun), and in other towns there are also big Jewish communities (Iași,[37] 34,000; Galați[38] and Bacău,[39] some 13,000 each, etc.). The fact is that the Jews are gathered in large numbers only in cities. In Bucharest alone there are 97,868 Jews today. Now, after

37. The capital of Moldavia.
38. A port on the Danube.
39. A town in Moldavia.

the completion of this comprehensive census, giving data on numbers, professions, financial status, education, etc. (for which the newspaper praises the Centrala), a Jewish statute is in preparation. The German newspaper gives yet other details. For instance, that of the Jews now living in Romania, 17,000 have kept their jobs in certain essential industries and occupations. All are exempt from forced labor until December 31, 1942. General headquarters, which is in charge of Jewish forced labor, is presently studying a project whereby the money paid by those exempt (approximately one billion, two hundred million lei) will cover the expenses of those in labor camps—food, housing, tools. The article concludes with amazing news: so far, the Centrala has completed the first stage of its work. Now comes its second mission, namely, preparation of plans for the deportation of Jews to Transnistria. However, as these plans have progressed so well, one can hope that 25,000 Jews will be sent to the Bug within the year. The deportation will be interrupted until spring because of the difficulties in transportation during the winter months. At any rate, by fall of 1943, Romania will be cleansed of Jews *(judenrein)*. And that will no doubt also put an end to the function of the Centrala.

Still, the Centrala eased certain matters. In Bessarabia (where its influence was missing), Jews were made to dig the graves into which they were to be thrown. It was done badly. Had there been some Jewish leadership for this sinister operation, precise measurements would have been taken, the graves would have been dug deeper, and as the work would have taken longer, the tragic end would have come a few hours later. That would have been the accomplishment of a local Centrala!

*August 15*

Great agitation among the Jews. Not only because of the effects of the *Bukarester Tageblatt* article, but on new and very real grounds: a number of Jews, who did not respond to the call to forced labor, have been deported from several towns to Transnistria, together with their families. Moreover, the situation of the Jews in Transylvania seems rather serious as, it is rumored, they too, or at least those in certain areas, are scheduled for deportation to Transnistria. Even here there are plans to draw up lists of people who will be forced to take the same road east. The news from the front, unfavorable to the Germans, as they themselves disclose, is no consolation to anyone. A threatening hand hovers over the fate of European Jews. Some still hope that everything will turn out well, others choose to disregard reality until it hits them, and there are even those who rejoice at the thought that not they but others are involved, and so don't worry. There are persistent rumors about trains passing through the northern part of Moldavia, carrying Jews from occupied France, sent by the Germans to the east. It is known that 20,000 Jews in occupied France have been recently deported from there, but no one could guess where they were sent. There are details: sealed cars, dreadful thirst, no food. But perhaps all this is merely a new version of last summer's horrors, when Jews were deported from Iaşi in sealed cars and died of thirst, without anyone heeding their screams for help all along the way.

## August 19

A sudden decision by the government that the Jews are to pay thirty lei for a bread weighing five hundred grams. While Gentiles and foreigners, who pay no taxes, buy no national bonds, do not contribute to public works, continue to pay fourteen lei. Why? Is there no flour? If sixty million lei are collected from Jews, will there be flour? Someone said that the government wanted to raise the price of flour sold to the Germans. The Germans refused and suggested instead that the Jews pay for the difference! This story is no doubt told in order to bring Germany in as the determining factor in all the measures taken in this country. At the same time that the price of bread was raised, bicycles and motorcycles were confiscated from the Jews. It seems other measures will be taken step by step, until the final one, deportation, which threatens the existence of the whole

Jewish population in the country. Meanwhile, the Jews in Transylvania have apparently been allowed to remain there.

A first attempt at debarkation by the British and the Americans was made at Dieppe, on the northern coast of France. They spent a day there, gave battle, took prisoners, caused destruction, then withdrew. Merely a demonstration that they can do it?

Days of fog and loneliness, like an ugly dream . . .

The unrest caused by the CNR's[40] eviction of Jews from their apartments continues. In some areas the city is covered with blue and red FOR RENT signs. Many interested parties go to see the houses. As a result, Gentiles will move from houses on the outskirts of town to more comfortable and conveniently located ones in the center, and, necessarily, Jews will move toward the outskirts, into houses owned by Gentiles, who will demand exorbitant rents. An interesting case is that of a magistrate who apologized to a Jewish friend for the illegal and inhumane act of evicting a Jewish tenant from his home:

"What can I do, my dear friend, Gentile landlords don't want to rent me an apartment. They all ask me first if I am a Gentile. They only take Jewish tenants!"

Some incidents worth recording occurred in the course of these difficult moments when people come to look at an apartment. The other day a captain went to see the apartment a Jew was renting on Strada N. It was early morning and the house was in disorder. The tenant asked the captain to be kind enough to come in the afternoon, during the hours specifically set aside by the Renting Office of the CNR. In answer to this normal request, the captain jumped on the tenant, grabbed him by the collar, and told him:

"I could shoot you like a dog! I killed fifty kikes like you in Odessa!"

There are amusing aspects, too. A dilapidated house, with warped doors, the paint peeling. A visitor exclaims in a loud voice:

"Just look how the kikes are treating state property!"

40. Centrala Naţională de Românizare, the National Center for Romanianization.

A woman physician, who is reading *Dreamers of the Ghetto* by the English Jewish writer Israel Zangwill, pointed out to me that the work is translated into German by Hans Heinz Ewers, the Hitlerist writer, leader of the National Socialist literary academy in Berlin!

## August 25

Whoever has not tasted reconciliation with the woman he loves, after a period of suffering and isolation, has missed a great and lasting joy. I am not talking only about that sudden clearing up, the unclouding of the senses, but particularly of its radiation into the cardinal points of existence. Everything acquires a harmonious meaning, like the impetuous blossoming of spring. The basic truth in life invades you warmly, overwhelms you. You understand the purpose of the sun, of your comings and goings, the sense of days, the mystery of nights. Stems grow from the depth of your heart. You hang true smiles on them, and stalled thoughts become fresh and fast horses, their manes full of flowers, like in a celebration.

The fierce battle for Stalingrad continues for the last several weeks. Yesterday, the German communiqué announced that the Germans are on the outskirts of town. Today the newspapers speak of stopping the fight and besieging the city, which has "great and powerful fortifications." Who knows how much longer this battle, so important for the Soviets, will last. The Germans will have to make a supreme effort.

## September 5

After one month, another bout with influenza, very high fever and unbearable headaches. While in the grips of fever and head congestion, I learn of sudden arrests in the city. Several hundred people, men and women, have been locked up in a few Jewish schools, miserable buildings transformed into prisons for the occasion. The stage director Sandu Eliad and the poet Alfred Sperber are among the prisoners. They are to be deported to Transnistria for mistakes committed in the past: they had applied for departure to Bessarabia, or have lent their names to now blacklisted cultural causes, naturally along with some Gentiles. Is it possible that the program of systematic extermination of the Jews is beginning to be carried out?

At the Cultura school on Strada Romulus, and two other schools on Strada Mămulari and Sf. Ion Nou, Jews are crowded together in rooms and in the yard, waiting to be sorted out for deportation. Relatives and friends keep pressing up to the fence while the guards disperse them again and again. The prisoners are relatively calm, smoking and looking out the windows or over the fence at the street full of sun and freedom, their eyes searching for dear faces among the people crowding the sidewalk. The children play serenely with stones and sticks, go on inventing games, unaware of their parents' worries. Three-year-old toddlers as well as people in their sixties. Alfred Sperber's head, like a frowning mountain peak, rises above the fence. He paces the yard and chain-smokes. Friends struggle for the poet's release. The writer Ion Pillat was asked to appeal in Sperber's behalf, but he only signed the appeal and left for his usual weekend in the country. Enormous sums of money have been offered for some of the prisoners, but there is little hope that anyone can be saved. Except for an actress, native of Bessarabia, who seems to have been freed. They wait, consumed by silent fear, under the gaze of the people on the other side of the fence, who ask themselves when their own turn will come.

We search for some reason in this sudden decision to arrest Jews. Their having registered long ago to leave for Bessarabia, or some petition they signed, is no justification for their present arrest. The government itself had authorized those registrations to avoid disorder, clearly indicating its wish that Jews leave the country. That was during the unforgettable period of Iron Guard persecutions, when a joint Russian and Romanian office was set up in Galați to facilitate transfers to Bessarabia and Bukovina. It was a time when the rich left for America, Australia, and Palestine, and the needy for Bessarabia, because there was no more work available here and they could no longer put up with the Iron Guard regime, which maimed and robbed them. Everybody knows that those who crowded in Galați awaiting their turn weren't Communists, but young people yearning to work, having been fired from their jobs here. And if those who couldn't leave are dangerous, how come this danger was realized only now, two years later? Is this the beginning of the program announced by the *Bukarester Tageblatt?* Then how is one to understand the small number of four hundred arrests? Will there be more, each week? The official Jewish press speaks of twenty-five thousand people around the country (of whom seven to eight thousand are in Bucharest) to be arrested by fall. The panic among the Jews of Bucharest is growing, and whatever the explanations, whatever the efforts not to think about it, anxiety poisons all the hearts already broken by sorrow.

All the Jews in unoccupied France, from Nice, Marseilles, Cannes, and elsewhere, have been deported to Eastern Europe. Paula heard the news during a conversation, and I saw her trying to hold back her tears: her sister with her husband and children were refugees in Nice! If the Germans managed to do this in France, where official resistance still prevails, where protests are voiced by foreign representatives and religious leaders, and where the population and even the police oppose anti-Jewish measures—what chance is there that they will show restraint here, in a country which has granted them much greater concessions than that of getting rid of some undesirable kikes?

The day after the departure from Romania of Dr. Funk, the Reich's minister of economy, a decree was issued cutting the Jews' bread ration down to four days out of five. The Germans must have succeeded in pressuring Romania to reduce its domestic consumption of grain. (It is rumored that Romania is to furnish Germany 20 percent of its grain and forty thousand freight cars of corn.) No doubt our economy is very strained. And as usual, here too, the first measure to be taken is one against the Jews. But does this solve the problem? Jews have been forbidden to consume cornmeal—yet since that decree was put into effect, the Gentiles fare no better; on the contrary, they have more and more trouble getting cornmeal, which has practically disappeared from the market.

### September 8

The Jews locked up in schools have been sent away from Bucharest. Those who saw them being loaded into trucks said it was a terrifying spectacle. Slaughterhouse screams filled the street. Passersby stopped, weeping, and threw cigarettes and money in the open trucks. Children refused to get on, while those left behind clung to the trucks until forced by guards to let go. The schools are being disinfected and soon everything will be forgotten. Sperber and several others were left behind, for a review.

The garden has wrapped itself in autumn haze. An unusual autumn, lacking that thrill of vegetal warmth when the sap is still alive and holds up the trees, drunk on solar gold. It is the sorrowful climax of the summer's drought. Never before was I so struck by the cancerous emaciation in a garden. The leaves started turning yellow in July and began falling, like a dance of prematurely withered bodies. The grass dried very early, flower beds grew bald, the tall dahlias didn't bloom, the earth is cracked, and over the vegetation floats an agonizing weariness, a sickly discoloration, a consuming sadness rising from the depth of the parched roots. The spiders have multiplied like never before. The greenery seems frightened, and from the window up here it looks even more tragic in the sunlight, which tries to breathe into it a last tremor of life.

The Bulgarians, too, are toeing the line: on the fifteenth of this month, their forty thousand Jews must deposit their money in a bank account from which they will receive only what they need for food; their enterprises will be confiscated, they will wear the sign on their chest and post it on their dwellings, etc., etc., in accordance with the rules of the new civilization.

## September 12

Everybody is talking about Churchill's speech in the House of Commons, in which he gave an account of his visit to Egypt and Moscow. It seems that he talked about all the problems of the war and that, for the first time, there was a note of optimism quite unlike the objective tone of all his previous speeches. He announced changes in the General Staff in Egypt, which had been weak, and guaranteed that resistance on the African front will continue for several months. Then he spoke about the Russians, praising their extraordinary fighting abilities, and promised that the western front campaign will be conducted impeccably. He concluded with the Jewish question, strongly protesting the horrors committed by the Germans, and solemnly promising, on Roosevelt's and his own behalf, that as soon as peace is reached tribunals will be set up in Germany and in all allied and occupied territories, to judge all those guilty of crimes, cruelties, and excesses against the Jews, so that future generations may see the punishment meted out to those who committed or abetted the most ignoble bestialities in history.

A Gentile passing through Strada Romulus stopped before the school where the Jews were imprisoned awaiting deportation. Seeing so many people crowded in the yard, scared faces, weeping children, disheveled mothers gathering their shabby belongings, he asked the guard at the gate who they were.

"Victims of fate," the soldier replied.

On Strada Sf. Ion at the corner of Mămulari, a truck with German soldiers stopped a few moments: the soldiers no doubt recognized, by the desperate faces of the people who swarmed in the yard, what their ethnic origin was. They laughed and asked the soldier at the gate who they were. They got immediate confirmation. When the truck was about to leave, the German soldier sitting next to the driver passed his outstretched fingers along his neck, moving them like a knife.

An old woman hanged herself at dawn, before the trucks arrived to take the prisoners to the train station. And on the way, a woman threw into the arms of a passerby her tiny baby, a piece of paper tucked into his diapers giving his name and date of birth.

A certain Dr. D., a Gentile married to a Jewish woman, who was on military duty somewhere on the border between the Russian territories under German and those under Romanian administration, spoke of the fate of the Jews over there:

"On the German side, every week forty, fifty, eighty Jews are gathered, a grave is dug, and they are shot. It's much better on our side: a Jew is shot only once in a while, if he has a ring, a good coat, or something else of value."

*September 15*

A funny one, overheard in a line for cornmeal. A woman exclaimed loudly:

"That's what our children die for on the front? To make a country for the Jews in Transnistria?"

The panic among the Jews is now permanent. Every night they are taken from their homes and imprisoned in schools, to be deported to Transnistria. The criterion of selection varies from day to day: those who shirked forced labor, those with police records, etc. The Jews, terrified by the waiting, invent every day a new criterion for deportation, and the spider web of obsessions, the anxiety, the doubts, the fear spread from one person to another, as they meet in the street, when they have a chat, at the table, at work, all day and all night long. No one speaks anymore of "the Jews' oversensitivity," of "the alarmists' hysteria," of "rumor-mongering," of "overheated imagination." The truth is confirmed each day and every Jew is in utter despair. Even the wealthy ones, who used to be secure in the knowledge that they'd always have the means to buy an arrangement, now shake with fear.

It does seem that the statement in the *Bukarester Tageblatt,* according to which twenty-five thousand Jews would be deported this very fall, is a serious plan systematically carried out. We don't know anything anymore. Each night we go to bed afraid that we may be awakened by the police, and in the morning we give thanks for another day gained. Meanwhile, life is torn between the bloody drama of the struggle for daily sustenance and vain illusions about the end-of-the-world catastrophe. In a recess of your mind a bit of optimism still glimmers, however threatened by uncertainty. During the hours of insomnia and in the long afternoons of moral torture, thoughts keep searching the distant place where death awaits you by so many other tombs. These persistent thoughts have covered with a heavy layer of resignation the expected moments of final horror. Yet, when you hear around you in what an absurd and arbitrary way an existence still full of inner life is destroyed in a few minutes, fear and rage overwhelm you and undermine the layer of resigned calm, plunging you into helpless despair. No doubt now is the moment when I ought to turn to poetry for its nourishing strength, its support which brings forgetfulness, direction, serenity. But today poetry comes very hard to me, although many times in the past it helped me in low moods and depression. If Arghezi, deeply rooted in a secure personal life, and isolated in his manor, can complain nowadays that his pen is idle, that he cannot read—what should I say, I who die and come back to life several times a day, merely hearing about the tragedies around me?

I went down again among those tired zinnias and marigolds, their yellow flame still alive. By the fence, cemeteries full of dry leaves. The chestnut tree has started its machine-gun fire with little, green grenades releasing the brown explosions of the chestnuts. The dahlias, barren this year, are bending on their stems, exhausted. We sit around on chairs with peeling paint and absentmindedly look at the bald spots among flower beds, which we sometimes forget to water, crushed by this grim present, terrorized by the specter of winter, which will bring its own, as yet unknown tragedies.

The poet Sperber is still waiting at the police station for a decision on his life. The poets Voiculescu and Pillat, Professor George Brătianu, the writer Walter Cisek, and others rack their brains trying to save him, but it is very difficult. His deportation has been postponed to allow for contacting high-placed officials.

### September 18

A second batch of Jews, rounded up and imprisoned for some seven days in a school, seems to have been deported to Transnistria this morning. They say there haven't been any screenings whatsoever.

Since the severe blackout enforced on the city, people have made a discovery: the moon. This old feature of rural life now has become priceless for the city people who are groping through the heavy dross of darkness. The moonlit nights are an immense satisfaction, an escape from the black purgatory where we pine for the relief of light. People go out into streets, into backyards, on balconies and get drunk on the light of a moon that no decree can black out. The city is white and intensely present in this generous silver bath—present with its lights and shadows, with its houses standing suddenly out like surprises, with an orgy of lunar white over its squares. The moon, that old goddess, has regained the ancient powers and glory that once held humanity in its spell and survived only in the poets' minds.

### September 24

The fierce struggle at Stalingrad has lasted for two months, and still the Germans can speak of no positive outcome.

*September 28*

A policeman's comment:
"There aren't as many Jews as there are reasons for their deportation to Transnistria."

As of tomorrow we are left without servants. The Jews may no longer employ Gentile domestics. There was hope that the decree would not be implemented until spring. So we will do the housekeeping ourselves. For the last two days our maid has cried continuously, won't touch food.

*October 2*

Hitler delivered another speech: a disappointment. A rehash of the same commonplaces, which have paled through repetition: Churchill and Eden are imbeciles, Roosevelt a paralytic, and the Judeo-Bolshevist plutocracy and capitalism are the plague which has set in motion Germany's war machine. The only serious threat he made—and this time in detail—is the extermination of European Jews, insisting that it will be fully carried out. But he said nothing about the end of the war, which he used to announce with specific dates; and—most serious—he promised the German people nothing, gave no hope from a military point of view. His whole exposé was an obvious sign of weakness, although on the surface it still had traces of his former shrill emotional appeal. It is interesting that he accused the Americans and the British of stealing his program, adding that no bourgeois state will survive this war. But perhaps this commentator's angle is purely personal. On the streetcar today a corporal told a companion, referring to Hitler's speech: "See here, it may be true that the Jews have stopped laughing. But now it's our turn to laugh at him."

Arghezi tells me about a maid who worked for twenty-five years for a Jewish family, was nursemaid to the mistress of the house. Now, she's got nobody, doesn't know where to turn. Wants to kill herself. And about another one, whom he knows; she told the people who employed her for eighteen years that she'd like to convert to Judaism.

For a long time, perhaps even to this day, the Jews from Germany scattered throughout the world feel nostalgic about the German places they have left behind. Thomas Mann, now living in America, is said to have remarked when asked whether he does not miss Germany: "Why? Am I Jewish?"

## October 6

Thomas Mann, I am told, spoke in New York the other day denouncing a new, incredible German crime: in occupied France, several Jews were gassed. He was in tears as he talked, and concluded: "At the end of the war, all nations will pounce on Germany seeking revenge. One people only will forgive: the Jews, who have always forgiven much."

Occasionally I come across an old issue of the *Tribuna Medicală,* the magazine Dr. M. and I edited for six years. I reread pages which bring back the feverish days of struggle in the Physicians' Union, days of freedom and honesty which have never recurred since. Those days seem so distant and so unlikely that sometimes I think I must have lived them in some other existence. All the ties are broken. I no longer meet any of my former comrades-in-arms. Sometimes I see across the street a face looking at me strangely, worried and remote, trying to avoid even the semblance of a formal greeting. Once, one of them was so close that I said hello—a Greek who has a prosperous career as a Romanian doctor, without worries and with all the delights of a victorious climb. He did not recognize me. I had to tell him my name, though not so long ago we sat next to each other during our working sessions. I left immediately. I haven't seen Dr. M. either. He has remained an honest man, I am sure. But he gave no sign of life, never asked after me, never called me. Memories, memories . . .

*October 10*

The first cold day of autumn. It rained all day. A curtain of darkness seems to have fallen over the weather, over hearts, over thoughts. We lock up windows and doors, we huddle in corners, and we begin to wait, in fear and solitude, for sad news, for dislocations, for hopes inspired by rumors. Last night Barbu Lăzăreanu and his family were arrested for deportation to Transnistria. But at the same time with this news we learned from official Jewish sources that deportations will stop and that the cases of those already deported will be reviewed. The joy of the Jews is still only a crooked grin with traces of fright. But perhaps there is some truth to this rumor. A Swiss magazine publishes all the protests of Catholic prelates and of German bishops. And today our newspapers announce that the papal nuncio in Romania, who had been recalled by the Pope, is returning to his post. The Catholic Church keeps protesting vigilantly. Whether the protests will have any effect on policies remains unknown. Still, a gesture of sincere goodwill is something, and perhaps forceful action will follow.

Last night our street resounded with desperate screams. No one could find out what was happening. Most people thought they were the screams of Jews who had to abandon their homes and be deported. In the morning we found out that thieves had broken into an apartment.

"Thieves!" people exclaimed with relief. "Thank God it wasn't the police rounding up Jews!"

The battle of Stalingrad, which has been going on for seventy-three days, can be considered lost to the Germans, even according to their own communiqués. The Soviets announce that, so far, the German army has paid for this battle the fabulous price of three hundred eighty thousand dead. Some wounded German soldiers who came here say that the whole field before the city is covered with corpses, raising a pestilential stink. Those alive must remain next to the dead. The seriously wounded cannot be moved and die in the field; only the wounded who can walk escape. The Russians rejected the Germans' request for a twenty-four-hour truce to remove the dead and the wounded. The extent of the horror there can be deduced from the hopelessness a German officer expressed when he said: "Send the Jews to Stalingrad, and we'll gladly go to Transnistria!"

A peasant woman came to sell potatoes in the neighborhood. She lifted her heavy sack, rested a bit, then stopped some soldiers who were just passing by:

"Where you from, dear? Did you happen to see Ion, from Regiment such-and-such?"

The soldiers shrugged their shoulders. Then the woman explained to a housewife who was buying some of her potatoes:

"Three and a half years since I haven't worked with my man shoulder to shoulder. For five months now I don't know where he is."

She sighed deeply and added:

"Maybe the Lord will take pity—kiss the soles of His feet—and will bring my man back home!"

## October 14

In the *Bukarester Tageblatt* of Sunday, October 11, an article entitled "Judenknechte" [The kikes' flunkeys] attacks the Romanians who support the Jews threatened with deportation. The angry tone and the transparent allusions are an indication that the government's measures to stop the deportations are not acceptable to the Germans, determined as they are to cleanse Europe of Jews. The author reminds us of Hitler's decision that there shall be no Jews in the new Europe, and that only those states which managed to solve the Jewish problem shall join the new European order. It would appear that the tribute in blood paid to Germany by its allies is not as important as their cleansing themselves of Jews.

The government's decision to stop deportations to Transnistria resulted yesterday in the freeing of all Jews detained in the buildings on Strada Sf. Ion Nou. Several magistrates went over and the gates were thrown open. The news spread like wildfire throughout the neighborhood. A huge crowd gathered to help free the poor wretches locked up for days in the filthy buildings from where they were to leave for Transnistria. Those present at the moment of liberation witnessed scenes of almost unbearable delirium. People jumped out of windows, throwing their luggage into the street, handing babies into outstretched arms, shrieking with the happiness of freedom. Some fainted with joy, unable to bear the emotion of having survived the most agonizing of shipwrecks. And they hugged one another, they kissed, asking over and over again if it were really true, their hands fondled the air of freedom, they kissed the ground. Within minutes, the city had heard the news of their liberation. And everyone hurried to share it with family, with friends, with acquaintances.

People wonder what the reason is for the sudden change in the government's position on deportation. Nothing whatsoever is known. Possibly there was pressure from abroad. The Vatican seems to have intervened in all countries where it has representatives. Perhaps there are new factors in the overall political and military situation of which we know nothing yet. Still, the general joy, the brightening up since yesterday of all Jewish brows, the sudden rise in optimism, are not entirely justified. Many expect graver, more comprehensive measures to be taken, to compensate for this unexpected easing. For a compensation will have to be granted the Germans, enraged by what they feel have been quite successful plots to delay the fulfillment of their destiny.

## October 17

Almost every day, I pass through Pitagora Street, unchanged in name and appearance for the forty-five years I have known it. My first clear memories are connected with this street. There is an old house, at no. 34, I believe, its ground-floor windows facing the sidewalk, sloping toward the Radu-

Voda bridge. In the middle, a couple of steps lead to a passage-
way opening onto a small yard and then out to the back of
the house where an empty lot, full of weeds, drops almost
vertically toward the Dîmboviţa quay. The house used to
belong to the former bookdealer Sfetea, the father-in-law of
the poet Coşbuc.[41] I don't recall whether the poet actually
lived at his father-in-law's, but I know that his son, Alexandru, spent all his time there. We became good playmates.
All day long we would climb among the weeds, down to the
river and up again, to catch lizards on its banks. They
would later be confiscated by an older boy, about thirteen,
M., the nephew of a Dr. P., who eventually went to America. The doctor did not practice medicine. He lived with his
mother, a poor widow who occupied one of the four apartments facing the yard. M. was a sexually precocious boy,
obsessed with erotic problems, and I vaguely remember his
diabolical initiations into secrets which Alexandru and I
were too young to understand. M. would bring from his
uncle's room human bones, show us mysterious engravings
in large, fat books, and tell us strange stories, blown up by
his sickly imagination; he enjoyed a curious pleasure when
he managed to scare us or arouse our curiosity. Our explor-
ers' vast domain was the hill of the Theological Seminary.
Alexandru was the fearful one. The deep silence spilling
over the wild weeds on the hill, the proximity of the church
and its mausoleum, gave us the shivers, particularly when
evening would catch us before we climbed down to the gate.
M.'s bizarre stories, the bones, the skull, and the pictures in
the medical books mixed together in our imagination, and
we would hold hands as we slipped by the tombstones of the
historic monument. Once when it got very late, Alexandru
told me: "Listen, don't you tell Father where we've been, or
he won't let us go anymore!"

At the foot of the bridge, by the firehouse, just as we
were about to cross it, the poet Coşbuc, looking worried,
stood waiting for us. He took Alexandru by the hand, and I
held on to my playmate. Coşbuc scolded him, but gently, in
an absentminded tone of voice. That was the first time I
saw the great poet—tall, his face drawn, thin, with a

41. George Coşbuc (1866–1924), one of Romania's foremost poets.

gloomy brow—although he was known in my family. He came to visit my aunts (who later left for America), brought by Mr. Fuchs and Mr. Goligher, two friends of theirs who were habitués of the literary circles of the time, where they had met Coşbuc. The visitors would recite his poems enthusiastically.

Alexandru moved some two years later, I think, when I began to attend elementary school. I saw him once more, in the street with his mother, then much later I learned he had died at twenty in a stupid car accident. The house in Pitagora Street has remained unchanged. I felt no particular emotion when I saw it again. Anyway, I have never experienced that well-known and much talked-about feeling of tenderness at the sight of one's childhood haunts. The Bucharest streets where I was born and where I spent my childhood always left me totally unmoved. I don't quite know why. The poverty and misery of those days? Actually, my memories are quite pale. The rosy and violet light of my first feelings is fogged over by hardship and turmoil, which no ray can penetrate. Or perhaps later struggles, different preoccupations, left deeper impressions on my memory.

The garden: a massacre of leaves, after the wind's ultimatum.

And still no one can figure out the reason for the government's sudden decision to change its position regarding Jewish deportation, and in particular the reason for the manner in which it was carried out. Perhaps, as some believe, the cabinet stayed the execution of the decree sine die, that is, pending the formation of a special committee to handle deportations and take responsibility. That this decision was made public may be explained by a wish to produce a certain echo in special circles. The rumored infighting and frictions between lower ranking functionaries, such as the officer in charge of the Jewish question, an undersecretary, a prefect, etc., cannot be directly responsible for the sudden and sensational change in policy. A more likely explanation is that America has intervened, through the Swiss minister, as have also Sweden and especially the Vatican, which seems to become an increasingly important

factor in the activities taking place on the borderline between war and peace. At any rate, this explanation is more
tenable than the one according to which our government
was reacting to the news that the Germans had killed some
of the Jews in the first lot of deportees. The government is
unlikely to have been moved by the murder of yet a few
more Jews after so many massacred since the beginning of
the war. There is also persistent talk of intervention by
Romanian politicians, an intervention that has aroused the
fury of the German leaders, whose views are carried in the
German-language daily *Bukarester Tageblatt.* All these in-
terventions, and perhaps some new information on the general progress of the war, may have prompted the decision to
halt deportations. But its suddenness, its immediate implementation—when the Jews imprisoned in schools were
waiting for their doom—is still hard to understand. A policeman simply went there, addressed the poor beings who
were petrified with the fear of living their last moments,
and finally told them: "You are free!" And the moment
when the prisoners expected to be crowded into police vans
turned into an outburst of joyous enthusiasm, everybody
singing the royal anthem and shouting "Long live General
Antonescu!" Since then, nothing of a serious nature has
happened. There was no response to Sunday's article in the
German newspaper, in which Killinger demanded that Romania be cleansed of Jews.

## October 19

In a collection of essays in honor of Rainer Maria Rilke,
a Frenchman, André Germain, gives a most original reason
for his appreciation of the great poet. According to Germain, "Rilke occupies a special place, mainly because he
and the great Stefan Georg are the only poets who are neither Jewish nor 'Jewified.' I have nothing against the
Jews," he goes on. "I find them interesting, picturesque,
necessary. But in Germany they represent the very opposite of the German spirit and, especially the opposite of certain German qualities which I appreciate greatly: the

dreaming, the conscientious searching, a mildness full of rustling woods, of lakes, and of fairies. I approve of and appreciate the dry irony of a Sternheim, the bizarre yet magnificent madness of Else Lasker-Schüler (Germany's Madame de Noailles), the patient and often artistic work of the brothers Thomas and Heinrich Mann (both 'Jewified' through their wives). But all these honorable and even brilliant qualities do not touch my heart. They are equally foreign to Germany. For, I repeat, the Jewish spirit is foreign to all Germans—both to the German spirit I disapprove of, the harsh and hungry fatherland of a Bismarck or a Luddendorff, and to the one I appreciate, the haven of well-balanced and profound intellects such as Hölderlin, Novalis, the Empress Elisabeth, Schiller, or Goethe."

André Gide, interestingly enough, speaking of Rilke who, during one of his visits to France, criticized the German language, which lacks a word for the palm of the hand, notes the fact that Rilke, modern Germany's greatest poet, is of . . . Czech origin! Actually, born in Prague, Rilke was molded by Russian sensibility, then lived for twelve years in Paris, where he wrote the bulk of his poetic work. When he came from Russia to France he brought with him *Das Stundenbuch* [The book of hours] and *Geschichten vom lieben Gott* [Stories of God], which he reworked and completed in France. Rilke himself admits that the years he spent in Moscow were decisive in his spiritual formation. What would he say, were he alive today, if he saw that city again?

## October 25

In a talk with a lady, an officer confirmed the truth of the horrors committed by Germans in the Russian territories that fell under their administration. The Jews are killed pitilessly. He himself was present at a terrible scene. A young girl managed to escape from a group of Jews being dragged to their execution and ran to the area administered by Romanians. Disheveled, her dress in shreds, a breast showing through the rags, dirty, barefoot. A German officer raised his rifle and shot her. When the Romanian officer got sick, the German told him, smiling: "Kamerad, es ist eine Judin!" [It's a Jewess, comrade!]

A month has passed since we live under the new ruling forbidding Jews to have Gentile servants. There are very few Jewish maids, and they are most demanding and expensive. So now we are doing our own housework. We clean up, wash dishes, carry wood, light the fire, etc. Of course it is hard, particularly as we are stuck with the difficult kind of household that was appropriate to our former bourgeois condition, with all the burdensome requirements—a professional office in the house, spaciousness, rugs, paintings—that have enslaved us. The physical effort needed to maintain them are beyond our strength, but we do get by, wearing ourselves out with unruffled serenity, until we reach better times. The other day, during a Sunday afternoon at Mrs. K.'s, as leisurely as in the good old days, we were four physicians, all of us describing how we tidy up, and bragging . . .

## November 2

People's personal belongings are of secondary importance, but each only by itself and in itself. The manner in which they combine—a sofa, a table, a shelf, chairs, and possibly a piano—determines what is known as a climate, that is, the atmosphere created by a person in his surroundings. This climate is not always easily achieved. There are some friends' homes we have been visiting for years, good friends, but homes in which the objects are hostile. We don't know why, and we can do nothing to fit into their unharmonious atmosphere. Usually this has nothing to do with the worth of those who live among the "untamed" things. If the people are stronger than the objects, our relationship with them continues, regardless of the objects. But when objects have a life of their own, they can sometimes be stronger than their owners through the specific life and harmony they achieve. We all know from our childhood and adolescence such perfect combinations of objects to which we were attracted. In the present circle of our friends and acquaintances there are one or two homes where the objects are stronger than the people, and we are drawn by the atmosphere their furniture creates. Perhaps we go there in order to find ourselves in those surroundings, that certain climate unchanged by the flow of time, telling calm, and strange dreams. The atmosphere of the living room where a physician's mother entertains, or that of a graphologist from Bukovina, with a grand piano baring its white teeth at the old sofas and armchairs, perhaps yet another room, somewhere, I can't recall, confirmed my feeling that objects brought together can lead their own intense life, one stronger than their owner's.

*November 5*

After a year and a half, the government realized that, in order to avoid great danger to the nation, it is not enough to forbid Jewish writers irrevocably from appearing in the Romanian literature and press. Their exclusion must be total. And so it issued an order to remove all Jewish writings from public and private libraries. The order does not specify what means are to be used. Are the books to be merely removed, that is, set aside and not lent to any interested reader, or sold (to whom? Jewish bookstores? Jewish collectors? There are some . . .), or perhaps gathered somewhere for an auto-da-fé? Lists with the names of Jewish writers are available in the larger bookstores. They must have been compiled from the Centrala's statistics, for all sorts of details are noted.

*November 9*

Rarely since the beginning of the war has the city been as excited as it is now: yesterday morning American troops landed in Morocco and Algeria, following Roosevelt's message to the French people guaranteeing the integrity of the two colonies and assuring them that the U.S. is coming over to fight for France and with the French army. The news sped through the city like a tornado, shaking everybody. Today's papers confirm it and one can read between the lines that events are moving fast and are, of course, favorable to the Anglo-Americans. General Giraud's case is rather amusing: after escaping from a prison camp in Germany, he appeared before the Vichy government, won its confidence, and was entrusted with the command of the French troops in Algeria. When the American armies landed on French African soil, he welcomed them and resumed command of all military forces in northwest Africa. According to official reports issued by the Germans, French resistance was merely a symbolic gesture. Even Marshal Pétain's appeal to resist seems to have been a half-hearted attempt made to impress the Germans with his firm stand only in order to save unoccupied France from German occupation. Now the reason for the massing of fleets at Gibraltar becomes clear: Rommel's army will be attacked from two sides, and it is doubtful that there will be time for evacuation and the return home of his soldiers. His popularity will be shattered; the next time Hitler speaks, he will probably no longer use Rommel's name to arouse the enthusiasm of the masses, who admire the young general of the desert. All of Africa will most likely fall into the hands of the English and the Americans, and then the Mediterranean will be at their disposal for all future landings they may choose. The winter offensive the Russians are preparing may then be the next and final blow. At any rate, all eagerness and wishful thinking aside, great events are in store. The thrill of fresh hope runs through all hearts, the optimists exult and the pessimists smile, relaxed.

Following Stalin's and Roosevelt's speeches, Hitler felt the need to speak again. It was pitiful. He rehashed, but without the brilliance of his former obstinacy, all his claims about Judaism, bolshevism, and capitalism; he recalled his offers of peace and assured his listeners that he would strike in time and win the game, again with the help of providence. He oversold "real" socialism, which—according to him—German soldiers have realized, exists not in Russia but in Germany; he maintained that he was not one of those leaders who, when the country is in danger, flees abroad; he appealed to the party; he promised he would not speak again except through weapons, and jolted the country with the warning that he is playing his last card, for life or death.

Professor I. told a friend about a trial in Iaşi: some Romanian soldiers were court-martialed for disobeying orders. It was in Bessarabia, and the soldiers had been ordered to move a crowd of Jews from one place to another. On the way they sold the Jews to some peasants for 500, 700, or 1,000 lei apiece, depending on the bid. The peasants led the Jews away, took their clothes off (this being the object of their purchase), and set them free, naked, on a highway. In other words, instead of taking the kikes wherever they were ordered to take them, the soldiers had sold them —thereby disobeying orders, and that is why they were court-martialed.

## November 12

What everybody expected has come to pass: the Germans have moved into unoccupied France, despite the armistice, under the pretext of wanting to defend the Mediterranean coast against Anglo-American landings. Still, there was an emotional reaction, Hitler issued an explanatory proclamation, Pétain—a message to the French people. Admiral Darlan took refuge in French Africa and has probably joined the Americans who have occupied all the colonies one by one. The French army in Africa has surrendered very quickly. The Americans are advancing toward Tunisia. But there the Germans have flown in troops and occupied Tunis and the port of Bizerte. London keeps predicting events of importance. On the other hand, on the eastern front there is almost no change. Stalingrad did not fall, and the Caucasus, with its oil, is still in Soviet hands. Winter is setting in at a dizzying pace. The German armies will be forced to choose positions to hibernate. For the time being, the opening of the African front suits the Germans because the spotlight is no longer on the eastern front, where they can do nothing any more. And now, the waiting and the winter. . . . The snow started falling on the same day as it did last year. Wet snow, damp and cold, cutting to the bone. The struggle for supplies grows worse all the time, anxieties and bewilderment over policies fill the days, which have put on the gray garb of mourning for the dying year. Just a little time left before 1943 begins, a crucial year of offensives and defeats, of efforts and undoings, but perhaps of ultimate salvation. This winter the soul of mankind will rot away.

## November 22

However great the despair and whatever the sentimental considerations, events are moving more quickly than expected. It seems that the war has followed the lines of a well-thought-out and perfected system, so that now it proceeds with implacable logic. The Soviets have broken through the German front at Stalingrad, advanced a hundred kilometers, capturing eighteen thousand prisoners and causing the Germans the loss of thirteen thousand dead and wounded, besides enormous quantities of war equipment. They have occupied Kalach, crossed the Don, are now in possession of its bridges, and the German army at Stalingrad is surrounded. In a few days the two Soviet armies north and south of Stalingrad will probably meet. It appears, then, that the Soviets have launched a full offensive, while everybody thought that now, when the Americans have penetrated deep into Africa, the Russians would rest after the huge resistance they put up this summer. All this when the Germans' recent significant defeat in the Caucasus has again revealed their desperate situation on the threshold of winter. In Africa, the English continue the offensive they started from Egypt. The Germans and the Italians are withdrawing and have reached all the way back to El Agheila, while in Tunisia, the Americans are cutting directly through to the sea, isolating the Bizerte triangle where it is said that German troops have landed. Rommel's army is discredited. Africa has passed into American hands, with the total support of the French, electrified by Darlan who, at the last moment, brought the Americans Dakar, with the fleet stationed there. The Germans cannot get over their amazement. Now we learn that Stalin and Churchill had made plans and set the date for the landing in Africa as far back as June. All the landings on the coast of France, including Dieppe, were diversionary maneuvers, as were the Russian interviews and speeches. Consequently, the Germans concentrated thirty divisions on the French coast, and fifteen in Norway, where they also had 350 airplanes. Perhaps the next step in the development of events will be an attack on Italy, the closest point for bombing and landings. December will indeed bring many surprises. Germany's confusion and collapse can be clearly seen. The end of the war is not far off. It may be that in April Hitler's ten years of National Socialism will be over.

I have returned to the warm atmosphere of work on the anthology which, as a matter of fact, I have not neglected a single moment. But as I came across a handful of new and interesting material, I plunged with relish into work. I must hurry and put the final touches, although the book can be considered finished as of now. One hundred poets and almost four hundred poems are collected in a volume with which even I am impressed. The poems are very varied and of unquestionable literary value. I still have to straighten out the bio- and bibliographical part, and I would have finished that chapter too, long ago, if Rabinsohn were not so disorganized. I am the only person who was ever able to put up with him for four years. He is unpunctual, has no sense of time or people. Truth reaches him only through the clouded filter of his imagination. He is a genuine poet, and he lives and feeds on poetry, but he is so terrified of events that he cannot find a stable refuge and consolation in it. He did, however, render me great services, which I value fully. I got over his shortcomings, and I am well, now, on my return from one of the most beautiful artistic voyages a poet can make. Particularly today, when no one can travel anywhere.

*November 28*

The situation is unchanged, but perhaps only for a short time. From one day to the next military events may hasten political changes. For the time being, although the Germans feel cornered—as is evident from Goebbels's latest article, where he speaks of a life-or-death struggle—there is no change in their outward appearance of self-assurance and bravado. Quite recently they asked us for thirty thousand Jews to be taken as hostages to Poland. It seems that after a cabinet meeting our government refused to comply. The other day, it was announced that the thousand Jews in Norway were declared bankrupt, their fortunes confiscated, and they themselves deported to Poland, where—according to unconfirmed rumors and censored official communiqués—several thousand Jews are murdered every day since July. At any rate, the acknowledged number of seven hundred thousand Jews killed in Poland has grown to one million. The number of people the Germans have massacred must have reached a terrifying figure, if we take into account all the horrors they committed in occupied Soviet territory. And the crimes continue. Here, it seems, there is some hesitation in enforcing anti-Jewish measures. It doesn't matter whether this attitude was dictated by events or by a sudden reawakening of human conscience. Or by the elementary obligation toward a population fully integrated into Romanian life. Jewish representatives were summoned by the government and officially informed of its wish to extend assistance to the Jews deported to Transnistria. Of the one hundred forty thousand Jews deported there (this figure is uncertain, and the Germans claim larger numbers), only seventy thousand are still alive. Our government made a special point of the fact that its decision was dictated not by events but by humanitarian considerations. It suggested that the Jews in Transnistria emigrate to Palestine, and asked for three billion lei to accomplish this! The Jewish representatives requested that the Jews in Transnistria be first brought over to some camp in Moldavia, and that their emigration be organized from there. But nothing has been done yet. Humanitarian solutions can only go so far, or perhaps there are limits to goodwill. Who knows what other difficulties arise when it is a matter of saving some Jews?

## December 1

Doctor Vătămanu, who writes the medical column for the *Universul,* has found an opportunity to disseminate anti-Semitism through popularized science. Speaking of "footwear and foot defects" he quotes the German surgeon Dr. Ropke, who practiced in Africa and who notes that flat feet are a deformity peculiar to city dwellers and very common *among Jews.* To this, the physician Vătămanu adds the following interpretation, by way of scientific explanation: "What is this phenomenon but an ossification that occurs in individuals who don't run or dance, but pace the floor in their dingy shops or before the door, to draw customers in?" According to this flabby brain, Gentile vendors in the marketplace, though they are city dwellers doing the same thing as the Jews, could not possibly have flat feet. The defect is therefore a demeaning one. On the pattern of this horrendous argument, one might as well claim that Romanian Gentiles develop conjunctivitis because when they take a bribe they look the other way!

Violent people live content because they dominate all spheres of life to their satisfaction and no one bothers them. Calm, gentle, and rational people don't oppose them, to avoid provoking violence, for which they are not armed, while other violent people avoid the clash between their own and another's temper. Thus, taking for granted their dominance, which is supported by the force of their violence, they go through life without suffering. In a friendship, violence is certainly not a pleasant element, and in no way does it promote deeper understanding, but it can be borne if it is compensated for by real qualities and if the weak partner is intellectually superior and has enough inner balance and harmony. Financial relationships with violent people are not desirable because they bolster the wish to dominate which, in turn, encourages violence. A feeling of inferiority is then created, which, even if not of a moral nature, undermines the balance of power. They say that, basically, violence is a weakness, but, alas, this is as true as the saying that poverty is . . . a virtue.

## December 11

Recipients of the Nobel Prize met in New York for a conference presided by Thomas Mann, who took this opportunity to make a speech with profound political implications. He expressed his personal wish to see the cooperation between the Soviets, the U.S., and England continue even after the end of the war. He thought that the deep friendship between the Western democracies and the Soviet regime must find the formula necessary to satisfy their collective needs. The aim of this understanding, according to him, should be the kind of peace that would be more than merely an intermezzo between catastrophes.

## December 17

For a while now the English and the Americans have given serious thought to the fate of European Jewry. Press reports and radio broadcasts (according to those who listen to them) carry news of the horrible massacres, and there are protests, threats of retaliation prepared as of now against all those who have committed the crimes, have aided and abetted, or have failed to object to them. Foreign papers carry Eden's recent speech in the British Parliament about the atrocities committed against Jews by the Germans and their acolytes in Poland and elsewhere. Although Jews have been massacred for almost two years, since the beginning of the war, it is only now that indignation has reached proportions leading to official commemoration of the victims, with the members of the British Parliament rising for two minutes of silence. Afterward, they read an official declaration issued by America, England, Soviet Russia, and thirteen other nations, stressing again their joint decision to punish once and for all the crimes committed against Jews. The protest is gathering momentum in neutral countries as well, particularly in the press. But in our country the press goes on with its racist fury. Our Mr. Prudeni wrote a commentary on "My Jewish Brother," an article published in a Swedish paper, full of his usual poisonous hatred.

*December 20*

A new Russian offensive at Voronezh, a breach of ninety kilometers through the German front toward the Voronezh-Rostov railroad. Loss of equipment, men, and prisoners taken. It seems that the German army is withdrawing to new positions in the south.

Someone gave me details (again, new details) about the bestialities committed by Germans against Jews. Neither profound conviction in racist policies nor discipline in carrying out orders can explain the cruel refinements with which they commit the crimes. There is a human limit which stops, modifies, or at any rate simplifies the deed. Not even fanatic faith in a man can justify the fury of individual acts committed in such a variety of ways and places. There must be some base pleasure, some delirious pleasure derived from crime which creates the thirst for another crime, a passion which incites imagination to invent further refinements of murder. Why does one speak of "bestiality"? Animals kill simply and directly, without fantasy.

In a novel by a woman, which appeared immediately after the last war (1914–18), there is the following passage: "America and Russia are two engineers who have begun to dig a tunnel, each at his own end and unaware of the other, and one day they will meet in Europe."

Will this Christmas be the last Christmas of war? One year ago we cherished the same hope, although we lay buried in huge drifts of snow, broken by insults and boundless hatred.

All roads were closed. The struggle had stopped. There was no hope in sight. This year, however, things appear quite different. There is a new theater of war in Africa, but above all there is a totally unforeseen Soviet offensive. From north to south, along the whole front, battles are raging and the Germans are massacred. The offensive from Voronezh progresses with giant steps toward Rostov, the Germans retreating all the while, leaving behind their dead and prisoners. Hundreds of depots of ammunition and food prepared for the winter have fallen into Russian hands. A whole series of new fronts, disrupting Germany's entire offensive system, faces the most optimistic Germanophiles with the dark problem of defeat. We still have to wait to see how things develop. But if you read Goebbels's Christmas message to the German people, whom Göring just a few weeks before had promised flour, butter, and sausage, you can easily see what is happening in Germany. He speaks for the first time of "our dead who, alone, must inspire us today," and insists that "the bereaved mothers can rest in the knowledge that their sons have not died in vain!"

*December 29*

Turmoil in the city. Many arrests, searches conducted for the first time by German and Italian officers who accompany the Romanians. They are probably looking for members of the Iron Guard disguised in foreign military uniforms. Might it be true that the Germans did, after all, give in to Romanian pressure and agree to liquidate all the Iron Guards who took refuge in Germany with its official consent? In that case, what is the price for this concession? The Jews have very good reasons to wonder.

I like the loneliness of late autumn afternoons. Or of gloomy winter ones, when evening comes quickly and seems to rise from the garden, by the trees shrunken in the cold. I suddenly wake up facing two large, heavy sheets of zinc fallen against the windows. There is no one at home, or perhaps somewhere, in some room, someone is sleeping. The room's loneliness, leaning on the stove, gives me a feeling of total hopelessness, as if drowning in the ocean of time. I stop working for a few moments and let myself get drunk on a kind of sadness so heady it feels almost good. Yet often I am soon seized, not by anxiety itself, but by the memory of similar feelings of anxiety when I was a child left alone at home. The days were rough and cold. Mother would go out to buy kerosene or try to improvise a dinner, leaving me locked up in the room. The wick of the lamp was turned down very low, the things around me had trouble finding their own shape and took the shape of all my imaginary creations. But what impressed me most of all was that quiet, rising from their soul like a shadow advancing to take me in its cold embrace. When mother returned she would always reward me with a kind word followed by a story, usually borrowed from her readings, and which was more often than not too difficult for me. I remember one winter afternoon when, come back from her struggle, she told me about the life of Colonel Dreyfus, whose tragedy was taking place at the time. The memory of that childhood anxiety, with its net of sadness and loneliness, is now a fertile ground for me. A short break, and I get back to work, well and gladly.

## December 31

End of the year, full of crucifixions of pain and waiting. Tonight is the fifth anniversary since Goga,[44] in his capacity as prime minister, made his famous speech inaugurating in this corner of the world the era of hatred and crimes against the Jews in Romania, already tried by the adverse conditions of their existence. It was the final call to arms of a bourgeoisie that saw with horror the writing on the wall and felt it had to defend itself as best it could. But the time is not yet ripe to draw accounts. The horizon is growing redder under the deadly fire. Shortages are worse, the waiting has become grimmer, fear is unabated, and everywhere the earth steams with cruelty, wickedness, poison, plunder; supermen throw their lives away for a better future for

44. See "1937," n. 1.

those who will survive, disfigured by disgust, sick with nightmares, and maimed by shame, but ready to recover and ready to proclaim a new happiness under the old sun. No end-of-the-year night has ever been so sad, so difficult, and yet so full of lonely hopes, despite the hopelessness it spreads over mankind's weary soul. We trust and we wait.

1943

*January 3*

Professor G., former nationalist and opponent of King Carol, donated over six thousand lei a month for the upkeep of two children in Transnistria, explaining in a letter that humane feelings were the reason for his generosity. Prince G. Ştirbei, too, it seems, has offered five hundred thousand lei! Now there are Gentile contributions for those ship-wrecked in the land of hunger and death. One might think that the Romanian Gentiles have just discovered what has been carried out on the country's border in behalf of na-tionalist and European ideals. Someone said that even the government declared it had no idea about what was going on in Transnistria and that now that it did know, it would take steps—that is, it would allow help to be sent and some freedom given to the starved and frozen shadows dying there, when the simplest thing to do would be to let them return to the homes from which it deported them.

A new restriction limiting even more the rationing of bread for Jews.

## *January 10*

It has been snowing ceaselessly since last night. The snow is almost two feet deep, burying the yards and the roads, and it keeps falling. The Jews are already on their way to labor. An earlier snowfall, light but followed by freezing weather, sent them out with their pickaxes to break the ice. The atmosphere of a year ago is exactly duplicated. Jews in a labor camp near Cotroceni,[1] many intellectuals among them, were beaten up yesterday by the soldiers in the regiment because of "insufficient output"—in the colonel's view and following his order. As of tomorrow the capital will be an immense Jewish workyard. "Snow" has become an unforgiving communal institution. If at least they would forgo brutalizing . . .

In our yard we have a so-called caretaker, an honorary title, one of the workers in the landlord's tobacco plant. Over sixty years old, healthy and sturdy, a passionate smoker and drinker, stemming from a village near Bucharest, where he has many children. Not a spark of intelligence, of life experience. He is a digestive tract, starting under a fur cap and ending in a pair of stinky boots. In summer he sometimes comes into my garden and sits down aggressively on a chair across from me, to start an argument. All his thinking is expressed in swear words. He lets loose a salvo, then a second one, or more, according to the number of problems discussed. And when this obscene organism has swallowed the leaders of the world, of the country, the plant owner, police inspectors, and other personages, he feels the need to complete his thinking with an expression of his feelings: he spits profusely through the gap in his

1. A suburb of Bucharest.

teeth, the spittle reaching impressive distances. My frozen smile and unresponsive silence don't hamper him in the least. Eventually he asks me for cigarette paper and leaves. On tipping days, he crosses the street to the tavern. Only twice a year, at Easter and Christmas, the digestive tract looks vaguely human: yellow shoes tied with string replace the boots, and a hat the fur cap. Thus decked out he goes off in a cart belonging to one of his sons-in-law, to visit his wife in the village.

## January 17

The Soviet offensive proceeds steadily, if we are to judge by the Germans' painful efforts in composing their communiqués. Their propaganda speeches and articles mirror their confusion over the way the war is going. It would seem that the German armies are totally on the defensive, hardly able to cope, while the Soviets have begun a definite and perhaps decisive offensive. The blows fall daily, to the north, to the center, to the south. According to a gentleman speaking in German to a companion by the public phones at the post office, the German front was broken through recently at the confluence of the Donets and Don, south of Voronezh, and at Milerovo, which seems to have fallen. Moreover, the situation in the Caucasus appears to be critical, as two Soviet armies are converging on Rostov. His companion informed him in turn of the German army surrounded between the Volga and the Don, where only some eighty thousand remained out of the two hundred thousand soldiers. The refusal to accept the Russian ultimatum to surrender, the freezing cold, the hunger recently caused the death of thirty-two thousand soldiers. Fighting has started again in Africa, while in Spain mysterious decisions are being taken. The pace of war increases.

On the streetcar, a German officer to a fellow officer: "Der Krieg—ein goldener Volksschmutz!" [The war—a gilded shithouse!]

*January 20*

Streetcar No. 14 is late arriving at the Cotroceni stop, as it often is these days. Slushy snow, damp cold. Two fairly young men, well fed, nicely fur-coated, well shod, furry caps pulled down over their ears, impervious to the freezing cold, waiting for the streetcar. I thought I'd listen in surreptitiously during the boring wait. But no need, they talked loudly, unconcerned.

"You see," one of them was saying, "Peter the Great and Lenin stand for pan-Slavism and bolshevism. Pan-Slavism and bolshevism are two names for the same idea: the conquest of Western Europe by the East."

The friend, playing the devil's advocate rather than trying to argue seriously, said:

"We-e-e-ll, doesn't pan-Slavism mean the union of all Slavs? Then what would the Slavs want with the Western world when there are no Slavs there? There may be some, hereabouts, in the neighboring countries . . ."

"But don't you understand that these fellows prepared for a European invasion, the West included!"

"Even if they did, fact is, they didn't invade. So how can you tell they were going to? The Allies now say they never knew those fellows were so well prepared!"

"That's why the Allies went ahead and supported National Socialism, to fight against Soviet bolshevism with its disregard for racial differences, with its collectivism, its animal instincts and love of destruction. The victory of National Socialism is going to mean the 'rebirth of the Western world'!"

"Why is it a 'rebirth' when it was never overrun by the East in the first place?"

"Well, now, because it was destroyed by the kikes! Even a child knows that!"

"So that's it! Now I understand!"

On the way home I opened the newspaper, which I hadn't had time to read in the morning. On the third page there is an article reproduced from the monthly *Berlin-Roma-Tokyo*. Glancing at it I find, word for word, the argument put forth by the fur-capped gentleman of the pan-

Slavic theory. Did propaganda work that fast? Had he learned the article by heart?

### January 28

A renewed outbreak of hatred against the Jews? I don't think so, but some people do. A young man showed me one of the fliers distributed in the city: printed on colored paper, they show a row of crosses and a woman kneeling before them, with the head of a Jew in an insert behind her and the caption: "Remember! The Jew did this to you!" The source of this attempt to revive old madness is unknown. The persistent tendency is to lay the blame at the door of the Germans. But here the anti-Jewish sentiments remain unchanged in the circles and the minds of those who never could think straight and who don't have the courage to dig into the marrow of the only truth which explains everything. There has been no new adverse legislation. In Bucharest, things are still kept at a so-called (good Lord!) elegant level. But in the provinces the Star of David, isolation, petty persecutions prevail. In Cernăuți the situation is terrible. The Jews can go out only between 10:00 A.M. and 1:00 P.M., they are beaten up on streetcars, and the Germans force children, six to ten years old, to carry their heavy suitcases and chests.

After almost four years of military victories, the Germans have reached the point of desperation when they must inaugurate what they call "total war." That is, the whole nation is mobilized: women between the ages of sixteen and forty-five, and men between sixteen and sixty-five. To wage this kind of war they have revived an old law, never enforced until now. Whoever deserts, whether from the military or the domestic front, can be shot by anyone witnessing the desertion. Let's see now how long this "total war" will last! The eastern front, they claim, keeps "folding back," is being "rectified"—in other words, they are retreating. Several Soviet armies are converging on Rostov, and the Russians have also started an attack in the direction of Kharkov, though intending to bypass this German stronghold. The German armies west of the Caucasus and along the Black Sea are also threatened with encirclement. The Germans themselves declare that "an army should be admired not only for its victories but also for the manner in which it takes defeat." As for the army encircled at Stalingrad, they admit that it is lost, while the Soviets maintain that normal life has been resumed there and that the railroads in the area are functioning again.

*February 1*

Someone showed me a letter from a Jew deported to Transnistria: ". . . I could not write them all this and I couldn't have written you either if the person who brings it to you had not assured me you would get it unopened. If you see them, tell them whatever you think fit. But at any rate, not about the death of the two old women. I forgot to mention that Angela and Maricica are also dead. They died of starvation, not of exanthema. If you meet Frieda, tell her that her brother-in-law and her two sisters are also dead. We were neighbors. Like us, they lay all day long in their rags on the floor and went to the toilet in a bucket in the room, if you can call the hole in which they died 'a room.' I couldn't even see them. They were taken out in the morning, and it was so cold that we were all crying under our dirty rags. What's the point of giving you such details? We weren't as lucky as we hear others were who fell into German hands and were quickly done away with. But perhaps we don't have much longer to go. I said good-bye to my youth, my twenty years, and expect the end any day. If only it would come soon!"

*February 13*

My Yiddish anthology is becoming something quite different from what I first planned. To familiarize the public

with Jewish poetry, I meant to translate some of the more
representative poets, that is, to limit myself to a number of
the best. But as some of the older poets represent turning
points in the evolution of Jewish poetry, I included some
lesser ones because of their historical importance. Then I
went on adding translations from all Yiddish poets, even if
they did not conform to my initial criterion of excellence.
Thus it has become a historical and critical anthology, a
fresco of the whole of Jewish poetry, leaving it up to the
reader to choose the genuine works of art. That is why
many poems are merely deserving, others didactic, yet others sentimental. Of course, if they are judged by contemporary poetic standards, they cannot pass muster. But for
those days, and in their historic context, they were most
interesting achievements.

*February 18*

The Soviet offensive, according to German official data
and echoes from Romanian circles, has become a march that
will be hard to stop. Panic is more and more widespread.
The Caucasus has been completely freed of Germans; Rostov, Kursk, and Kharkov have fallen, while north at Orel,
and south toward Stalino, the Russians advance systematically and faster each day. From what I hear these days, all
the Romanians agree that the Germans can no longer organize resistance except perhaps on the Dniestr, and that the
Russians' strategy is to surround the German positions one
after another, giving no respite to the enemy armies. Someone said today that a group of Jews has been sent to Transnistria to dig trenches. But what is surprising is that many
intellectuals have started speaking about the Soviets in
completely different terms than they did a year ago. The
Romanians taken prisoners are being released and sent
home, and most of them have nothing but good things to
say about people whom only yesterday they considered sav-
ages. The fear of Soviet occupation still persists, as does
speculation on all the political and military possibilities, indeed, it contributes to the general bewilderment. Moral re-

sistance, it seems, is lower in Germany than anywhere else, and lower than one would expect in view of the so-called total war. Enthusiastic articles, encouraging speeches, terribly sincere confessions—all these weapons are used in the struggle to create maximum resistance, the exaltation of despair, and a supreme effort.

Commissions composed of judges from the Court of Appeals now sit on appeals by Jews requesting exemption from forced labor, or rather, extensions of their earlier exemptions. (The first time around about 80 percent were rejected, all of whom appealed and had to pay a tax of 5,000 lei—unprecedented anywhere else in the world, where the right to appeal and to review grievances is granted free of cost.) To appeal, each Jew must submit all personal documents and data, and a memorandum explaining why he solicits the exemption. Naturally, two photographs must be attached. In one case, when the presiding judge picked up the papers, he pricked his finger on the pin holding them together. In his fury, without another look at the documents, he pronounced the sentence: "Denied!" Another authentic case: the president of the commission looked through the dossier and glancing at the plaintiff's photograph said: "Son of a bitch, look at him laughing!" And he threw the papers to the court clerk, declaring: "Denied!"

## February 20

Goebbels's speech yesterday in the Sports Palace in Berlin, three months to the day since the Soviets unleashed their offensive, caused great commotion. By the moment chosen, its contents and its sweep, it is actually a speech by Hitler. But a speech Hitler could not deliver since he would not be able to project a mood of despair. The press carried only excerpts. Those who heard the speech on the radio say it sounded like the howling of a caged animal and that its only topic was the Jews. Everything Goebbels said resounded with hopeless rage. It was a desperate appeal to the whole of mankind, and a warning of all sorts of catastrophes to come if the indifference of all nations allows the now openly admitted military disaster in Russia to continue. The fact that it is no longer possible to hide from the Germans the truth about the situation in the east gives much food for thought. The call for help to England and America, although concealed behind a show of presumed superior force, again reveals what Germany's present fear is. The panic that emerges from the speech is like a direct physical panic, a need for personal rescue, like the fear of an animal at bay. The "execution squads" Goebbels sees behind the Soviet armies in their victorious march are nothing but the legions of ghosts, the ghosts of the looted, massacred, and crucified populations in the territories conquered by the Germans. And then the criminal daring of his open confession: he doesn't care what others believe, the Germans will exterminate all the Jews, who are the cause of the great misfortunes of the world. But the most extraordinary part of the speech was its conclusion, when he asked the audience, considered as representative of Germany, ten questions: "England says you have lost confidence in victory. Speak up: is it true?" And the audience shouted "No!" Etc., etc. And once assured of the determination of those present, that is of Germany, to make all the sacrifices, immediate sacrifices to save the country, he concluded prophetically: "People, arise! Let the storm rage!" As a man said on the streetcar, commenting on the speech: "The storm has been raging a long time, and the people have been trampled into the ground." While a German declared: "I believed in Germany's victory, however hard it seemed, but only until yesterday, when Dr. Goebbels spoke!"

An interesting note: the day Goebbels announced in Berlin the decision to exterminate the last remainder of the Jews, our country made public its decision to repatriate from Transnistria the Jews deported from the Old Kingdom. The ruling has not yet appeared in the *Monitorul Oficial* but was forwarded to the Centrala[2] and included specific information on its implementation.

2. See "1942," n. 11.

*March 5*

I had the opportunity to talk to V., writer, lawyer, politician. His large round head with sly eyes, his mustache, and his striking girth have often tempted the cartoonist's pencil. A typical example of the Romanian politician of yore: democratic, humanitarian, civilized, politically active not because of ideology but for the welfare of individuals, and ably struggling to get a firm foothold in the Romanian bourgeoisie with all its privileges. Lacking depth, ignorant of social and political sciences, but up-to-date on the bestsellers, the man nevertheless told me interesting and surprising things. His latest evolution led him to embrace the National Peasant party, from whose leader he picks up information on the course of local and world events. He claims that the Americans, the English, and the Russians will win the war, and that our situation will be solved by a British invasion. Until then he feeds in solitude on his unquenchable hatred of the Germans, who have destroyed Romania. He fights wherever he can colleagues and acquaintances who are Germanophiles (and, according to him, pathological characters). He cannot see how a genuine Romanian patriot can fail to understand the drift of Hitler's classification in *Mein Kampf* of nations and people into "Herrenvolk" and "Untermenschen," which places Romanians in the latter category. On the other hand, he said, all the peoples forming the Soviet Union have maintained their name, their culture, their language, their traditions, according to specific data he quoted. Thus, whatever might happen under the Russians, he would still keep his identity as Stan or Ion, while if the Germans won, he would have to become Kurt Kramer. He is convinced that after the war communism will be modified and that its European formula will be different from what it is or was in Russia. I presented him with several objections against the communist system, whereupon he declared his preference for a national democracy, but then expressed his conviction that the phenomenon in Soviet Russia and Stalin's emergence represent the most important historic event since Ramses. That is why he believes that after the war Romania will have to draw closer to Russia, which is its strongest, most lasting enemy on the eastern border, and with whom it will be possible to establish a perfect understanding.

He is not anti-Semitic (but then, all Romanian politicians maintain the same thing) and he opposed the horrors committed against Jews, believing that most of them were the work of the Germans. He promised all his support to build a dam against them. And he understood that the solution to the Jewish situation depends on the solution to the general situation in the country, the Jews being genuine Romanians, and not Romanians by force of circumstance. I often smiled, surprised, while he talked, but particularly when he waxed enthusiastic about the Malthusian theory—that population growth is the only real cause of the catastrophes that have befallen mankind. The shallowness of his thinking and his professional deformation suddenly surfaced, and the garden variety of the Danube politician produced by the climate of our recent history appeared clearly sketched with all its basic features.

A distinguished biologist told me that a rat consumes sixty grams of grain or its equivalent, a day. Last week, a Jew got 100 grams of bread a day.

*March 9*

There are days when coincidences bring a great amount of suffering to the fore. On my way I met several acquaintances.

"How are you?" I asked one of them.

"They refused me a permit for exemption from labor."

"So what will you do?"

"I don't know. I'll have to join some camp of quarry workers or road builders in Bessarabia!"

At the next corner, another one:

"How have you been? How are you doing?"

"My application for exemption was approved, but it's a tragedy."

"How come?"

"I must pay twenty thousand lei in tax, and I don't have it. I'll have to give up the exemption."

A man from Iași, on whose brother-in-law I performed surgery a few years ago, came out of a fruit stand. I asked him how this relative of his, a very nice man, was doing.

"You don't know? He died!"

"When?"

"He was murdered in Iași, two years ago, together with his father-in-law, two brothers-in-law, and a nephew."

I was in front of the post office when a woman called my name: a Polish refugee, a talented poet, involved now in all sorts of activities to help her unfortunate compatriots.

"How are you?"

"I'm really miserable!"

"What happened?"

"Lilly is dead."

"Who's Lilly?"

"A friend of mine from Warsaw. The most beautiful woman in Poland: an angel-faced blonde with the body of a Greek statue. This morning, a man who came from there told me. It's horrible, you know? . . . They put her in a truck with other women from her street, crowded like animals to the slaughter, they covered them with a canvas sheet, then they put some watchdogs on top. They took her somewhere and shot her."

When I reached the corner of Strada Lipscani, I tried to avoid an acquaintance wearing a black armband. But he stopped to greet me.

"For whom are you mourning?" I asked.

His eyes filled with tears and he swallowed a sob. Then he said, bitter, grim:

"My family—my mother, my sister, my brother-in-law, and a nephew. They were executed somewhere on the Bug."

I returned home with a splitting headache, under a warm sun, a sky heralding spring. Near home, a few Jews—ragged, dirty, exhausted, were shoveling the black, wet garbage nowadays called "snow." One of them, dark-skinned, sweating, with huge eyes, walked up to me and asked:

"Could you spare a cigarette?"

Someone said that the mayor of New York declared March 9 a day of commemoration for the two million Jews massacred in Europe.


## March 16

A Swiss was asked what his country's position was in the present war.

"We Swiss are neutral," he replied, "it's all one to us who defeats the Germans."


## March 25

Hitler broke his promise not to speak again and made another speech. A curious speech, which I couldn't quite figure out, although it contains many refrains from his old record with its political views and repeated prophecies. Something strange, a tiredness, some rambling broke the firm line and attitude, almost as if someone else talked through him. But at any rate, nothing new and nothing about the end of the war or its future development.

At the same time Churchill spoke in London, although he was not expected to speak until after Eden's return from America. He only discussed the political setup after the end of the war. At this moment of enormous strain and anxious waiting for the outcome of the offensives in Russia and Africa, this man who knows so much offered no sign of hope, nor the consolation of a vision. Everybody imagines there will be news on Eden's negotiations in America, and European circles interpret his hasty visit in the most contradictory ways, guessing about plans to hasten the end of the war, in other words, plans for a second front. In Churchill's speech—nothing but the strange declaration that the Germans will be defeated in 1944 or 1945! But perhaps this silence about immediate realities is just a cover for military plans to be carried out shortly by the Allies and be kept secret right now. Or something else? I don't understand anything anymore.

A diarist can in no case be considered a graphomaniac. Graphomania is a pathological need to write without having the foundation, the vocation, and especially the need to publish prodigious quantities. One of the graphomaniac's strongest urges is thirst for immediate notoriety. One might conclude that a diary writer is a kind of graphomaniac who cannot get published or who expects to find in death an assured, though tardy, editor. But this too is a completely unwarranted pejorative interpretation. The diarist, usually a contemplative rather than an action-driven nature, writes only to the extent that he experiences, and with no other need than that of intimate and solitary daydreaming. Perhaps precisely because he wants to avoid contact with society.

There is perhaps some cowardice in keeping a diary, an easy acceptance of immediate consolation, except of course in the rare cases when the diary represents the crystallization of a struggle, or when, under certain circumstances, the diarist decides ahead of time to jot down everything he experiences, knowing that this activity is absolutely necessary. This is the common case, when one records simply and continuously one's experiences as they occur. Being perfectly conscious of one's mediocrity, he avoids the confrontation of a literary work with the public, he gives up verification, and writes whatever he pleases, stopping wherever he likes, and gains peace of mind by speaking sincerely, without making the effort necessary to transform the material into a work of art.

## April 2

While waiting for a friend to return home, I had the unsought-for opportunity to see his wife making up. The living-room door was open and I could see in a mirror by the window all the phases of beautification the woman underwent. I have known this woman for some twenty years. But in these moments when she performed the complex and difficult ritual, not of improving her looks but of establishing her daily appearance, she seemed a complete stranger. Her face kept changing time and time again, not in progressive stages but as a strange, almost terrifying game, as if she were putting on a series of different heads for a macabre ball. The boxes and jars performed frightening magic. Alcoholic reds, mortuary violet, sickly pink, and other nuances of mixed colors placed terrible masks on her face as she labored nervously and with feverish despair. At one point, thanks to a plunge into a grease bath, all the previous heads disappeared to be replaced by a hideous grin. Then, drowned in flour, the same face looked like a grimacing clown trying to seem tender. I wondered whether what I saw was really a make-up scene or the absurd and bizarre reflection in a series of concave and convex mirrors. But the woman was calm; the transformations of her face didn't even make her wince.

There is no worse tragedy than this twilight of a woman's youth. But does any woman believe in the effectiveness of her efforts to improve her looks? One often wonders why women persist in prolonging their youth. Is it out of inertia that they go on emptying the boxes and jars of storebought illusion? There is a mask of aging which gathers from within and which cannot be covered up by an outer mask. Women do not want to understand that the instability, prejudices, neuroses, fixed ideas created by their femininity, the immense terror of approaching loneliness, is what really constitutes aging.

## April 4

The whole city is buzzing: a trainload of Jews from Salonika has stopped at the railroad station on its way to Poland. A repetition of the same things that happened with other trainloads of Jews, whether from someplace in Romania or in transit from other countries. We all know what fate awaits them in Poland. But while here, they were forbidden to get in touch with anyone. The Germans made it totally impossible to supply them with food or beverages, or ing.

to give them any help. Who knows whether these details are merely the product of exaggerated fantasy or an analogue of similar occurrences? Nothing entitles one to believe in a softening of the Germans' methods of torture. The old shudder of fear hovers in the air again over all Jews here. Again people wonder what the mysterious reason is for today's special situation of the Jews living in this patch of Europe, the Old Kingdom of Romania.

One of the Centrala members, when asked whether it was really true that forty carloads of Jews from Greece stood in the train station, replied: "Why, not at all, it's not true. There are only twenty!"

And meanwhile the Jews are jubilant at the humane advantages created for them by the new law on rents: the Jews will pay the same rent increases as the Gentiles, except for an extra 15 percent, payable to the state. The legislation applies only to those Jews whose landlords are Gentiles, and not to those renting from the CNR.[3]

## April 9

A lonely, sleepless night. It started to rain against the window by which I sleep. Suddenly. And close to me. It seemed as if the rain had climbed up to the window, propped up its violin on the lamp post and, like an old fiddler, played in my ear.

While washing the dishes Marguerite tells me she's written a new poem. Suddenly, she rinses one hand and runs into her room; when she returns, with one hand in the water, squeezing a sponge, and the other holding a sheet of paper, she reads to me her "Spring." It was an amusing scene: two poets, one with a hand in dishwater, the other with a coffeepot in his hand, their thoughts traveling with the poem.

Great civic concern has been recently accorded to washing the streets of our city. The work is performed by Jews who scrub the sidewalks with special brushes from seven

3. See "1942," n. 40.

o'clock in the morning until three in the afternoon. As the city's water pumps spray water in abundant waves, the improvised sanitation workers push it with the brushes through gutters until they reach an opening into the canal. Today, on Strada Batiştei, three Jews were doing this job. Suddenly a speeding car appears and splashes the townhall's water on the sidewalk, spraying some ladies who happened to be passing by. One of them exclaimed, indignantly: "Blast these dirty kikes! They swamp the place and mess you up so you have to go home to change!"

## April 13

A war incident worth recording. A Polish Jew, doctor of law, caught here by the war, received desperate letters from his family in Poland begging him to do whatever he could, at this eleventh hour, to save them from being shot. The man struggled until he found a way to rescue at least his eight-year-old son: a German officer agreed, for a certain sum, to bring him over by train in a basket. The child traveled the long distance from Poland to Bucharest without betraying his presence. For a frail child to have the willpower to bear up under such conditions, aware that the slightest suspicion would cause his death—that is a heroic deed which will never appear in the chronicles of this war!

Rumors, rumors . . . as always when one stands at the crossroads in times of strained waiting. Now, in the fourth year of bloodshed and gnashing of teeth, the moment separating the events of last winter from those of the coming summer seems uniquely tense. On the one hand, the end of the campaign in Tunisia, while on the other the great and decisive European offensive. Is it being coordinated on the basis of a comprehensive agreement? Will there be at the same time Anglo-American landings, Soviet forward pushes, and the entrance into the war of new belligerents? Who can judge things objectively? We always seem to lack some piece of information essential for any estimate. In the meantime, we chew rumors, our daily food, which merely increases our worry.

*April 19*

The cat spends all her time, alone, in the kitchen, in a box which served first as a labor room, and now as a lying-in bed. Two grayish balls you could stuff into one glove, weak and blind, slowly drag themselves through the scraps of rugs lining the box to reach their mother's nipples. When they fail, they squeak like mice. But the cat is bored. She has gone through this experience a couple of times before. She sits resigned and dozes off over the helpless little balls and washes them sometimes, fulfilling all her biological obligations. But she is bored. Then suddenly she tears herself away and goes into the living room, jumps on the windowsill and spends a long time looking into the yard, at the garden in bloom, at all that moving life which would interest her so much were she not caught up in her dreary duties. She is envious of the dogs at play and especially of the tomcats' freedom, who spend immense fortunes of laziness under the April sun. Suddenly she seems to remember that she is a mother, quickly jumps off the windowsill and rushes into the kitchen to climb over her offspring, thirsty for her nipples. Then she lies down in the box, with an air of supreme exhaustion, as if wondering: "How much longer?"

After so many decades circumstances have forced me to adjust to life in one of the peripheral neighborhoods of Bucharest, which haven't changed too much since my childhood. The tobacco shop is a center of cultural and political life where residents come to discuss the events in the neighborhood and in the world. This is where we find all the newspapers, gather all our information, and swap rumors. The relationships with the shop owner (now a retired captain, a handyman and a landlord) are most intimate. Everybody knows everybody's jokes, gestures, tics, personal affairs. People ask each other's advice, discuss the war. The grocer, the butcher, the two pub owners are important personages around whom daily life evolves. People go to one or the other pub according to their affinities. Police officers and citizens meet there on neutral ground, expressing their likes and resentments. In the yards, the squalor of daily life is remorselessly exposed. In a large, black kettle the laundry boils on heated bricks. The smoke rises up to my room. For days, linen and underwear are left to hang on lines that block the view of the garden and the street. Discussions are heated and commentaries ample on the households' most intimate details. Anything can spark off a quarrel and send it rolling over, loud and peppery. Children howl all the good day long. A pitiless stream of deliveries to each household: the kerosene vendor with his cans, the tinsmith who takes away leaky pots and pans and brings them back all patched up, the vegetable man, the Gypsy with her popcorn, the yogurt vendor. Every few days, someone spreads out mattresses and pillows on the fence, de-lices them, scrubs the wooden boards with washing soda. The level of spiritual life hasn't risen by as much as a millimeter since my childhood. The music they listen to now on the radio is the same as the one gramophones used to grind out decades ago. The women put their hair up in pin curls, the men read *Universul* and drink. Politics is limited to anti-Semitism. If in these special times you happen to be the neighbor of a tobacconist, a grocer, and a baker, you must also put up with the racist plot that hurls the most vulgar swear words through your window; you must even give up the bit of grass planted in a garden for consolation and for some quiet isolation. In many ways the outskirts of Bucharest are still Gypsy country.

## May 1

The atmosphere of the school where I serve as a physician and as an instructor of sorts[4] reminds me of the Jewish high school set up at the turn of the century. I was a student there. The need for it arose from the difficulties for Jews to be admitted to public high schools. A group of enthusiastic Jewish university students initiated it under very difficult conditions, lacking the official support of Jewish organizations, which at the time were not centralized. The cultural and philanthropic life of Bucharest Jewry

4. Following the exclusion of Jewish students and Jewish teachers from Romanian schools in 1940, several Jewish high schools were organized in Bucharest.

took place in committees which headed various organizations and were at odds because of rivalries and disproportionate ambitions, each of them with its own social status props: banner, rubber stamp, sashes. The action of the modest students in an outburst of great energy bore fruit for many years to come. The school was set up in a fairly large building, suitable enough for its purpose. One can still see today on Strada Mircea-Vodă a rectangular yard, with the old elementary school Iacob şi Carolina Löbel on one side and the high-school building opposite; on one of the narrower sides, a luncheonette, and on the other—the building which houses the Jewish Funeral Society. A sad yard, without a tree, without flower beds, the ground trodden down by generations of school children and high-school students. The second and only floor of the high school used to be the residence of the now deceased rabbi, Dr. Beck; he was also the principal of the elementary school, which I attended for four years. The neighborhood resented the school because of the noisy, prankish school children. When we would see the venerable old man, with his long locks of hair, his impressive sideburns, and eyes of sharp steel, coming down the stairs and going toward our school office to attend to complaints, cold fear gripped all of us and we quickly locked ourselves up in classrooms or hid in the remotest corners of the yard. Besides being the principal of the elementary school, Dr. Beck was also a teacher of Hebrew, or rather, of religion. He was dull, tiresome, and imposed strict discipline, not so much for pedagogical reasons as out of malice. The young group of university students who were our instructors opposed him, but had to give in because he was very influential in the Jewish organizations of the time.

The high school had been in existence for two or three years when I began attending it, had outgrown somewhat the initial improvisations, and overcome some of its difficulties. It had soon acquired a reputation for excellence because at the end of each year its students passed state examinations given by old and renowned teachers. Our own instructors were young, inexperienced, had not yet received their certification, had no supervised practice, but their enthusiasm and willingness more than made up for the lack of specialization. Most of them are still alive and some have continued teaching, eventually turning to good account their classroom experience of many years. The high-school principal was a medical student, or rather, had completed all requirements but postponed taking his finals, maybe because of his obligations as principal, maybe because of difficulties in setting up a private practice. He taught mathematics and was a skilled instructor, the students' favorite. Tall, gloomy, morose—his smile was a rare feast for the school, which respected and feared him. His name was Saidman. He got his degree very late and opened an office on the same street, Mircea-Vodă, where colleagues and former students would visit him often. A few years later, at about the time when I started my own medical studies, he had a stroke and was left paralyzed in both legs. He went on practicing, with great difficulty, sitting behind his desk in an apartment over a store on Strada Lipscani. His face was completely changed. A great inner light flickered, and a permanent smile blossomed in the large, dark eyes; his icy voice had acquired kindly inflections and a warm, humane tone.

The geography teacher was also a medical student. A poor young man beset by great family problems, he had a blondish head with curly hair, a penetrating glance. He taught with passion and brought to his teaching an erudition far beyond the set requirements. His friendly, vibrant voice, was most suitable for communication. Our young teacher made full use of the new approach to the teaching of geography and would talk to us at length about the customs of different nations, spicing his lectures with the comments of a sentimental socialist, a rebel against an unjust social structure which held him back in his intellectual aspirations. I still remember his mildly sad smile and the way he would pass his hand through his full, shaggy hair. For most of us he might have remained the picture of the ideal teacher had we not met him later in life: he had become a physician with a prosperous private practice and a horse-drawn carriage, most successful despite his mediocre scientific preparation, a slave to his job, without any interest in intellectual pursuits, in reading, and without any enthusiasm. We, his students, were disappointed, because we had considered him fit to be our generation's leader.

A third medical student was the instructor of natural sciences and, in a pinch, of physics and chemistry. Baruch by name, he was one of the leaders of the young generation of romantic Zionists, with Isac Leon, the great Zionist activist of the time, orator and poet. Instructor Baruch was nervous and brutal. He flogged us out of a need to release his tension and sometimes, when using the rod, his heavy hand would crush the boys' tender ribs. He showed an excessive, total, absurd sternness. A magazine called *Tribuna sionistă,* published at the time, was distributed from the Jewish hospital. Every two weeks, I seem to recall, he called me and another student over to address envelopes, lick stamps and labels, and drop the load into a mailbox. He never explained to us what Zionism was. I remember one Sunday afternoon when he called me over to the office of the magazine. After the job was done, finding him smiling and in a good mood, I shyly asked him—what is Zionism? He frowned and replied: "None of your business, boy! Keep your nose to your books!" Eventually, he got his diploma, married the daughter of a Pitești merchant, opened an excellently situated office, and practiced for many years, while being involved in Jewish politics and turning a pretty penny which enabled him to move to Bucharest. Here, too, he was active as a physician and a Zionist and joined the leadership of the Jewish community as supervisor of schools. We met again and he expressed his admiration for my career as a writer to which he was happy to have contributed. I never found out how: through the services I rendered him as a mailing clerk—or through his flogging?

There was yet another medical student at the Jewish high school, Bernarduş Marcus, dark-haired, slender as a reed, who taught gymnastics in the gymnasium of the Aurora Society, which had its headquarters in our high-school building: a large hall, dark and cold, but well equipped and maintained by the young, Jewish middle-class members of the society.

The teacher of Romanian language was an unlikable pedant, who thought no one was his equal in knowledge and complexity. He had a constant adversary in the person of Finkelstein, the French teacher, who considered himself a specialist in the same subjects. Finkelstein was not particularly brilliant, but he was a good teacher, and although demanding, earnest, and unfriendly, he taught us French grammar much better than it was taught in public high schools. Still, there was a great gulf between him and his students. His distinctive profile, his baritone voice spilling over in sonorous cascades, the authority he emanated effortlessly, destined him to be a manager. And indeed later, when he escaped the difficult job of Jewish teacher, he went to work for a bank, then became the director of several commercial enterprises where he proved to be an energetic and conscientious leader. Although a young man, he flogged us just as hard as did old A. S. Gold, who taught us Hebrew and never walked into the classroom without a rod in his hand. But even more vicious and cruel was the notorious Stambler, teacher of drawing and calligraphy, an illiterate who spoke like a slum dweller and who considered himself a great artist fallen so low as to teach in a Jewish school. He had a pumpkin head, its baldness covered by heavily greased hair he combed forward from his nape, and was disgustingly potbellied. A confirmed bachelor, he was exceptionally elegant; everyone who knew him remembers the distinguished gentleman in a bowler hat, with cane and leather gloves, who at five o'clock in the afternoon sat down at an outdoor table at the famous Café Ionescu, on Sf. Gheorghe Square. More often than not, a woman would transform his coffee hour into a rendezvous, which the students would notice, as they went silently by.

Mr. Segal, instructor in history and Latin, nowadays drawing a pension from the Sephardic community as the former director of its elementary school, was quite undistinguished. A conscientious teacher, intuitively good at his job, he taught us a great deal. He, too, demands recognition from his former students who made a name for themselves in literature, although his connection with belles-lettres was entirely nonexistent. On the whole, none of our teachers ever rose above what they accomplished in those early years, none produced a groundbreaking work in his field, nor was any of them culturally active or innovative. I refer, of course, to those who remained in the teaching profession, the others having joined the medical ranks.

Perhaps that explains why my years in high school appear to me like some gray, sad, monotonous river. Except for the brief moments of festivities, school life offered nothing to our childhood, spent in the dust of Bucharest's outskirts. At the time, the radio and the movies were yet to come, the national theater's performances were rare and beyond our means, and as for sports—all we had was an occasional ball game. The town, drowned in dust, held no opportunity for entertainment. The only amusements were an occasional "excursion" to the out-of-town Grozăveşti bridge, where the iron railing along the Dîmboviţa River stopped; or some escapade to the Cişmigiu park, where we stared through the trellis of a summer theater at performances by magicians, jugglers, and popular singers; and, very rarely, a walk in the Filaret meadow, full of swamps and marshes. People sat down on the grass in clusters, the children caught leeches and lizards, the oldsters picnicked and drank cold millet beer or lemonade warmed up by the sun, while the affluent devoured *rahat lakoum,* sunflower seeds, or candies. The only recreation was books, cheap editions of popular works, and some translations, printed on dark paper with sad, ugly letters.

There was only one extracurricular activity, developed by the juniors (the terminal class, as there was no senior class, for lack of students): we published an underground literary review. It was called *Seven,* the number of students in that class. The editors-in-chief were myself and a classmate, Eduard Alscheck, who later practiced medicine in Paris (where he died of appendicitis). One of our contributors was Enric Algazi (later contributing editor of the Paris newspaper *Le Temps*), who submitted prose and poetry. Among other columns we had a humorous one in verse, where we sneaked in some innocent obscenities. In order to avoid detection we wrote it in a special alphabet I invented. The signature signified the solidarity of the whole class—*Alflali Lobeco*—composed of the first letters of everybody's name. It was I who wrote out the whole magazine with red ink, in printed letters, decorating the borders with festoons and imaginative designs. At one point we were nevertheless found out, betrayed, if I'm not mistaken, by a lower-grade student. The issue was confiscated. I was called up into the office and asked to disclose the key to the secret alphabet. I stood my ground. I was not shaken by the threats of dismissal because the whole class was behind me. A special meeting was called and Mr. Baruch, professor of natural science, demanded the most drastic sanctions. Eventually, we got a light punishment and the magazine was suspended.

That is when the French teacher, whose father was a friend of my father's, found out that I wrote poetry. During one of his subsequent classes, frowning and dictatorial, he demanded that I bring him a sample. I remember that at the next session, my heart as small and jumpy as a flea, I approached the teacher's desk proffering a sheet of paper on which I had copied a poem entitled "Spring." He liked it, apparently: his face relaxed as he read it and he had to make an effort to maintain his stern look. Then, with a ferocious air, he looked me up and down and returned the poem, shouting: "It's very beautiful, but don't let me catch you writing poetry again, or I'll break your hands!"

A few days later, he sent word through my father that I was not to write poetry any more, for that way "lay poverty." How right he was, my former teacher! Still, in the sumptuous offices of the "Discom," where he directed the country-wide production of tobacco, whenever he received me, a modest physician who had still not given up the bad habit of writing poetry, he would boast about this former student of his to all the magnates and distinguished gentlemen present.

## May 8

The Anglo-American armies have taken Bizerte and Tunis. The American landing was launched six months ago to the day. No doubt the German communiqués will be couched in the same old style: they are giving up those positions no longer important. The news has spread incredibly quickly throughout the city. Many bets have been made. The pessimists are forced to revise their political and strategic views. Everybody tensely awaits the coming events.

Many people have noticed that the sparrows are not back yet. They try to figure out the reason, and one of the explanations is—a boycott against a Europe troubled by war! Others account for it by the air warfare in Africa, even though only a small strip of land is involved, in Tunisia. But as the war in Africa is over, this explanation is no longer valid. We are waiting for the swallows.

Some friends sighted one. But one swallow does not make spring . . .

## May 12

After so many expenses the Jews had to bear, the Centrala was asked for 100 million lei to settle the various litigations arising from the requisition of personal effects enforced two years ago. To be completed by May 15. The Centrala has immediately increased all contributions by 25 percent. On top of taxes on snow, work permits, and others. Now there is a rumor that Jews will be asked for four billion lei (?!). Again, the Centrala will be entrusted with this action, as it has been with all others aimed at the despoilment of the Jewish population. All these measures seem to fit into the atmosphere of the eve of an offensive on the eastern front. The press has resumed its campaign against bolshevism and has intensified anti-Semitic propaganda at a time when the government is taking new measures against the Jews, even if it is not following a broad, systematic program. Tension has increased tremendously in the last three to four days. The liquidation of Tunisia inspires all sorts of fantasies and impatience concerning a landing in Europe, which many Germans discuss ceaselessly, obsessed by an unadmitted fear. There is talk of air raids. A gigantic struggle is about to break out in the east. Meanwhile, the search for supplies has reached dramatic proportions, and a lot of money is needed for anything, even for waiting, merely waiting. Any problem that arises becomes a huge problem, and the sums its solution requires are astronomical. The French saying "plaies d'argent ne sont pas mortelles" (financial wounds are not fatal) has never been more untrue than now. You may have to pay with your life for your lack of money.

## May 15

Somebody told us today that, in the Tunisian part occupied by the Allies, all those who insulted the locals, be they

French, Muslims, or Jewish, must wear an armband marked "profiteur." The French remain to the end elegant and polite.

Paula, pacing up and down the long, silent rooms baked by the sun:
"Nothing is happening! Nothing is happening!"

A Jew's anxiety when he sees a policeman. If he is talking with a friend, he stops suddenly, or discreetly signals to him, and if he is alone, he crosses to the other side of the street for no reason. Always, automatically, he feels the pocket where he keeps his papers. But that is not a recent reaction. At all times and almost everywhere the policeman has aroused a small, involuntary response, like an unwelcome presence. He is the element that disturbs the landscape of a street or the dreamy solitude of a square. I remember Jules Renard saying somewhere: "My age and my being a mayor are of no avail, when I see a policeman, I worry."

## May 21

Some women carry their breasts as if they were offering two hearts.

I spend most of the hours of the day at my desk, often without working. Just to sit next to it quiets me. There I become serene, make decisions, chew on an idea, despise myself, or kill myself. Many of the few good things I have written come from the climate created by my desk, which is often inspiration itself. Sometimes at twilight the desk becomes a transatlantic liner, or an airplane on its way to the stars. My desk takes all the shapes of my dreams.

## May 24

Horrible details about the massacres in Poland. It seems the Germans gassed the Jews of Stanislav and Cracow and then turned to those in Warsaw. The Poles gave the Jews weapons with which they fought the Germans, killing several thousand. Resistance is said to have lasted several days, and then the assassins came with airplanes and tanks.

The shade of the old linden tree, tall and bushy, covers the garden, the yard and the street. It is the most venerable resident of the neighborhood. When people stop under it, they take their hats off.

Nothing . . . just a light ash-gray dust from the depth of memory settled like a small snowfall.

"Aren't you coming?"
"I can't, I'm very busy."
"With what?"
"Being alone."

## May 26

Poison gas, the most horrible of all the weapons prepared for this war, has not been used to this day. None of the many belligerents dared to unleash it, however tragic or desperate their military situation. It seems it has been reserved for one enemy only, the Jews. Recently, we keep hearing of the gassing of Jews in various countries occupied by the Germans. But despite confirmed reports and testimonies, people refuse to believe that such things are possible. How can the most deadly of weapons be used against the most defenseless of people? Some feel that there must be a little hesitation even among those who have sunk to the lowest level; others think that in bestiality itself there must be traces of a human law; and very many believe that these rumors are merely exaggerations of an imagination deranged by the unbearable war conditions. And yet it is the whole truth and it must be recorded together with the endless list of crimes committed until now.

Formerly, when I used to live in the center of town, perched on the third floor between stone apartment buildings, a garden was a need which I managed to satisfy almost every day. I wasn't too lazy to go down to the Cişmigiu, where I wandered on the paths, among flowers and trees. Now, all I have to do is look up from my desk and I see the tips of the fir trees, linden trees, and elms in the garden below. I don't even go out for days at a time. I am content with the rocking of the branches and the sky's light glancing off them. A beginning of reality is enough.

The lemon vendor sat leaning against the fence of a public building. An impressive head, with a patriarch's beard, and two reproachful eyes like two dark hollows; he wore a tattered jacket of navy blue cloth, on its left side a row of shining war medals. With one hand he held the basket with lemons half-propped up against the fence, and with the other he absentmindedly stroked a rough-hewn pipe, puffing on its cheap tobacco. A gentleman in a raglan coat, his hat at a rakish angle, carrying a sumptuous leather briefcase, stopped by the lemon basket. He was a price inspector.

"So you're speculating, eh?" he asked in a tone midway between sternness and goodwill.

The old man shook his head, no. The inspector bent over the basket to choose some lemons.

"Your papers in order?" he asked tentatively.

The vendor nodded, yes. Then he took an identity card out of a pocket of his war veteran's jacket. The inspector opened it without much interest. I, too, looked at it over his shoulder. The photograph showed a beardless man, vaguely resembling the lemon vendor.

"Where's the beard?" the inspector asked.

"I put an older picture in," the old man explained, hesitantly.

The inspector chose two lemons, paid, and left.

I started to search through the basket, looking carefully at the old man. Something in his speech, although he had only said one short sentence, and something in his features, I don't know what, gave me the idea that he must be Jewish. But his coat with the war veteran medals? How to find out? What if, insulted, he reacts violently?

Suddenly, I blurted out in Yiddish: "Are you Jewish?"

The old man shook his head, no . . .

I choose the lemons slowly and start a conversation about life, the hard times, the difficulties for some people, and eventually I gain his confidence. The old man has a daughter in Transnistria who left her two children in his care. He used to make some sort of pretzels and sell them in the Jewish quarter. One rainy evening he was on his way home when a man jumped at him out of the dark and stole his papers and all the money he had on him—two thousand one hundred lei. Unable to scrape together a living, miserable, he struggled in such torment that he even considered killing himself, as well as his two grandchildren. But one day, he found salvation. In his neighborhood there lives a Gentile war veteran, a sick old man who spends most of his time in bed. And since he never got dressed anyway, he offered him his veteran's jacket so that, protected by it, he could do a little business in a more central location. The picture on his identity card bore a great resemblance to the old Jew.

## June 2

By chance I came across and reread some of my old drafts, dating five years back. I was seized by a disgust that nothing can overcome. A smooth, glossy surface, a calligraphic style, everything pretty and superficial, good and uninteresting. I will have to build a big fire and throw all my old manuscripts in. Perhaps I ought to pile on top many of my printed books. I will keep a few poems. Surely I ought to have been a journalist instead of writing literature, a sin I must admit in all honesty. Perhaps only this diary . . .

## June 4

Prime Minister Kallay's declarations in the Hungarian parliament have made a deep impression on all Bucharest circles. He stated that Hungary has withdrawn its troops from the front in Russia, with whom it has no quarrel; he considers that Hungary's armies must be used only to defend her own interests, and intends to live in peace with her neighbors; as to certain territories which had not belonged to the Hungarian crown—they were his government's inheritance from a previous regime.

Regarding the Jewish question, he said that in Hungary there is a rather large number of Jews (some eight hundred fifty thousand), but that their problem cannot be solved at the moment and must await a solution to be reached in agreement with other nations. Until such time, the Hungarian government intends to take no measures against them, and anyway Hungary, being a Catholic and Christian state, never did take any such measures.

The Jigniţa Garden,[5] which saw the development of some of the most important chapters in the history of the Jewish theater, Romania being its cradle, is now the business place of a coffin manufacturer. The coffins are actually stored on the stage . . .

Arghezi[6] was detained by the police for four days to give evidence about a column he had contributed to the newspaper *Informaţia* concerning Filderman's deportation.[7] Curious, this outburst of the poet-polemicist in defense of a politician, when he never showed such chivalry toward some Jewish intellectuals, victims of hatred and injustice.

## June 7

The first real day of summer. The city seems to have blossomed again and turns its blond, laughing face toward the sky. The women are out in brightly colored dresses. Old memories flutter in the folds of their silks, new dreams sparkle in their eyes. Every street is a song.

People rushed to judge too soon. I read Arghezi's column and it didn't strike me as being an unexpected defense

5. A theater located in the heart of the Bucharest Jewish quarter, where the famous Yiddish troupe of Abraham Goldfaden performed from 1877 to 1879.

6. See "1942," n. 17.

7. See "1940," n. 47.

of some Jewish political heroism. The poet himself immediately contested the misunderstanding and even hastened to clarify in writing his position. The man he defended is a mere journalist who happens to be Arghezi's editor. The bombastic and extravagant tone and the flowery style certainly seem out of all proportion with the stature of the person eulogized. But Arghezi always writes in the same way about anyone who happens to hold the purse strings at the moment.

## June 12

The Anglo-Americans have occupied the islands of Pantelleria and Lampedusa, and now that the way across the Mediterranean is open the war is nearing the coast of the Italian kingdom. During this time, there has been no movement on the eastern front. Roosevelt sent the Italian people a message asking them to overthrow fascism, assuring them that he has nothing against them, and promising to respect the country's territorial integrity. This is the latest and hardest moment Italy is living through. According to recent articles and some news releases, a break in the Axis is not far off. During every summer of this war we expected decisive events, but in no previous summer did we have as vivid a feeling of forthcoming breakdowns. It is quite possible that by the end of the month extraordinary things will happen, confirming the rumors and forebodings. What will our country's position be in the final moments of the tragedy? Who can tell? I have the feeling that even our leaders know no more than the man in the street; the solutions will come from elsewhere. And how will we Jews fare during the last hours? This, too, cannot be foreseen. We might escape if there is trouble among the Germans themselves.

## June 21

The play I am writing has no connection with present contingencies. That is precisely the reason why I decided to write it. A broad problem in human psychology. But while working, I keep wondering: Is this a legitimate preoccupation for a writer nowadays? Who can be interested in the drama of an ugly woman? How can it appeal to a reader or an audience eager for the new, stirring problems determining our future? Thus, new hesitations are added to those of creativity proper. You want to isolate yourself, to flee the present. But do you have the right to do it? The spirit stands at a crossroads and the pen takes this opportunity to justify its failures.

The linden trees in the garden have bloomed . . . the street, the yard, and the rooms are invaded by their heady fragrance, which has always made me slightly dizzy. But since this diabolical war invention—linden tea we drink at breakfast with bread and jam for lack of Russian tea—I don't know how to avoid the smell of the linden in bloom. The dizziness has grown worse, becoming unbearable, and nausea has settled in.

The commemorations of Yiddish writers, held in order to boost the morale of the Jewish masses, have reached the proportions of an epidemic. Almost every week there is a commemoration in some synagogue. The spectacles are worse than mediocre and the public is beginning to tire of them. At any rate, the possibility of producing the Romanian works of Jewish writers is being seriously considered. These writers live in isolation, cut off from professional writing because most of them can no longer make a living with their pen. The intention is to organize a literary gathering. I think it will succeed in spite of all obstacles from the authorities which do not allow a free selection of the writers and the works to be presented. There is enough energy available, but one must always accept a format which delays and weakens the expression of the initial enthusiasm. We shall see whether the end of July is a suitable time for a Jewish literary event. The month of June has gone by full of tensions such as we have not felt since the beginning of the war. The Allies' landing in Europe is discussed feverishly, tensely, with an anticipation reaching exasperation. Some people think, however, that this endless wait has to do with Italy, which is on the point of finally capitulating. The optimists count the days, fearing that "there will no longer be time for a decisive offensive." And we are waiting, waiting . . .

## July 10

When I returned home I learned of the Anglo-American flash landing in Sicily. Excitement has reached its limits. Today's greeting consists of announcing this news. We are deeply moved, our thoughts are in an uproar trying to work out the possibilities which will put an end to the mighty world struggle. All bets are on Italy's imminent capitulation. But this is very unlikely to happen right away. The military action is massive and definitive, according to news releases, which are categorical. Who knows, perhaps Sicily will be the door through which peace will enter this dark and mangled Europe! At any rate, it is now possible to see clearly the beginning agony of Nazism and fascism.

## July 15

A friend who just came from downtown brought me the news of E. Lovinescu's death.[8] I haven't seen him in years, although many colleagues kept bringing me his reproachful reminders. For about one year, some twenty years ago, I used to visit him assiduously. After that our contact was limited to chance meetings in bookstores. Writers and intellectuals are deeply moved by his passing. He was unique in Romania's intellectual fauna: for several decades he presided from his armchair over a generation of writers who filed by, especially beginners, and often even hacks or graphomaniacs, who later sobered up. He is a singular case of monumental patience and passionate love for the phenomenon of writing—certainly an unusual occurrence in Romanian society where any fairly bright professor or pushy little lawyer would dash onto the remunerative road

8. See "1940," n. 35.

of politics. No doubt his temperament helped him: he was not a fighter. The battles he fought were with his pen, from his desk, and only in the arena of literature. Nothing but the mystery of creativity interested him. He had no long-lasting friendships, he was incapable of any emotional commitment. Even the human being behind the writer interested him only mildly, and the occasions when he brought himself to extend a helping hand were very rare indeed. He didn't love life, he didn't love people. Inevitably, he suffered the dire consequences: everything he wrote is a mere intellectual game, a cold and artificial product, lacking sap, lacking the real breath of life. That is why, despite his numerous attempts, he was not successful as a creative writer. For if you do not love life and do not experience it yourself, you cannot be a writer. A man of classical culture, he wrote in a clear style, he was even-tempered, coldly elegant, objective, and hospitable, and spent his life in a feverish but subdued obsession with the discovery of great talent. And he did discover quite a few talented people, that is, those whose gift for literature had been recognized by others and who would come to him for confirmation. But his great, impatient expectation was all in vain. The undiscovered genius did not knock at his door, and he died, his hospitality spent on minor successes. Still, in a city where people chase after empty goals, he achieved a climate of lofty dreams and preoccupation with literary criticism, in the island of his room, where he officiated over beauty, simplicity, and honesty.

## July 20

Romanian humor. A scene on the streetcar. A Jew stands up and offers his seat to an old man.

"I'm not going to take a seat that has been occupied by a kike," the old man announces fiercely.

Another Gentile, standing near the old man, asks him: "You don't want to sit down?"

"I certainly don't."

The second Gentile takes the seat offered by the Jew. After two minutes he gets up again.

"There, you can sit down now," he addresses the old man, "the seat has been Romanianized."

Was Lovinescu an anti-Semite? Most people can't make up their minds. Anyway, he was objective, more objective than many others, and polite, civilized, most hospitable, or at any rate as hospitable with his Jewish as with his Gentile visitors. The Jews who visited him assiduously considered him a benevolent friend. Still, those who discussed the Jewish question with him remember statements that indicate a clear anti-Semitic stand, expressed coldly, amiably, simply.

I took up this problem with him many times. When he wanted to be nice, he smilingly skimmed over convictions he did not dare to state bluntly. Several times, however, he expressed himself more precisely, though appearing to be a political dilettante, and one time he had an outburst that betrayed him completely. What is more, he wanted me to know his views. It happened the year I wrote *Conversations with My Horse.* He asked me over on a weekday (his literary circle met only Sundays) to read the whole work for him. He refused to give me his opinion before my reading at the next Sunday meeting, but he assured me that the character of my poems, which did not fit the nationalistic tastes of his guests, would not cause me any trouble. That Sunday, there was an incident with Rebreanu,[9] who kept shuffling papers while I was reading. I lost my temper and told him that no one was being forced to listen if he didn't feel like it, but that a guest in that home ought to respect its customs. What I read pleased some and displeased others, according to each writer's attitude toward the political and social problems raised by the war. A couple of days later, alone with me, Lovinescu told me to my face what he had not dared tell me before:

"That is why Romanian literature will never fully accept you Jewish writers: because you write this sort of thing. I was in the war too, but I wrote about it differently, I wrote in a patriotic spirit, warmly and objectively."

9. Liviu Rebreanu (1885–1944), a prominent Romanian novelist between the wars.

"I doubt you were really in the war," I replied. "And it also depends on where you were. You were stationed in Iaşi, as a censor. I agree—from there, the war could only appear the way you saw it. But I was on the front, and on the front war looks different. Cruelty, misery, revolt, injustice, death—an artist cannot envision all this unless he experiences it, without the falsifications and patriotic demagoguery of the man remote from it!"

Later, the cynicism of his views appeared transparently in some notes of his *Memoirs*. Still, he continued welcoming Jewish writers and beginners, and always maintained his equanimity. He was searching for an outstanding talent who would be his disciple and whom he could mold in his capacity as a teacher of literary creativity. Unfortunately, no great hopeful arose, even from among the young Jews. And the new generation could no longer knock at his welcoming door. Perhaps somewhere there is someone . . .

## July 26

The most astounding event since the beginning of the war was announced last night: Mussolini has resigned. We learn from an inconspicuous newspaper report that on the night of July 25, 1943, fascism has collapsed after a rule of twenty-one years. The consequences are incalculable. . . . Everybody, from the little boy who brought the news in the folds of a paper, to the highest man in politics, is shaken as if by a geological shift. The king of Italy has reassumed his prerogatives. Marshal Badoglio has been named premier, and proclaimed that he will continue the war. But this will be impossible. The war is Germany's war, not the Italians', who, since a few hours ago, can only wish for peace. Italy will undergo a number of convulsions and will capitulate. Then the war will go on between the Anglo-Americans and the Germans, until, sooner than we expect, Germany will collapse in a huge military and political catastrophe. But henceforth, the political front has primacy over the military one.

## August 1

The first American bombing of our country, similar to those of Italy and Germany. Some one to two hundred bombers dropped bombs on the Ploieşti[10] refineries. No news about the damages, but they seem to be great. The air alarm lasted two hours and included Bucharest, where we immediately learned of the disaster our oil center suffered: fires, victims, everything we have read has been happening for such a long time elsewhere. The dread of worse damage to Bucharest is now greater and more justified, and people are fearful. The expected political easing in Italy has not yet occurred. The people want peace, the unrest continues, and the war follows its course. Things will clear up, but no one knows how or when.

## September 1

The days, the running around, the worries, kept me away from this notebook. I haven't forgotten it. But sometimes the thought of its uselessness defeats me. Life is so dry that you cannot bend over a page of jottings, even for one moment. I thought the same thing might happen that happens with tobacco: if you don't smoke for three weeks, you may give up smoking. But here I am, solitude has enfolded me again, and I am back. Tired of people, saddened by what is happening. I should have noted new disappointments in a friend. A friend? I am still not certain about the definition of this word, and life does its best to mix me up. Violence keeps pace with untruth, spiritual values beat a retreat. Struggle . . . Naturally only those who fight are right. But it still involves people. Egotism hides under clever masks. Thoughts and actions . . . Behind them are people, that is elbows, brutal elbows shoving to make room for themselves. If at least there would not be the day's sadness, bringing with it the shiver of an old and wasteful restlessness.

10. A town in southern Romania, the main center of the oil industry.

*September 6*

End of summer and of a long, hard road. The offensive launched by the Soviets two months ago has gone far. Essential changes have occurred along the whole front. In the center they have broken through at Orel, Kharkov, and Bryansk, and the Donets is now in their possession. They are heading toward Smolensk in the north, Kiev in the center, and Crimea in the south. All German positions have crumpled and they keep announcing territories ceded, falling back, and other actions to maintain a mobile front. On the Italian front, Sicily has been completely occupied by the Allies, who have even landed on the boot, in Calabria. Perhaps there the war will not last too long, for Italy will soon have to capitulate. So it is still possible that by the end of this year we will be drawing nearer to peace. Important events will happen any day now.

*September 10*

Although anticipated, still a sensational event: Italy has offered to capitulate and Eisenhower, commander-in-chief of the Allied armies, accepted! It is interesting that an armistice was actually signed on September 3, so that the landing in Calabria was a subterfuge to keep the agreement secret from the Germans. Henceforth, events will unfold as in an adventure movie. There are already developments. A rival fascist government in Germany. Fighting in the areas occupied by Italians and Germans. The Italian fleet leaves. Allied troops land. And then, as in a murder story, Mussolini's beheading . . .

*September 20*

"Yiddish Works in Romanian Translation," a recital I have been preparing, finally took place yesterday downstairs at the Baraşeum.[11] I became unavoidably involved with that

11. See "1940," n. 37.

gang of exploiters. But it was a complete success. My introductory lecture, an outline of the development of Yiddish language and culture, with observations on its future destiny, and with such political allusions as I could make within the bounds of the strict censorship—immediately won over the audience. Even G.'s remarks, which I patched up and edited by one-half, were well received. My readings of translations from Yiddish poets aroused unexpected enthusiasm. The well-disposed public enjoyed the recitations, the popular music, the concert, and listened in rapt silence to the whole program, which lasted exactly two hours. At the end of the performance there were loud ovations, which convinced me that we have overcome the public's hostility toward literary and artistic festivals, a hostility bred by the previous writers' festival, a pitiless, four-hour-long massacre. The warm hall was filled to overflowing, despite the sabotage attempts by a few friends, with whom I will settle accounts someday.

*September 29*

Now, at the beginning of this fall, the military and political situation is quite changed from last year's. Then, the Germans were at Stalingrad, today they have withdrawn a thousand kilometers. The Soviets are at Kiev, along the entire bank of the Dnieper, while in the south they are cutting off Crimea and mastering the lower Dnieper. The Germans are terrified by the possibilities that will open up to the Russians if they conquer the whole river. They fight desperate defensive battles. In Italy the Germans continue waging the war, but under difficult conditions, naturally, because the political, social, and economic situation after the capitulation brought chaos to the country. The Germans keep occupying new towns, new positions, since they can't trust the Italians, while south, at Naples, their front will have to give in to Anglo-American pressure. The present moment is, as have been all others so far, under the sign of Soviet superiority, their offensive power determining the whole course of the war. More landings, bombings, rebellions are expected. The end? Everything will be postponed until spring? Or will we be rid of the Germans by the end of this year? And how?

*October 2*

The whole city is in an uproar over Arghezi's satirical piece published in the newspaper *Informaţia* and entitled "Dear Baron." It refers to the German ambassador Killinger, and the experienced satirist poured into it his purest venom. Arghezi was arrested, naturally, but only after the paper sold throughout the day, which justifies the current suspicion that everything was done with the government's consent. In which case, Arghezi's courage is less admirable.

The initial surprise gave way to an excitement which quickly spread to all circles. Baron Killinger raised hell, which resulted in friction, coinciding—accidentally or on purpose—with certain difficult moments for our government: rumors of Iron Guard arrests and of agents provocateurs in the pay of the Germans. The rumors created panic both among Jews and Gentiles, a panic superimposed on the worry over the stormy progress of the Soviet armies toward the Ukraine. . . . We are heading toward the last hours of the war.

*October 22*

What does it matter that I jot down dates? Is there any difference between sorrow that bears a date and that lost in the void of time? One should record only the moments of victory over oneself, the completed stages of evolution toward serenity, toward renunciation of egotistical preoccupations. If this is not possible, then the scrap paper called a diary is worthless.

*October 27*

Chrysanthemums—summer's rear guard. The last flowers to fight against autumn's heavy offensive.

As the Germans withdraw from the south of Russia, one wonders about the fate of the Jews in Transnistria. Persistent rumors have it that the Romanian government might consider their repatriation. But nothing, so far. Some families from the Old Kingdom, especially from Muntenia, and a few of those deported because they were remiss in fulfilling their forced-labor duties, have returned. Their stories are horrifying.

Lightning-fast Russian advances on the eastern front. They attacked Kremenchug and took the Dnieper loop as far as Krivoirog, then conquered Dnepropetrovsk, forming a triangle for broad encirclement between these three points. At the same time, they took Melitopol on the Crimean border, and their armies are also advancing toward the peninsula from Nikopol and Korsun. People are tensely awaiting the outcome of this decisive chapter in the offensive.

Various rumors keep reaching us. Today I heard a bizarre one concerning Marshal Antonescu's remarks during his recent tour of inspection: he encouraged the peasants to form communes similar to the kolkhoz, although the commune is of Romanian origin and has only a superficial resemblance to the kolkhoz. He praised statesmen who adopt their enemy's worthy institutions and serve their nations by forcing them to introduce similar changes into their own economy. Then he urged industrialists to improve the lot of their workers before being forced to do so by legislation, because soon, the war over, they will face the workers without a Marshal Antonescu on their side. German circles, too, feel the pressure of the inevitable.

Speeches . . . Churchill's, about the war and how much longer it will last, setting its end in 1944. No mention of the discussions in Cairo between Eden and Menemencioglu, Turkey's foreign minister. The rumors that Turkey will enter the war have subsided somewhat. But people still expect a change to come from the south of Europe. Then a surprise speech by Hitler, who had promised not to speak anymore. Although still obdurate, he mostly argued with those who recently brought various accusations against him. He underscored his belief in God, his steady nerve, and his determination not to give in to the very end. And he reiterated the stale leitmotif of Judeo-plutocracy and

Judeo-bolshevism. On the whole, a pitiful performance, far from sounding the clarion the way he used to when he imagined he would dominate Europe through military might. No information about the war, its progress, his plans, the end of fighting. Those who heard him on the radio maintain that the press did not carry everything he said. For instance, he is supposed to have stated that if Germany loses its will to fight and is defeated, she will have deserved her fate and he will not feel sorry for her. He imagines that, at this last hour, the German people yearn for his tears! His speech also revealed that there are domestic rifts and rebellions in Germany, which he qualifies as "the actions of criminals," whom he will not hesitate to liquidate, at a time when so many people are dying on the front! But we still have to wait. And the optimism of those who expect peace in a few weeks is not justified. Right now, the most impressive side of the overall situation is the dizzying speed of Soviet advances: the Russians, having taken Kiev but yesterday, are now heading west and north, while in the south they have reached the mouth of the Dnieper.

Constant death statistics: it has been officially disclosed that, to date, 3.5 million Jews have been massacred in Poland. About the size of the Jewish population in that country before the war. During the same period, all the Jews in German-occupied Italy have been deported to Germany and will probably go on to Poland, the great Jewish slaughterhouse of Europe. Before leaving the Russian towns about to be reconquered by the Red Army, the Germans massacre tens of thousands of Jews. No nation fighting in this war has suffered as many losses as the Jews, who are not belligerents. But death statistics will go on . . .

## December 15

After the Moscow foreign minister's conference—between Molotov, Eden, and Hull—Stalin, Roosevelt, and Churchill met secretly in Teheran. It seems that at this meeting, disclosed only when it was over, they decided on drastic steps to shorten the war. People wait for them, some pessimistically, others with unshakeable faith. The question is whether the promised European front will be opened this winter or in spring. As of yesterday, there are forebodings of new events. Perhaps the planned, concomitant front . . .

Yesterday, two workmen in front of a tobacco shop, discussing a newspaper headline announcing in big, fat letters: JEWS BANISHED FROM SOFIA.

One of them asked: "What's that for?"

"What, man?"

"This business with the Bulgarian kikes. Why are they being kicked out?"

"Look," was the answer, "if the Bulgarian kikes live in Sofia, down below the Danube, the Germans can't beat the Bolsheviks up there on the Dnieper!"

"And if the kikes are 'under house arrest,' like it says here, will the Germans beat the Russians?"

"Well, we'll see later."

"What if they don't beat them?"

"Well . . . Then they look for other kikes to kick out somewhere else, until they chase away the Russians."

"So . . . It's still the kikes' fault!"

"Well, I guess so."

"Sure it is. Don't you think so?"

"I guess so."


## December 23

A very crowded streetcar, nervous people. In the middle of the car a tall German, so broad he takes up all the space between the rows of seats. Behind him a lady, resigned to being jostled, but eager to escape the crush.

The conductor keeps insisting: "Move ahead, please, move ahead."

The lady, panting hard, says: "How can I move ahead with this ox in my way?"

All of a sudden, the German turns around and enunciates clearly: "You also—ox with teats!"

# 1944

## January 3

The beginning of the year coincides with the beginning of the Soviet winter offensive, which is merely the continuation of the military action started last summer. After thwarting von Manstein's counterattack at Korosten-Fastov, the Soviets followed up with vigorous attacks, recaptured Korosten and Zhitomir, crossed through Berdichev, and are now drawing close both to the Polish border and to our own. The invasion of Italy and the extraordinarily heavy bombing of Germany, particularly Berlin, cause new panic and raise very serious problems for our country. As the front draws closer, the Jews live in fear both of the bombings and of German persecution or even executions. According to those who have returned from Transnistria, life under the Germans spells total disaster.

Still, no one can foresee how the forthcoming military actions will turn out, actions which seem to be decisive in ending the war. "Decisive" is a word used frequently throughout the over four years of war. Still, this much is sure: decisive events will take place, sooner or later. Perhaps this coming spring. Meanwhile, the Jews find consolation in the thought that this political and military juncture (underscored in all the New Year speeches, whose tone and contents convey serious reservations and painful reappraisals) may have a favorable outcome.

It seems that the new head of the Centrala,[1] Dr. Nandor Ghingold, who maintains categorically that he is not Jewish although he has undertaken to save the Jews, cabled New Year's greetings to General Antonescu, who replied: "I thank you for your wishes and extend my wishes for the health and prosperity of all good Romanian Jews." Some wags hastened to interpret "good Romanian Jews" as referring only to those six or ten Jews declared ethnically assimilated through special decrees published in the *Monitorul Oficial*. Our eminent leader, nevertheless, takes full credit for Antonescu's cable, boasting that it is the result of his honest dedication to Jewish causes. (A while back he refused to allow goods and clothing to be sent to the miserable exiles in Transnistria, but recently he issued an appeal to collect these necessities.) Thus, burdened by taxes and documents, by downgrading of status and forced labor, we await dramatic turns in an unknown future.

He fought so hard the obsession with death that he had no strength left to fight life.

Some evenings seem like assassins, lurking by the window.

## January 10

The official as well as the private news that reaches us from Berlin about the air raids is horrifying. One-third to

1. See "1942," n. 11.

one-half of the city has been destroyed. The human mind cannot imagine the fires, the collapsed buildings, the extreme shortages, and the population's grief. But what is incredible—something we have just learned—is that cards rationing sleep are being issued there. Every person is entitled to five hours of sleep. Each citizen goes into a room, or perhaps a shelter, where he sleeps five hours, then gets up to give his place to the next in turn. And the war goes on. . . .

Sometimes all the sources of patience and energy dry up and the soul is empty, almost ready to sink into indifference, and perish. Then a new spring of optimism wells up, feeding the waiting, and you begin to hope again, even to work. But work, too, is only a palliative. Nothing original, nothing personal—everything remains a superficial effort. Deep down you feel the weight of the war like a sickness which must end, but you can't see when. The life of the lowliest being depends on the outcome of the war, and the writer is no exception.

## January 30

I seem to have neglected the pages of this notebook. Life, drained of meaning over so many years, is growing even more senseless without intellectual pursuits. You read very little, you see very few people, and those you do meet exude an emptiness, a dryness, a desperate stagnation of spiritual vitality which mirrors your own. Since a commemoration of Eliezer Steinbarg[2] seems likely, I started revising the translations of his fables, begun many years ago. The work goes very well, perhaps because of the intimate contact with Yiddish poetry I had over the last five or six years. There are, however, difficulties specific to Steinbarg's work. Although some people attribute a superior quality to his language, it is a difficult one, with many inversions and an enormous percentage of Hebrew words never used by other Yiddish poets. He also relies on too many diminu-

2. See "1940," n. 3.

tives, perhaps because of his own infantilism: he was short to the point of deformity, had a child's voice and, some of his intimate friends say, was psychologically arrested as well. I was very surprised to learn that Steinbarg had no contact with nature, according to Hecht,[3] one of his closest friends, who occasionally took him outdoors.

## March 31

Again, after several weeks' pause, I am returning to these pages, with the same feeling of weariness and uselessness. . . . I spent almost all of my time on the excessive amount of work required by the preparation of materials for Eliezer Steinbarg's commemoration. Errands, meetings with people, endless typing of copy, with periods of sadness and incurable regrets, of useless revolt and productive persistence. Soon, all the illusions with which I await the end of the last, lingering cold days will be over. During this time epoch-making events have taken place. The Soviet armies have reconquered all of the Ukraine; have crossed the Bug and occupied Transnistria, part of Bessarabia, Cernăuți, and the Prut; and have entered Romanian territory. The German armies have been routed and are withdrawing in disorder. The information brought by countless refugees from the north of Moldavia, if it is to be trusted, indicates utter havoc. The German soldiers are selling their military wear, begging for bread, and deserting. A refugee from Iaşi told us that, just as he was about to leave his home, two German soldiers walked in the door and requested permission to take a bath. Afterward, taking advantage of their host's momentary absence, they helped themselves to civilian clothes and fled, leaving behind their uniforms. The waves of refugees are rising.

The Russian armies have reached Iaşi and the passes of the northern Carpathian mountains leading to Hungary. They are also closing in on Lemberg. To the south, having occupied Nicolaiev, they are marching toward the shores of the Black Sea. For strategic purposes, the Germans have

3. Helios Hecht, a Romanian graphologist, born in Bukovina.

entered Hungary by surprise, and have begun to impose
their infamous reign of terror: more than one million Jews
there, including many refugees from neighboring countries,
endure the horrors inflicted by the Germans throughout
Europe. In our country, we are totally confused and appre-
hensive of the future. Soon, we too will be engulfed in catastrophe.

## April 3

Yesterday the so-called Presentation of the Yiddish
Fable took place, to commemorate Eliezer Steinbarg, in the
tiny *Baraşeum* studio, naturally, where I managed to introduce some staging devices. Even the most finicky critics
found the show impressive. After a prelude—a violin lul-
laby—the actress Beate Fredanov recited a poem by Rose
Ausländer,[4] dedicated to Steinbarg, movingly evoking the
death of the poet. Then I gave a talk on "The Fable and
Fabulists," followed by a recital of Steinbarg's fables in my
translation, and finally, by short pieces from his famous
"Alphabet," acted out by elementary-school children. The
show was enthusiastically received by a public that filled
the hall to overflowing, confirming yet once more my belief
that a single individual with a clear idea of what he wants
is much more effective than the most brilliant committee.

Dr. Ghingold, leader of the Centrala, has resigned from
the "high, self-sacrificing position" he held in order to
bring happiness to the Jews of Romania. They say his blood
was one hundred percent Romanian (being a hematologist,
he ought to know what this means), and consequently he
requested appointment to military duty. No one can figure
out what prompted him to desert at the eleventh hour.
Whose wrath did he seek to avoid? Where does he want
to hide? The Jew who spread tonight the news of this
appalling resignation used swear words beyond the worst
expression of hatred. And a great many others shared his
feelings.

4. Rose Ausländer (1907– ), a German-Jewish poet, born in Bukovina.

## April 5

Yesterday we too were introduced to the scourge called American air raids. At about 2:00 P.M., several hundred bombers flew over Bucharest and, with the sun shining on, showered us with bombs. It was horrible. In the hail of bombs, I headed for my civil-defense post. Back home, my family went down to face death in the shelter. Across the street, some twenty meters away, a bomb fell on the grocer's house, blowing his family to bits and hurling them into the store next door. Seven dead there. Bombs fell every few hundred meters on Mărăşeşti Boulevard. The whole city sustained shocking losses and destruction. The railroad station, the Triaj car barns, Calea Griviţa, are unrecognizable. Innumerable victims, incalculable devastation: heavy damage at the Athenée Palace and Splendid Park hotels—the latter a German headquarters—at Dorobanţi, at the Obor train station, and at other points in the heart of town. A large area of the Cotroceni district was heavily hit. Many died in the air-raid shelters when these refuges took direct hits. Life is completely disorganized. There is no water, only partial electricity, no more streetcars. People fetch water in buckets from the pumps next to the various factories. Since the bakers have no water, bread is hard to find. I keep getting phone calls about new victims. The house of one of my colleagues from Cotroceni was destroyed, he is left destitute. A young man delayed at lunch downtown came home to find everybody in his building dead, eleven people in all. Several hundred more died in another shelter, in Obor—some two hundred dead, according to one estimate. With windows and doors broken, we wander around our house, bewildered and terrified, awaiting new misfortunes. Nerves strained beyond endurance and our minds stunned, we record absurd rumors. We wait . . .

## April 6

The day after the American air raid over Bucharest a new wave of airplanes hit Ploieşti,[5] bombing it even more

5. See "1943," n. 10.

violently. The town is ravaged beyond belief. Entire streets
have become mounds of rubble. People died in their homes.
Rescue teams rushed from here to Ploieşti, but found no
one to rescue. The Germans, they say, released artificial
clouds when the alarm was sounded, but the American pilots dropped their bombs through them. The right wing of
the railroad station is destroyed and the shunting yard is
out of commission. Trains cannot run. Here, we go on clearing the debris and removing corpses, whose number has not
yet been established. A visit to the Griviţa district is nerve-
shattering. It seems that the American pilots, starting over
Chitila, dropped hundreds of bombs all along the way to
the North Station, pulverizing the entire district. They
dropped only a few bombs over the rest of the city, to de-
moralize the population. Terror has frozen everybody. No
one works any more. Most of us stay close to home, to be
near a shelter.

One may die at any moment. Life has shrunk to a handful of fears and useless defiance. The population reacts in
different ways: many are indignant that the government
does not hurry to conclude a peace treaty, while a minority
rages against the aggressors, although it does have some
understanding for their actions. And this cold spring with
its leaden sky will never lighten the frightened faces and
the terrified eyes.

*April 12*

Another air-raid alarm, at about midnight last night.
Crazed people rushed into the shelter down in the garden,
groping in the dark, shaking with fear and cold, bumping
into one another, desperately searching for one another,
calling one another. But the air raid was not meant for Bucharest: the planes, they say, were headed for Constanţa[6]
and the Cernavodă bridge. Sleepy and resigned, people
stayed in the holes they no longer trust, ever since so many
shelters have been hit. It was an autumn night, with an ex-
asperating rain pricking you to the very bones. I raised my
collar and slipped away like a ghost to the civil-defense sta-

6. A Romanian port on the Black Sea.

tion. At about two o'clock in the morning I fell asleep. And so another day went by.


## *April 14*

Perhaps Claruța will write her memoirs some day, in Hebrew, no doubt. Meanwhile she spreads around shockingly vivid descriptions of the tragedies in her brief life. Claruța is nine years old and is one of the several hundred orphans returned from Transnistria, expecting to be sent to Palestine. Her small body, as if stunted, bears the stigmata of undernourishment: swollen belly, thin legs. She has a boy's haircut. Large eyes, lively and intelligent, feverishly observing her surroundings, reflect old wisdom from the ashes of past sorrows and a saint's resignation. She was born in Bucharest. When she was six, her parents took her to visit an uncle in Cernăuți. There they were caught by the sad circumstances which led to their deportation to Transnistria where she lived for three years. Now she is staying with some friends of ours who have clothed her and are lovingly taking care of her until her departure for Palestine. They brought her over for a visit. I spent a whole afternoon with her, listening to her memories and comments. She is an old person. Suffering has worn out all the spontaneity of childhood and dried out the sources of feeling. Her tales can yield social and political data for the most strictly objective history of the deportation.

"So all the Jews from Cernăuți left?"

"No. Those who had money and could pay, remained. But it was only an illusion. They bought the right to be deported three weeks later."

"And how did you live in Mogilev?"[7]

"The wealthy ones lived well, the poor ones kicked the bucket."

She speaks about death with chilling detachment: "What's the difference, life or death? Every day when I woke up I saw dead little boys and girls. I stepped over corpses. I don't know how I escaped!"

---

7. A Ukrainian city, site of one of the concentration camps set up by the Romanian government in Transnistria.

They ate grated beets and potato skins; she is nauseated when you offer her borscht or any potato dish. She knows medicine, hygiene, understands the psychology of people, and gives everybody advice. But what is really terrifying is her hatred for Gentiles, to whom she reacts with physical terror. A friend came to visit Marguerite. Claruţa saw him go to her room and suddenly ran to us, screaming:

"There's a Gentile there! Quick! Throw him out!"

"He's not a Gentile, child! Why do you think he is?"

"He speaks Romanian!"

She absolutely refuses to speak Romanian even though she went to Romanian school both in Bucharest and in Transnistria. She learned Yiddish especially in order not to use the Romanian language: "I don't want to, one mustn't! I am Jewish, and no Jew should have anything to do with a Romanian or a German. A Jew must go to Palestine!"

Her image of Palestine is tied to the hunger she struggled against: "There are figs there, and dates and oranges, and you can eat well and a lot!"

Suddenly, in the midst of a heated conversation, she grows silent and, lost in thought, stares at nothing. She misses her parents. She says so, simply, and she consoles herself with the thought that her mother will come for her, although she knows that her mother is dead. At other times she starts singing by herself, a heartbreaking song about a child who begs its mother to take it to her. She sings it without any emotion, searching with great interest the faces of the listeners to see how much they are affected. Noticing an empty candlestick, she vehemently demands a candle.

"What for?"

"I want to light it up for Hitler and sing his funeral song!"

And again she starts telling stories in Yiddish. Cernăuţi, the bridge over the Prut where the train derailed, the ghetto, the orphanage, sickness and death. Claruţa knows many things. As do all her comrades in whom suffering has sharpened intelligence just as it has blunted sensibility. She holds back a smile as she talks about two thirteen-year-old girls who had big bellies from eating beans. "The officers were nice to them," she adds in a dead, colorless voice.

*April 16*

Yesterday, on the eve of Easter, we had another air raid, at noon. While a squadron was bombing Ploieşti, it seems that several planes were detached to fly over Bucharest. Our shelter and the whole earth around it shook as if in an earthquake. The center of the city was hit: the university, still burning, the central baths, Palatul Sutzu, Palatul Generalei, the Union and the Stănescu hotels, the school of architecture, the Excelsior cinema, and other buildings nearby. You can see large holes on Brătianu Boulevard, by the statue, in front of the former pavilion for the Transnistria exhibition, its plaster fallen down, exposing the grin of the wooden beams. Again bombs fell by the railroad station. Very badly hit was the slaughterhouse neighborhood, on Strada Mărţişor, with its many run-down buildings full of poor people. My first-aid team had to work throughout the whole afternoon, removing sixty dead, thirty-six wounded, and people in shock. Although the street was teeming on the eve of the holiday, there were less victims than there might have been but for the early warning thanks to which people could take refuge in time. For two hours the city stood frozen under the deadly attack. Ever since the shelters have been directly hit, people don't trust these wooden tombs in which they hide, terrified. The atmosphere there is often hard to bear because chance crowds together all sorts of people, each with his own psychology and cultural makeup. A groaning old Jewish woman calls out *"Shema Yisrael!,"* a working woman kneels and crosses herself, a young boy moans and frets, others turn white or green, huddle in solitude and wait in the throes of death. Your dear ones are close to you, they await death with resignation, yet each faces death alone. The sharp swish of the falling bomb bends your head down, one more second left to live, two . . . three . . . that's it. It wasn't your turn this time around. Where did it fall? And the game is repeated again and again until, finally, if you are left alive, you go out into the sunlight, nerves shattered, heart as if drained of blood, all signs of life gone from your face. And the planes will keep coming. London, they say, has made an official announcement to this effect. That is why the city is so empty: three hundred thousand people have left. The wealthy, the war profiteers, those who benefited from the political regime, landowners, etc. Only the poor, office employees, artisans, intellectuals, and Jews are left. The Jews are not allowed to evacuate Bucharest. Some wealthy ones, though, managed to bribe the mayor or the chief of police, and settled elsewhere. But since Jews are not allowed in rural areas, many are now being sent back. Still, even if Jews were allowed into rural areas, it would be inadmissible to let them leave Bucharest: how could civil defense function without them? Most of the physicians, demolition crews, office heads, engineers, stretcher bearers are Jewish —and indeed services work to perfection.

## *April 18*

The air raids continue over the whole country. Several alarms in Bucharest, too. People just don't leave the house anymore. Life is restricted to home and the shelter.

## *April 21*

At daybreak this morning I looked out of the window by the bed in which we went to sleep last night, full of heavy thoughts. There was no alarm during the night. The sky is gray; it's raining. A calm, contained rain sliding down the window like a caress on a cheek. The gloomy weather puts me in a bad mood, but makes me think that perhaps today we will be spared the terror of bombs. We shall have to resist for a long time yet. The nerves are still all right. The heart behaves. All conversations tread obsessively around the same subject: the bombings. And there is no end to the ever new details about the dramas and misfortunes around us, always with the same idiotic conclusion: it is all a matter of chance. In the meantime, it's raining. The girls are still asleep. There is time until noon. Perhaps we will be spared again today.

We were not spared. At about twelve o'clock, a new air raid, which we endured in the suffocating ditch in the garden, crowded by more people than usual. To help matters, some workers gave encouraging explanations about the flimsiness of the structure. We don't know yet where the bombs fell, perhaps Pipera or the Obor train station . . .

At the entrance to our shelter there is an apricot sapling in bloom. When the end of the air raid was sounded yesterday and we came out, the young apricot tree was shining, victorious, in the sun. Only the birds kept running around, restless and as if indignant that their blue, airy empire had been taken from them.

## April 24

Today, the fourth bombing of Bucharest. It was the heaviest air raid to date—some five hundred planes, they say. The raid lasted much longer than usual, thirty-three minutes, and the alarm—two hours. Ploieşti was bombed at the same time. When the end of the raid was sounded, my civil-defense team was called to the central station, together with all the other teams. About sixty physicians with their assistants and medical supplies were taken there in three buses. Teams from other sectors were present as well. We just sat around in cars and on the curb until six o'clock in the evening. We were not needed, although there was great havoc there. Everything was disorganized. The bombs had fallen thick from the Grant bridge to Chitila, in Dămăroaia, and as far as New Bucharest, causing great destruction. The Griviţa plants, the locomotive depot, railroads, many residential buildings. I saw the Griviţa district for the first time after the bombing of April 4. It looks like an abandoned town. Every second building has been almost totally destroyed. A student of mine stood on a ladder in the middle of the street, cutting with a saw the streetcar electric lines. With shovels and picks, demolition teams kept appearing at street crossings, headed toward the destroyed area. People holding children by the hand and carrying suitcases crept silently over the clods of earth and the debris scattered over the gutted street. The small households on the side streets were mounds of bricks and planks. A poor man picking out his rags from a pile of old woodwork —all that was left of a small house in the middle of five bomb craters—asked me in a voice shaking with rage: "Come, Doctor, come look at a military objective!" Twelve people, crowded in a tiny inner room, escaped miraculously. Domeniilor Park, the area around the Arch of Triumph, and Filantropia, the Jewish cemetery, were also hit. Finally, the fifty or sixty physicians returned to their posts, having rescued three wounded and dropped them off at the hospital.

## April 27

All assemblies used to be forbidden, until the air raids began. Not even family reunions could be held without special authorization. Now, the shelters provide opportunities for gatherings of various numbers of people. And the alarms, lasting sometimes as long as two hours, untie tongues. One person makes a remark, another one replies, and so discussions and arguments are born, whenever the talk is not about the horror of the bombing. Public opinion can thus be polled, up to a point, since there is a random sampling of different social classes. We hear many interesting remarks made by people from various backgrounds. The hatred against the Germans has spread and risen enormously, and it seems that there are increasingly many defectors from the present regime. Everybody wants peace and very many don't care under what conditions. All they want is to escape the terror of the bombings, which have disorganized life and deeply demoralized everybody.

An autumn day with a heavy, ashen sky, ceaseless rain, and cutting cold. The raw green of the foliage seems a painful contradiction. Yesterday, too, the sky was cloudy, and people welcome this weather thinking it stops the planes from coming. Still, you are stuck at home, fighting the temptation to light a fire in the stove and waiting for some bombing schedule which never fits yours. You have accepted an estimate of the days it will take for the war to end, but you come to realize that these few days have to be lived. And there is a void you cannot fill either with memories or with reading. An absence of your self made worse by being cut off from everyone, by going over the same thoughts, when you lack information and often cannot push the cart of optimism out of the mire. If tomorrow brings good weather, the lilac will bloom and the bombs will fall.

### April 28

On the whole, the atmosphere at the civil-defense stations where the Jews are working is quite good. The leadership has become aware that the Jews respond promptly, working earnestly and with dedication. They say that the prime minister has personally congratulated some teams. Now and then there are reports of sharp anti-Semitic remarks in the outskirts. There are still people, even in the centrally located, elegant shelters, who believe that the American air raids are made with the help of Romanian Jews, and who loudly accuse the Jews of rejoicing when the city is bombed! Still, the shared danger and the comradeship of death have toned down the anti-Semitic reactions that were so violent until just recently. That's the most one can say. One of my colleagues in the Moșilor district shares a shelter built by the Jews renting apartments in two adjoining buildings and also used by two Gentile tenants, who were not asked for any financial contribution. Still, during one of the recent air raids, these two Gentile families loudly complained that they could not stay with Jews and demanded that the Jews leave the shelter.

### April 30

Claruța is leaving for Palestine with the group of children from Transnistria. She came today to say good-bye to us. She looked completely changed: pink cheeks, relaxed, wearing new clothes and shoes provided by the family with whom she spent her last days in Bucharest. She went to live with them without any feeling, simply for material advantages, as everybody realized. But this does not mean that she has become immoral; it is rather the conscious result of the clear-headed, practical maturity brought on by past suffering. She parted from us without any regret, in a matter-of-fact way, happy to return to the orphanage where preparations for departure are being made. Her obsessive desire to go to Palestine is unswerving. I talked with her and read her a short fable in Yiddish verse by Eliezer Steinberg. She didn't seem to understand it too well and immediately asked: "How can the wind talk? What does the wind or the star know? Better tell me a true story!"

"What is a true story?"

"My life in Mogilev is a true story!"

"But that is past!"

"The air raids on Bucharest are a true story!"

At the end of her visit she shook hands with everybody, and wished each of us one by one the same thing: "May you too come as soon as possible to Palestine!"

Before going out the door she asked that we buy her an orange, the fruit that fascinates her, that of the sun toward which she is headed.

Raining, the last couple of days. Ceaseless rain, as if it were late fall, and it is cold. The planes awaited by the people of Bucharest did not appear at their usual time. The joy of this breathing space compensates for the desolation of the weather, the humidity, and the sadness in the air. What will happen tomorrow? According to rumors, the English keep announcing that they will intensify the air raids over Romania. And Bucharest grows emptier each day. On every street you can see carts and trucks loaded with old belongings and suitcases, headed for the neighboring villages. The fear is unabated, although newspapers praise the exceptionally good behavior of the city dwellers. That's how history is written. After the unparalleled bombing of Berlin, the German press spoke of the courage and good mood of the city's inhabitants, claiming that the resistance and the morale of the Germans will improve. They even published some photographs of Berlin citizens laughing after a terrible air raid. But if you listen to the men in the street, in Bucharest, on streetcars, in tobacco shops, in pubs, they sing another tune: "Who's behaving?" they say. "Some have run away to the country, and those who are left behind are shaking in their boots. And why not? What can you, a defenseless man, do against armed men? You must rely on luck. What helps you is not civil defense, but God's will. In the three years since the war began, they didn't even manage to build a couple of hundred decent shelters in the city. They dug up boulevards, marketplaces, squares, they demolished houses with rooms which could have served a good purpose, now that so many dwellings are destroyed. Open trenches, infested with filth, that's what they prepared, so you die buried, asphyxiated, or shelled. There are no concrete shelters, like the papers say we ought to have. All that's left for us to do is take refuge in holes lined with wooden planks. God's will!"

The quiet before the storm continues. But everybody, the local and the foreign press, claims that the landing in the west is to take place within the next few days, at the same time as a new Soviet offensive.

The widespread news is that the Russians have amassed enormous forces and equipment on the southern border, that is, toward the Carpathian mountains, Iași, and further south of the Dniester, toward Tighina. Military events will come hard and fast in May. Without a doubt there will be more air raids. The Germans are trying to channel against the Russians the Romanians' anti-Semitic feelings. It is rumored that they demanded the deportation of Jews from Iași, and when the Romanian authorities refused to comply, they asked that at least a ghetto be set up. While official opposition to these demands seems to be firm, treacherous German propaganda among the population on the outskirts of towns has been spreading the idea that the American air raids are carried out in behalf of the kikes. It is the kikes' fault. That is, the Romanians are punished for having mistreated the Jews. There is some talk about it here and there, but it is not likely to catch on. They also say that there is some activity among the Iron Guard, probably incited by the Germans. But events have reached such a point that there will no longer be time for political diversions which have no hold on the Romanian people. The only important and decisive thing is the attitude of the government, so far unwilling to revive the Jewish question. Let's see what the beginning of May brings us tomorrow.

Last night we had what might be called an opening night: the first air raid by the British, who, they say, come only at night. So there is a division of labor over our country too—the Americans in daytime, the English at night. The raid lasted for a very long time, some forty-five minutes. The city was lit up by parachute lights as if it were noon. Many bombs spread over different areas of the city. At the civil-defense station we were again kept idle until 4:30 A.M. My endurance is still good, but I am very tired. I am stubbornly clinging to my translation of Steinberg, which I want to complete. Yesterday I worked on one more piece, which I finished today, laboring painfully after the air raid. A small fragment of eternal art opposing death, which preys from the air. And still, we hear nothing, we know nothing of what is yet to come. There is no news whatsoever. Offensive, landing—anything can happen at any moment. For several days now we have been chewing over the same speculations . . . Tomorrow?

*May 8*

The situation has reached a peak close to madness. Since the night of May 3, the alarms and air raids have not stopped. Day and night without pause. Thursday night was a night of terror unique in our experience. The planes dropped bombs all along our street, just before our shelter. We thought we had reached the end. A brick fell off an adjoining building on our shelter and broke part of our air vent. We all jumped out, driven mad by fright, and people began to howl. Toward dawn, dizzy and drained, we came out. No one went back to bed. The streets teemed with peo-

ple, a night like the unforgettable night of the earthquake.
I didn't sleep or even undress for two days and three
nights. The waiting at the civil-defense station stretched
out indefinitely. We live in a continuous waiting for the
alarm, which is sounded twice a day. Saturday night we
changed shelters and went to the one in the clinic across the
street, thinking that there we might not hear the whistle of
the bombs over our heads or their explosion nearby. A huge
crowd, suffocating heat, and the fire brigade with its phone
connected to the watchmen who kept calling in information
about the progress of the air raid. Still, it was by far more
bearable than our former shelter. We had no idea that a
bomb had fallen right in front of our house, breaking the
water pipe, and another one behind, on our landlord's factory. Yesterday morning, another air raid, the worst, they
say. The planes came in seven or eight waves. But though
there have been innumerable fires, the number of victims
keeps getting smaller—at least compared to the first raid,
on April 4. The despair is beyond bounds. Evacuations to
the country have risen. The Jews still don't have the right
to leave. Thousands of people assault the shelters in town,
standing around from nine o'clock in the morning, waiting
for the warning to be sounded. On every street, streams
of people, suitcase in hand, some headed for the Banca
Naţională shelter, others out of town. Transportation
means are very scarce; for a trip out of town, you have to
pay what amounts to a poor man's fortune. This scarcity has
also affected the aid to victims. The civil defense has no
vehicles to transport the wounded. People come to my station carrying their wounded on stretchers, in search of a
hospital. Indeed, there were violent protests. Accusations
were openly voiced: all the upper classes, high-ranking ad-
ministrators, expensive call girls, and other important personages get into their cars and run away as soon as the
alarm is sounded, while we, the poor, must stay here, to be
killed, or, if we are wounded, unable to save our lives because we lack the means of getting to a hospital. And thus
we wait for an ending, with no sign of it in sight. My life
has shrunk to a simple format: between home and the civil-
defense station across the street, to find out if there is any
likelihood of an air raid, and between home and the shelter,

to wait in front of the entrance, suitcases on the sidewalk. A few hours' sleep, and the rest—a state close to total prostration.

## May 10

Poor Dr. Verea, an old friend and colleague, was killed by a bomb that hit the shelter on Bulevardul Domniței. We all gathered at the cemetery, horror-struck and deeply moved by memories. A day of purple clouds and silences woven with fears and excruciating waiting . . .

## May 13

Tense hours of waiting: on the one hand, for the air raids, on the other for the western invasion and the eastern offensive, which are to bring about a final settlement. But meanwhile, for about a week, no air raids.

As of today, a great change in my home: a radio, after three years. Jews of the second category and former officers —my case—are allowed to have one. This is by no means a sign of generosity, although we sense a tendency toward repentance and conciliation. I was told that, as two or three hundred thousand people had evacuated Bucharest and suspended their radio subscriptions for several months, the network's income dropped so low it could not even cover the employees' salaries. And that is why the Jews—who are still not allowed to evacuate the city—were invited to become radio subscribers again! I felt a certain twinge as I reestablished contact with the world.

In the last few days there has been a strong current of humanitarianism and reconciliation in the press. *Curentul* quoted the letter of a country priest who complained that, of the hundred families who took refuge in his village, only two attended services; and he went on to preach the equality of all religions in the face of death and bombings. An editorial in the *Ecoul* recommends the brotherhood of men, regardless of their ethnic origin. Between these two extremist publications, all newspapers paraphrase the same idea, probably prompted by higher authorities. Even the commercial, nationalist *Universul* carried an article to the same effect on its front page where, for so many years now, it has spilled waves of poisonous ink, with criminal ill will. "Many useless horrors have been committed, of which mankind will be ashamed," declares the cynical lead article, and goes on to plead, suddenly, the case for generosity and understanding among people. Reading this novel, pathetic literature, you are overwhelmed by an incurable disgust. Everything started with the idea of giving Jewish and Gentile Romanians the same right to evacuate Bucharest. But some newspapers speak of the "errors" (innocent euphemism for "crimes") which must be forgotten in order to begin a new life! And the village priest's invitation to come to church clearly includes Jews, God being one and the same for all mankind! While on the very day when this solemn and pious invitation was issued, all the Jewish families were chased out of Berceni and forced to return to Bucharest on foot! And more: proceedings are under way to prove that Jews are involved in politics, or otherwise guilty, in order to establish legal authority for sending them back home. Perhaps the new spirit of reconciliation (equality when it comes to death, but not when it comes to life) will continue to spread. But it is obvious that this spirit does not come from the heart or from a sincere conscience, but is a decree which must be imposed by force. And until there is a radical change in the world it will be hard to reach through the moral hardening of so many beings who by now have grown used to extreme violence and convenient hatred.

## May 14

All the lilac flowers have wilted on the greening bushes. No one asked for them, no one stole them. The irises raised their violet candlesticks through rain-soaked layers of earth, but nobody looks at them. Spring is sad and chilly, abandoned by people. And the summer will be the same.

## May 18

After eleven days of quiet, another air-raid alarm. Whether it was because we had grown unaccustomed to them or because of news about the latest bombardments elsewhere, I don't know, but this time the city was gripped by panic and unchecked hysteria. As soon as the alarm was sounded people rushed out as if they had just escaped from a madhouse. Within a few minutes cars were careening madly on the city's main exit roads. I suddenly found myself in a tourist bus before my station, with my family and the lieutenant's wife, headed toward the Olteniţa road. The road was a terrifying sight. Hundreds of cars, with people sitting on top, hanging onto fenders, running boards, and bumpers; clusters of people clinging to phaetons, carts, trucks, all sorts of conveyances, in an apocalyptic flight toward the farthest villages, seeking shelter. Scared animals barely escaped the threatening wheels as each vehicle tried to overtake another. Every once in a while, stalled cars, screams, curses, and every few hundred meters hands would stretch out begging for a few minutes' hospitality. We passed the Popeşti-Leordeni airport, got out and sat under a young tree that stared in wonder at the puffs of clouds playing in the sky. We returned an hour later: they had air-raided Ploieşti, Belgrade, and Nish.

The problem of Jews evacuating Bucharest has not been solved. The newspapers are full of articles on humaneness, while Jews continue to be chased away from villages. Yesterday Ilie Rădulescu[8] asked in *Porunca Vremii* how many million lei this sudden press campaign for "humaneness" had cost. The censorship allows this kind of article too, side by side with those on humanity and equality. Today I had a chat with someone who had evacuated his family to a neighboring village. He rented a house, settled down, then a peasant—his landlord—came over to question him:

"Tell me, are you kikes?"

"No, we are of the Mosaic religion," the evacuee replied. "Why do you ask?"

8. See "1941," n. 5.

"I'm sure glad you are Mosaics and not kikes. You see, the kikes speak through the chimney with the airplanes, telling them to drop bombs on us. So if you're kikes, you see, we couldn't let you live here!"

This is the state of affairs just a few kilometers out of Bucharest, where people live without latrines, with cattle in the house, with garbage in the yard, with all kinds of infections, without gas, without wood—and with this pervasive mentality: the Jews conspire with the airplanes through chimneys.

## May 22

Ever since the air raids have started, that is, ever since we too have entered the arena of warfare, life has acquired a supreme and unique meaning. Natural death no longer exists. You die only because of the bombs. If, nevertheless, an acquaintance departs from this life because of illness or old age, people are caught by surprise, bewildered, even bored. And if they do think about him, they do so for a day at most, often just as long as it takes to read his obituary. All efforts tend to rescue the victims of air raids or of war. The only important thing is to escape the war. Afterward—life will begin for all, young or old, in the perspective of immortality. Everybody shares this feeling that after the war nothing bad can happen any more. There will be no more sickness, nor sadness, nor battles with time, nor the doubts the years bring. Life has been cut in two; all memories have dried up. Hatred and death have swallowed all uncertainties about living; and, where life could occasionally be a senseless burden, it has now become an immense reservoir of unsuspected meanings and magical values.

## May 27

The days of May, humid and chilly, have gone by in an exhausting waiting for developments. Military action now centers on the Italian front, where in less than two weeks the two German defense lines have been broken. The Anglo-American armies have fought their way through rocky mountains, starting at Monte Cassino, to join at the last moment the troops landed at Nettuno. Soon they will reach Rome. But people, lacking information and yearning for a quick end to the war this very summer, imagine that, once Rome is conquered, the great offensives from the west and the east will bring the curtain down. Meanwhile, the eastern front is totally inert. The Russians' preparations are completed, huge preparations which are particularly worrisome to Romanian circles, deeply concerned as they are over the outcome.

Political unrest has not stopped. On the contrary, there is talk of opposition forces being greatly reactivated. But the formation of a unified political front to meet all contingencies seems more likely than ever. People are torn between all kinds of images, more or less false, created by incompatible propaganda sources, by comments, with their various interpretations, by the difficult German military situation, and by so many interests at odds with one another. The fear of a final accounting, the concern for humanity and justice, become more and more persistent in rumors, in discussions, and flutter through editorials. Perhaps the moment of great changes in our country is not too far away. Certainly these changes will not live up to the imaginings of the naive or the scared. Probably, once the war is over—one way or another—and the Germans gone, a democratic form of government will be installed, but we shall have to live through difficult, chaotic times, times of shortage, of painful adaptations, of dressing wounds and patching up. Those of us who have no money will have an uphill fight from day to day. I don't know how long this will last, but as for myself, I expect it to be quite hard. Provided, of course, military events do not lead to unforeseen results, and provided we live through the air raids. One needs courage and lots of money! On the whole, one might say, you can be optimistic if you have at least five hundred thousand lei! Where can one get that? Nevertheless, people are optimistic, optimism being a kind of currency that circulates even without any backing.

## June 5

Last night the Anglo-American armies entered Rome after a battle begun three weeks ago. This moment was awaited not as a final step but as a stage to be followed by other decisive actions. The fighting in Italy goes on, progressing toward the north. It is still believed that both a new Soviet offensive and the opening of the second front will begin soon, Rome being only an intermediate step in the war. Still, from a strategic point of view, the blow to the Germans is an important one.

## June 6

The echo of the liberation of Rome, triumphantly celebrated in its streets, has barely died down when the long-awaited event of this war took place. At dawn today, between 6:00 and 8:00 A.M., Anglo-American troops crossed over from England and landed on the northern shore of France. All pessimism has vanished in a huge breath of relief. So the invasion did take place after all! This thrilling and crucial moment of the war has overshadowed all other preoccupations. Even the air-raid warning, sounded just as we heard the news, made no impression on anyone. Everybody wanted to stay home, to hear more, to discuss, to rejoice.

The landing took place between Le Havre and Cherbourg, while paratroopers jumped from planes and gliders behind the German lines, and four thousand ships and eleven hundred airplanes bombarded the coastal regions. General Eisenhower has issued a moving appeal to the people of Europe, saying that the hour of liberation has come. Churchill spoke in the House of Commons, and, one after the other, the exiled leaders of German occupied countries appealed to their nations at the moment of the opening of the second front. It seems that a bridgehead has been established at the point of landing, a preliminary step, according to Eisenhower. The Germans, too, have announced the landing, launched, according to them, "at the request of the Soviets! . . . The Germans will receive the invaders warmly and fight them passionately, Germany being aware that she must save Europe from the invasion of the barbarians!" The city is buzzing as it used to during the great moments at the beginning of the war. The people's enthusiasm strains their nervous system. Their awe seems to overpower their resistance. They know, but they don't grasp it, they hear, but they can't believe. And now we begin to await developments. Weeks? Months?

*June 12*

In just a few days, the Allied invasion has made impressive progress. They have established solid bridgeheads, conquered several towns, and now they are heading toward the military port of Cherbourg, where it will be possible to land much equipment and many troops with the help of large carriers. The myth of the unconquerable Atlantic wall has disintegrated. At the same time the Russians have begun an unexpected offensive in Finland, toward the Karelian isthmus. Other great military developments are expected in the days to come. Meanwhile, air raids continue everywhere, although a huge air force is deployed in the west.

On top of it all, every once in a while we have to put up with anti-Semitic remarks. The other day, next to me in the shelter, a captain was talking to a civilian who had arrived collarless and without a tie at two o'clock in the morning:

"All the kike women worry about their brats, sir! See them? I'd put them all in a concentration camp! We're going to be be slaughtered anyway, so what does it matter? Look at those kikes—I'm sure they have radio stations that warn them when the air-raid alarm will be sounded. That's why they all have ties on, while you, who live just upstairs, didn't have time to put one on!"

"No . . . I live at a hotel farther away!"

A few steps away, the wife of a physician, a colonel in the reserves, was saying to an acquaintance: "We don't understand: the members of their tribe bomb them with their own money! Why do they bother to come into the shelter?"

*June 19*

A quick glance at the present military situation, as compared with that in past years, gives the following impression: from El-Alamein the English have neared the north of Italy; from Stalingrad the Russians have reached Poland and Romania; while in the north of France the expeditionary Allied forces have landed some three to four hundred thousand men. Recently, the Russians have launched an attack on Viborg, in Finland. Nevertheless, the Germans are still on their feet. But to cover up their tragic agony, a task their former propaganda system can no longer accomplish, they have launched a new weapon, a plane manned by a robot rather than a pilot, which drops the most powerful explosives. They started out by hitting London very badly with this new weapon. Their propaganda is now shrill with past slogans, drowning out all news of current military developments. Chased in Italy, overwhelmed in France, and threatened in Russia, they use their new weapon as a last-minute diversion, for it does not constitute a viable or decisive weapon in the actual struggle. As for its worth as a means of reprisals against the British, the sensation created by its mystery will fade within a couple of weeks, when either a replica will be developed or a way to cancel out its effects will be found. Right now, the battle for the port of Cherbourg has begun. Will there be another landing, or will the Allies try to conquer France with the forces already landed? Will the Soviets then launch a general offensive? Barren of thought and unproductive, people look ahead worriedly at the summer days that pass without resolution. Silent, with fear, with calculations, with agonies draining the spirit, the brain, the arteries . . .

*June 22*

Military actions unfold hard and fast. The map changes from day to day, and hopes become accomplished reality. One waits. . . . Everybody is overwhelmingly preoccupied by the outcome of the Russian thrust toward Moldavia. Soon, difficult days will be upon us. Meanwhile, I lit another little star on the boring sky of everyday life: I translated "The Question Mark and the Exclamation Point," an original piece by Steinberg.

## June 24

In the fifth year of war and with conditions as they are, with the Germans being hit from all sides, bestial acts are being perpetrated in Hungary, similar to those at the beginning of the war when the frenzied confidence in victory led to the most degrading actions.

We learn that recently, after ghettos had been set up and several thousand Jews were gassed, a celebration of a medieval nature took place in Budapest: five hundred thousand books by Jewish writers were destroyed. The members of the German embassy were also invited to this cultural event, where they fully enjoyed this outcome of their civilizing influence. When the time for reckoning comes, the Hungarians will no doubt plead innocent on the ground that the Germans forced them to commit this final savagery, as do all those responsible for the pillage and crimes committed in the course of the war.

The Jews are leaving for Palestine. Countless numbers have placed their name on a waiting list set up as a result of intervention from abroad: an American society to aid European Jews has sent funds. Three ships in all, formerly used for regular traffic, are now waiting in Constanța, and constitute the sole basis for this exodus. The scandal has reached my ears, but I don't feel like remembering the details. The departures for Palestine on ships which sometimes reached it, sometimes sank, were always based on dirty commercial deals. And now, during these difficult moments, when efforts are under way to send orphans from Transnistria, millionaires are buying up the places of these unfortunates to save their own precious hides and their fortunes. The Jewish population here will remain without any support, for the wealthy emigrants give no thought to what will happen after they desert. They give even less thought to what is likely to happen wherever they are going when the war is over and the world settled again. No doubt they will proceed farther away, to Australia, to America, and Palestine will be rid of the sediment deposited there by a society in decomposition.

An interesting incident at the shelter for Transnistria orphans, when the president of the Centrala went to pay a visit. Claruţa came forward to meet him and asked to say a few words. She spoke the truth in a clear voice:

"I know why we are not going to Palestine: because the rich ones have bought up our places with lots of money. But I want you to know that we are more deserving than they. Because we gave our health and our parents, who died of illness and starvation!"

The president, Ghingold's successor, must have squirmed, particularly as, terrified by his responsibilities, he himself is racking his brains to find a way to slip into the promised land where he hopes to hide. He will succeed, of course, if he joins his Romanian millionaires, while Claruţa and her like are left behind. E. F. is leaving. I don't know why. No doubt to qualify for a pension which will assure him of a materially secure old age. But Rabinsohn,[9] too, is going. For him, the transplantation is most appropriate: he writes poetry in Hebrew, he teaches the language, and he will find proper employment there, although it seems to me he is closer to Yiddish than to Hebrew. The latest poems he read to me were very beautiful and had unprecedented vigor. He leaves me at loose ends with my anthology, but the remaining additions and the bibliography are no longer unsurmountable difficulties.

## June 29

Yesterday morning Bucharest was very heavily bombed. The Văcăreşti prison was hit and sixty-four prisoners, almost all women, were killed. The shelter for the prisoners there is a long, open trench.

9. See "1940," n. 6.

In the evening, another air-raid alarm, but only Giurgiu was bombed. This time we took refuge, both in the daytime and at night, in the basement of the dispensary, where a multitude of well-behaved and quiet citizens spend their time, entranced by Major Nisipeanu, the fire commander, who is in touch with the other commanders throughout the city. He is an impressively kind and calm man who, with a well-placed joke during moments of terror, manages to inspire hope in the people around him.

The military situation changes from day to day. The extraordinary success of the Soviet offensive on the Germans' fortification at Vitebsk looms largest. It seems that everything there points toward a total decomposition of the German front, which no longer has any clearly defined line and no chance of reestablishing one. After heavy German losses, the struggle for Minsk has begun. Ten German divisions surrounded, thirty thousand dead, and many units surrendering without fighting. No one knows whether this rush will stop at the border of the Soviet Union or whether it will go on into eastern Prussia or Riga, to surround all German forces in the northern area. This disaster raises the serious problem of Finland, where, despite the agreement with Germany, there are upheavals whose outcome may cause a surprise, especially after the resignation of the minister for foreign affairs.

The conquest of Cherbourg was immediately followed by a new thrust, and the Allies' advance in Italy continues. Only Romania raises no problem. Here we await the Russian offensive quietly and confidently, although the Mannheim and Vitebsk lines have been shattered in a few days. Vague rumors and political preparations to meet the new situation—that and nothing else. Otherwise, just the struggle with everyday occurrences. The bombings, food supplies, and chewing over the news that flies around.

The Jews still fear a last-minute tragedy. The example of Hungary, where unspeakable crimes are being committed, is a permanent reminder of terror and death. The other day the press announced in fat letters that a large number of Jews had died in Budapest as a result of the air raids. In other words, "their English and American brethren" (the

Romanian term for the Allies) did not accede to the Hungarian Jews' request that they be spared the bombing. The Germans have set up the ghetto in the heart of Budapest's industrial center, they say.

The vocabulary and the style of the press have a certain tone, a note of mystic nationalism, which underscores the political interests and the individual rights of each country. Lead articles discuss problems in general terms, dwelling on humanity as a whole and on the need to find a way of reaching harmony in the exclusive interest of the masses. Nevertheless, many of them fall back upon the old style, often incompatible with the initial intention, and arousing nationalist enthusiasm and local patriotism. For instance, there is a great deal of talk about "blood." This liquid plays a very important role in the war. I read in a newspaper the following account of the death of an officer: ". . . and a thin streak of pure Romanian blood ran down his forehead." What does "pure blood" mean? Biologically, it means blood free of germs. Rhetorically speaking, the officer's blood can be nothing but pure, since Jews are not allowed to serve in the army, and the mixture of Armenian, Hungarian, Slavic blood, or blood of any other origin, is of no significance when it comes to labeling this precious liquid. I also noted the following commentary on the death of a German officer: "That his blood is proud can be explained by its exceptional nature, since it is Teutonic blood. And the proud German blood was happy to be spilled." I doubt that any laboratory test could prove the peculiarity of this blood. And how can one establish as a fact that this blood was "happy" to be spilled? Only the unhappy officer could have testified as to the feelings he had while hemorrhaging; but he is dead by now. Even more interesting is the characterization of Slavic blood. I remember this line: "The Slavic blood, full of élan." Biologically, there are two kinds of hemorrhages: venal and arterial. Arterial blood spurts powerfully, that is "with élan." Is that what the nationalistic Slav meant to say? At any rate, it is an interesting kind of blood: quick and devilish. If the war goes on, who knows what new characteristics we will discover? Perhaps they will find a new classification to indicate tripartite unity and talk about "satellite blood!"

At night, while waiting for the air-raid alarm: the small machine guns of the crickets.

*July 1*

Someday the world's churning waters will settle down in a quiet river bed, and the war will become a dark memory that everyone will try to shed. The events we are experiencing today, massive and relentless destructiveness, will be bygone. The collapse of whole cities, hecatombs of the dead, airplanes falling, persecutions and crimes, all will be forgotten. Mankind will seek other outlets, in creative work, "children will again laugh in the sun," as the poet says, and the world, now in the throes of hatred and death, will relax and smile at life and love. Years will pass like the sound of bells. I hear their chimes across the meadow of brotherhood. A dream? But why not? The master builders of future peace are already drawing plans and discussing details. So why not start dreaming?

The city is in an uproar. Early this morning a plane landed with three thousand people, three choirs that had won prizes at the Vienna Folk Music Festival, broadcast throughout the world. The three winning choirs, Russian, Spanish, and Romanian, are touring by airplane fifteen European capitals. From down south, from the Balkans, innumerable ships following the Danube have reached the port of Bucharest to attend the festive concert. The years go by, sounding like holiday bells. Factories hum with enormous production. The earth is spilling over with golden wealth. Planeloads of visitors glide over the north of the country on their way to the Moscow harvest feast. A bridge between Calais and Dover has been joyfully inaugurated, and French and English sportsmen cross back and forth on their bicycles. A stage director from Leningrad has landed in Bucharest to produce the play of a French dramatist, who introduced it personally at a public conference. It's spring. Fifty thousand Bucharest children are on their way to a two-weeks' vacation in the mountains. Five theaters accommodating five thousand people have been built in Europe, and their performances are being broadcast on television. Thousands of people have gathered in one of Berlin's squares. Who is this young man facing them from the stage? He is called Mann, grandson of Thomas Mann, a sculptor in the forefront of the young German generation, about to inaugurate his statue of Heinrich Heine, the poet of liberty and of social revolt. The years go by like the ringing of bells . . . 1970! . . . twenty-five years since the end of the Great War . . . We will be some seventy years old by then . . . Will we be still alive? Still around? We will be quietly asleep under the earth, with no memories . . . Let's dream *now,* let us conjure up visions, let us have joy . . .

## *July 4*

One air-raid warning after another, this morning, last night, and the night before last. To date, Bucharest has endured eleven air raids.

The Germans are suffering complete military disaster on the eastern front. Before reaching Minsk the Russians caused them twenty-five hundred casualties (dead and prisoners) within just one week. Very many soldiers surrender, generals fall one after the other, and the losses in equipment are enormous. Last night Minsk, the great center of German resistance in Belorussia, fell, and the Soviet armies are heading toward Poland, northeast of Vilna-Riga, and southwest of Baranovici-Brest. The road to Prussia is effectively open. Everybody is overwhelmed by this unique military feat. The Russians' achievement is indeed awesome, though still not decisive. However, the Germans, having to fight on three fronts, are bound to reach a final stage. For the time being their resistance has not collapsed at any point, though it may at any moment. They have no soldiers, no railroads to move troops and equipment, insufficient fuel, and they have lost their former moral unity. But they are unswerving in their bestial actions. In Hungary they labor with their criminal missionary zeal at the total destruction of the Jews. The news from there is maddening. Recently we learned of yet another of their unconscionable deeds: young Jewish women and girls are being sent to the front, with a label pinned to their breast declaring them "war prostitutes!" Only when we learn how the Germans treated the population in lands they occupied temporarily, can we realize what they have allowed themselves with the Jews. And yet they dare to announce serenely that the populations followed them when their towns were reoccupied by the Russians.

## July 7

I have completed the Steinberg translations. I chose about fifty of his fables, the best ones, I think, the most representative and valuable to world literature. It was difficult work, and I am glad it is finished. I think I have succeeded in giving them Romanian citizenship. But I wonder when they will be published. . . .

## July 20

Two Hungarian envoys went to Ankara to negotiate with the Allies. What did they want? Medical supplies and transportation equipment in exchange for . . . the Hungarian Jews still left alive. (Still left!) Naturally the instigators of this official mission were the Germans, inspired by the cynicism of criminals who have nothing more to lose. It is hard to believe, though you know full well that nothing is beyond these people. It is also hard to believe that the Hungarians accepted to undertake this mission, presumably in behalf of their people, though fully aware that Hungarians offered the Jews shelter, took their money and jewelry in payment for saving them from the German scourge, only to end up by denouncing them! The Hungarian envoys did not ask for an exchange of prisoners but only for medicine and vehicles so that the Germans can continue the war, much-needed merchandise for which they offered to trade Jews.

## July 21

Last night, July 20, a friend of mine, a reporter with the Radar news agency, brought me astounding news: there was an attempt to assassinate Hitler!—an unsuccessful attempt. All through the afternoon the city was in an uproar. Within a quarter of an hour, I learned all the details. Things were indeed more complicated, as I suspected. A certain colonel, Count von Stauffenberg, placed a bomb in the Führer's general headquarters, which wounded several officers while Hitler suffered only some superficial burns on his face and a mild contusion. He made a speech after midnight, as did several other Nazi leaders. It appears from their speeches that the situation is very serious. The attempt on Hitler's life was neither a Judeo-Bolshevik plot nor the action of a madman. There is a revolution in Germany. Several generals, probably from among the many Hitler dismissed, formed a government and planned the assassination. To begin the overthrow of the regime they informed officers and a select group of civilians that the Führer was dead. Orders were issued, probably a strategy was set up in detail. Göring made a speech and so did Doenitz—but not Keitler. They all pledged allegiance to Hitler and issued stern decrees against the clique. (A very small clique of irresponsible people, according to Hitler, who made a speech to let the German people know he was alive.) Himmler has taken over as commander-in-chief of the Reich's armies. Nobody can get on a plane any longer without Göring's personal permission, or Stumpf's, the head of aviation. All air flights must now be used only for domestic travel. They say there have been actual clashes between troops faithful to the Reich and those of the rebel generals, whose names were not disclosed. Telephone communications with Sweden have been suspended. History, it seems, is playing the last act of the tragedy which has raged through the world for almost twelve years.

A decree applying to the whole population of this country: everybody is under legal obligation to donate shirts, underwear, and socks for the soldiers. According to each person's income and, naturally, in accordance with the basic principle of this regime's legislation: the Jews must contribute double the amount. But this is the first time that Gentile Romanians are also included as contributors. It's a matter of patriotism. On the streetcar today a Gentile gentleman who, judging by his elegance, must have dozens of sets of underwear in his closets, said sharply to a companion:

"Can you imagine, sir! If a country can't afford to outfit its soldiers, it shouldn't go to war, should it? What? Wage war with the underpants off my behind? No way, sir!"

"What if they take them only from the Jews?" his companion asked.

"That's another matter! But you can't take from them either anymore, most of them have been left bare!"

Then, wiping the sweat from his brow, he concluded: "It's immoral, sir, that's what it is, immoral!"

I didn't quite get what was immoral—taking underpants only from the Jews, or going to war in the Gentile Romanians' underpants.

### July 22

A three-hour-long air-raid alarm. According to the official count, the twenty-eighth alarm since April 4, and something like the fourteenth air raid over Bucharest. We spent the whole time in the shelter. The attack was aimed at the Ploieşti oil refineries, apparently as part of an overall offensive on oil-producing centers throughout southeast Europe. Our city has been spared for quite a while. But terror has not subsided, not in the least.

A dialogue in the shelter:
"Sophia has not been bombed for a long time!"

"What is there left to bomb? It has all been leveled to the ground. They didn't have big apartment houses, although they did have Jews."

"And here we cursed the Jews for building apartment

houses! What would we have done without them? Of course, we would have gotten rid of the Jews, but we'd have been cleaned out too!"

In order to put up with daily existence, some people choose melancholy over despair.

## July 28

We have gone through the twenty-ninth, the thirtieth, and today, the thirty-first night of air-raid alarms. This time around, the bombing was terrible, reminding us of the first ones, in April and May. Again we took refuge in the basement of the Bucur dispensary. We felt the shaking when bombs fell nearby. Great panic. The whole city was hit, especially the center. Innumerable fires and victims. The city was lit up as if by daylight, the sky red with the burning buildings. The air full of smoke and dust. We went to bed toward dawn.

Seven German strongholds on the eastern front fell in one day. The Russian armies are at the gates of Warsaw and at the foot of the Carpathian mountains, near Czechoslovakia and Hungary. The Germans, still bewildered by the upsets caused by the recent attempt at assassination and revolution, have announced "total mobilization"—the second call for *total* mobilization, for there was already one a year ago! I have the impression that here we will soon face a Russian offensive in the north of our country, the last one for the general offensive to be complete. The beginning of August will bring important developments.

## July 31

This summer is unique. People live with the terror of air raids. We have almost lost the sense of sight. Only the sense of hearing remains, strained to the utmost. In all the streets, wherever you go, you hear the same noises, the official music, and a medley of marches, waltzes, and tangos broadcast by the Bucharest radio station, filling the city between communiqués on air raids. The women, dressed to go out, work in their kitchens, ears glued to the radio, starting at the noise of every passing car or truck. Telephone conversations amount to sharing the same waiting tension. Everything is suspect—the hurried steps of a passerby, a shout, the distant sound of an awning rolling down, too much silence, a sudden commotion. There is no escape. And that is how days and nights go by . . . For how long? The day after tomorrow, on August 2, we expect to learn Turkey's position in this, the decisive month.

*August 4*

We have lived through yet another air-raid alarm, the thirty-second, with intense bombing in the north of the city, while waiting for August 2 to bring the expected developments: Turkey has broken off diplomatic and economic relations with Germany. It did not declare war, pending Germany's reaction. Germany will probably take no steps likely to lead to a military confrontation. It is playing for time while studying Turkey's official note. It may withdraw its troops from the Balkans, being in dire need of soldiers and also in order to avoid yet another front. Particularly since the Finnish president's resignation may result in the installation of a new cabinet willing to conclude peace with the Russians. Political changes are bound to happen. Here it is rumored that we will capitulate or conclude a peace treaty. New political solutions float around, involving adaptation to the realities of recent developments, particularly since Churchill has again announced that Romania is within the Soviet sphere of influence. It is a fact that German troops are withdrawing from here. They have been hastily moved to the Polish front where the Russians have entered the suburbs of Warsaw, after having crossed the Vistula river, occupied a long stretch of it, and reached the Baltic Sea near Riga. The general impression that we are living the last moments of military conflict grows constantly stronger. What with the collapse of the German front in Normandy, the isolation of German troops in the Baltic countries, the Russian penetration into East Prussia, the crossing of the Vistula, and Turkey's entrance into the political arena, but especially with the internal unrest in Germany—it may be that we are nearing the last stage of the war.

Consistency of an anti-Semite: There is a total shortage of razor blades in the city. A gentleman asks for some in a drugstore on Take Ionescu Boulevard. The salesgirl gives him a pack. The gentleman looks at it and then, angry but his voice controlled, says: "No, thank you, miss."

The salesgirl insists: "They are very good and they are the only ones on the market."

"Thank you, but no, thanks!" And he rushes out the door.

I had a look at the blades to see what was wrong with them. They were marked: "Made in Palestine."

## August 8

To sleep eight thousand nights next to a woman and to feel the presence of her exciting body with the same fresh emotion—is one of the rare affirmations of happiness.

## August 15

I come back to these pages with a burning head and a taste of ashes in my mouth, while the syrupy songs on the radio fill the air and the rooms in the intervals between broadcasts. Today, another important military event: the Allies have landed in the south of France, between Toulon and Nice. They met with no opposition and keep unloading troops and equipment. Of course the Germans declare that the attempt failed. This time around, the news created less of a sensation: people have grown accustomed to landings. It does seem, however, that the Germans' situation in France has deteriorated. The Allies have cut a narrow cor-

ridor of some ten or fifteen kilometers between Falaise and
Argentan. The German armies caught in the pocket
managed nevertheless to sneak through, south and east, toward Paris. While in Brittany they will be forced to give
up their fortified positions, one by one. People say that the
battle for France has begun and that it will end with the
Germans being driven out. But before the end, several battles remain to be won: the battle for the Baltic countries,
the battle for Poland, the battle for the Balkans. The Germans are tense with rage in their last hour of agony. Despite the defeatism of so many of his military leaders, Hitler is still issuing orders. He still calls heads of state to his
quarters, and still mesmerizes enough naive ones by his tall
tales of secret weapons to be used shortly. And he still orders his soldiers to fight to the last man. He has gathered
the remainders of his troops from all over Europe and concentrated them in Prussia to stop the Russians from entering Germany. The Russians have arrested their advance in
order to regroup. No doubt they will soon launch their
offensive. Perhaps the last settling of accounts will be postponed until September. People are very curious about the
outcome of Churchill's talks with Tito, talks that took place
in Italy at the time of the landing on the Côte d'Azur.
Here, rumors about efforts to reach a peace agreement continue, as do those about renewed efforts by the opposition to
thwart them. The people yearn for peace, but the leadership
still has other considerations. White bread has again been
made available to us. Might this gesture cover up some new
economic concession to the Germans? Yet one more day, yet
tomorrow, yet a little while longer . . . Money, illness, bombing . . .

Miron Paraschivescu[10] acquired the right to edit the second page of the *Ecoul* and gathered around him a whole
slew of young Jewish writers who contributed articles
under Romanian pseudonyms. He imposed a certain political nuance which he underscored in the column of replies to
his readers. At a given moment, this second page became an
actual Jewish paper, signed with fairly transparent noms-

10. Miron Paraschivescu (1911–71), a Romanian journalist and poet.

de-plume. The editor himself wrote articles with shrill leftist overtones, which gave the impression that he wanted to
cover up or atone for some errors, so as to reestablish a
former reputation, to create an image as a promoter of
noble, generous causes, and of artistic integrity. Despite his
articles, in which general ideas are twisted and drowned in
prolixity, Miron Paraschivescu has shown great enthusiasm
and a sound feeling for genuine poetry. His correspondence
with young poets is refreshingly daring; it shows an intui-
tion and a deep sense of poetry unprecedented in the columns of a literary review. As a result, and following his
announcement of a forthcoming literary section in the
*Ecoul,* the new generation of poets gathered around him
and prodded him to organize a literary contest. The outcome? The authorities in charge of reining in the Jews' eagerness stepped in, the masks of pseudonyms were removed,
and the creative drive was . . . Romanianized.

## August 18

The battle for France has progressed surprisingly fast
in the last two days. The Allied armies are at the gates of
Paris, at Rambouillet, and they may enter Paris tomorrow.
The Parisians can hear the cannons on the outskirts of
town as they listen to messages urging them to go on a general strike and giving them advice on what to do during the
last moments of German occupation. They are sharpening
their hatred of the Germans for all they suffered during the
last four years. The German armies in the north of France
are withdrawing; the few remaining troops are under the
command of the same marshal who has already conducted
the withdrawal from Russia. The Germans, it seems, will no
longer be able to offer any opposition on the Seine.

The Allied armies that landed in the south of France
have penetrated deep into the country, while French forces
storm garrisons, take prisoners, cut off all the Germans'
routes of retreat.

The Russians have begun their offensive in East
Prussia, and Bagrinoff, Bulgaria's premier, declared in the

plenary session of the Sobranie that Bulgaria's symbolic war has cost enough, that the people want peace, and that the government intends to do everything in its power to give satisfaction to the Bulgarian people (whose existence and demands for happiness have been finally discovered and acknowledged!). At the same time, Finland's shift toward an armistice becomes more evident: Marshal Keitel and a German general are meeting there in an attempt to save a situation which Mannerheim feels cannot be resolved except by an immediate break with the Axis. In our country, we hear of no change. Just rumors and more rumors. The air raids are getting much worse. In the last few days, air-raid alarms twice a day. There is also talk of military action on the Dniester. Might a Russian offensive start there?

It is possible that life is alike in all air-raid shelters. Still, as the people vary from one neighborhood to another, there may be differences in the shelters' population also. In our area, the largest shelter is that of the Bucur dispensary. The siren on its roof shatters eardrums as people begin to gather. It's almost always the same people, so they know one another. Some come quite seldom; they are the ones who do not trust the sturdiness of the structure and stay there only when there is no way to leave town. At the apartment block across from the courthouse, for instance, the crowd is a select one, made up primarily of the tenants there, dignified gentlemen, intellectuals, and politicians, finicky and patronizing, the women dressed to the nines and bored by this brutal interruption of their pleasant existence. The dispensary, on the other hand, draws the rabble. Here they go, as the sinister siren sets off—an old, regal-looking woman with a heart condition, panting and leaning on her cane, accompanied by her daughter; another old lady, overweight, heavily made up, smiling; the pub owner dragging along his matronly wife and a suitcase full of money; the cheerfully resigned tobacconist; a regiment of women in their dressing gowns, interrupted in their household tasks. Then a lame man, hands clasped over his ears, and neighbors who greet one another with frozen smiles, rushing by as if invisible hands were propelling them on wheels. Most of them are Jewish: women, more women, groups of children snatched away from their games, the local doctor with his slovenly wife, the little lawyer from around the corner, and a crowd of poor people from the neighborhood. After they have put up with the shoving of the firemen and the curses of the administrative personnel, they go downstairs and sit on benches, spread out into the adjoining rooms, into the laundry room, into the boiler room, and even into the waiting rooms of the sick. In the large hall under the main staircase are the phones connected to the firemen's station in the charge of Major Nisipeanu, the battalion commander. Everybody waits for him as if he were a protective divinity. He is the core, the soul of the shelter. People look into his eyes drinking in peace and security from his wise and calm being. They start to chat. Suddenly, a long hissing sound, and deadly silence. The alarm is sounded and the major receives the first news from his scouts, who are spread throughout the city: "The planes are over such and such an area." Everyone's thoughts turn to a house, a friend, a relative living in that area. The planes are nearing. The major is quiet. He speaks in a whisper and smiles. Suddenly, all the people who had spread through the rooms facing the street crowd into the small main hall. The major's family—his smiling, brunette wife with her silken voice, a woman of rare kindness and discretion, his mother, and his sister—quietly inquire about the danger. Stony silence. The reports keep coming in. Outside, things must be quite bad, and even near by. Are these the sounds of antiaircraft guns or bombs? The roar is still distant. The occasional "guests," who regret having come to this shelter, sit around in consternation, head in hands. A discreet cross appears in someone's fingers. The Jewish women sigh, having given up inopportune religious manifestations. The tension is at its peak. Nothing. Suddenly, a shiver, like a frozen wind, goes through the whole shelter. Two doors have been slammed by a strange din. Terrified, people jump off their benches. Several women faint. A voice shouts: "Keep still! Nothing happened!" It's over. Silence again. What was it? A bomb fell nearby. Through the window we can see now the flames of a great conflagration. The telephone gives precise information about its location. The major goes into the room by the street to light a cigarette.

The heat is stifling. Those who have not moved have congested faces, wet with sweat, terrified eyes. Time flows like thick glue, as we wait for the end of the alarm. Sometimes, whenever the commotion subsides, the children play games. One child, the star among them, is called Silvica: a three-and-a-half-year-old girl, with the head of an elegant little doll, devilish eyes, two braids down her back. She can sing all the latest popular songs. Her greatest admirers are the Nisipeanus. They lift her up on one of the tables in the laundry room and Silvica needs no prodding to launch into her repertory. She has the hoarse voice of a chanteuse, rolls her eyes as she hams it up, and the contrast between the ribald words and her childish innocence draws tears of laughter. Even the inspector sitting in the corner lifts his head up from the air-raid alarm report he is drafting.

The precocious child sings with ease and grace, sometimes sketching a few dance steps. Paula distributes quantities of candy, for which all the little spectators clamor, and everybody showers compliments and kisses on the performer. Silvica accepts them unimpressed, like an old trouper, ready to start again at the slightest invitation. A lady goes up to her and asks: "What's your name, little girl?"

"Silvica Herşcovici," the artist replies, innocently.

"It's okay," the lady tells the maid who guards her child, "she can play with the baby, he doesn't know the difference."


*August 23*

This evening, at 10:30, after listening to the moving sound of the "Marseillaise" celebrating the liberation of Paris, I heard the announcement that an "important message" would be broadcast. Twenty long minutes passed and, suddenly, King Mihai proclaimed that Romania was no longer at war with the Allies, but had gone over to their side in order to take Transylvania back from Hungary, and that liberty and equality for all were reinstated. The announcer then read the list of members in the new government, composed of Liberals, National Peasantists, Communists, and Socialists, headed by General Stănescu and including Maniu,[11] Dinu Brătianu, Lucreţiu Pătrăşcanu, Titel Petrescu, and several generals. Pătrăşcanu, the representative of the Communist party and minister of justice, then read a proclamation of amnesty for all political prisoners, with the exception of the Iron Guards. The communiqué lasted a little over a quarter of an hour. That was all. Twenty minutes to turn over an epoch-making page in Romania's history.

We went out into yards, into streets, where we all stood around exchanging good wishes and shouting with joy. Some neighbors asked us in to drink champagne. Then, unable to sleep, we went to visit some friends. Who could sleep that night? Everybody, people on foot, on motorcycles, in cars, were screaming at the top of their lungs: "Long live peace!" But on our way back home, at about two o'clock in the morning, we were met with a shower of machine-gun fire near Carol Park. We ran through the square and, panting, stole carefully by the buildings on Mărăşeşti Boulevard. My heart tightened. The inebriation of the first night was over. I began worrying over what the Germans' reaction would be. I did not quite share the hope that they would withdraw quietly. I fell asleep at dawn.


## August 24

Indeed, there has been a reaction. The Germans began bombing the city at 10:30 this morning, descending every thirty minutes with a vengeful rage on streets, on houses. Their planes keep diving and dropping bombs on the same spot. People have taken shelter, terrified. No one knows anything whatsoever. Telephone communications have been cut off, as has been the water, following a rumor that it has been poisoned. The radio is dead. Just once in a while it plays some Romanian melodies. Still, some newspapers have appeared, just a few: *Poporul,* the inhuman, Hitlerist, anti-Semitic paper, has added an innocent subtitle to its banner:

11. See "1937," n. 2.

"The Working People." *Informaţia* flaunts its editor-in-chief, Tudor Arghezi, and reprints his satirical piece, "Dear Baron." The race to show off one's radicalism and to make penance has begun. But I hear that *România Liberă*[12] has also appeared! At last we shall be able to read it in the open! Still, we can't get it in this particular corner of Bucharest, where we are surrounded by fearful people lacking information and direction. The air raids go on with periodic vigilance. One can leave the shelter for a few minutes, only to go back in again.

The vehicles for transporting the wounded have not yet arrived and we still have time to look around. I get onto an ambulance going from Dealul Spirei to Piaţa Puişor. I cross the almost deserted city, which looks as if it is ready for hand-to-hand fighting in the streets. At every crossroad, in every square, soldiers with machine guns. Here and there cannons camouflaged by branches. Airplanes circling above. Again the antiaircraft guns go into action. The massive destruction wreaked by the Germans is everywhere. The Academia area has been seriously hit. Up on the hill, four Romanian soldiers disarm two German officers, who hand over their weapons with a request that they be allowed to pick up their belongings. Over a broad area, in Piaţa Puişor, ruins and fires. Three dead. No wounded. We drive back to start out elsewhere. I learn that the Germans are holding out in many buildings and in the suburbs. Rumors fly, numerous and absurd. Still, the unrest leads to increased tension. The big question: What if the Germans take hold of the city? We know nothing for sure. Vague assurances that the leadership is optimistic. In the shelter, the crowding, the steaming heat, and the smells are unbearable. Over a thousand people have gathered here, with food, blankets, and pillows. It's like a transatlantic ship, fourth class, in a storm. People await impatiently the arrival of the Allied armies. Everybody offers a guess as to the precise point they have reached in our country. Most of us wonder at the absence of the Americans, whom they would like to

12. The official newspaper of the Romanian Communist party. It was printed and circulated illegally.

see arrive with hundreds of planes to save the city. But it seems that the Germans are surrendering all the positions they hold. They are putting up resistance only at Băneasa and at a few peripheral points. The news about their situation is contradictory. We keep hearing bombs dropping around us. Panic. The night is darker than ever. In the shelters we huddle on the steps of an iron ladder, next to some machinery, and wait for the dawn.

*August 25*

A single German airplane terrorized us all night long, as it kept coming and going. All the news about the Germans still being strong have proven false. Nevertheless, the air raids continue. Announcements of new instances of destruction keep coming. The emergency hospital has been destroyed. The Athenée and Royal Palace hotels have been hit. Bombs have also fallen on the Jewish quarter. We are living in the shelter. There is no time to eat, to wash up, to sleep. A strong wind sweeps through the city, spreading fires that swallow everything unless firemen intervene quickly. We know nothing about the overall situation. Young Jews are being drafted into defense units, with special weapons and uniforms. The American prisoners interned at the National School have run away from their camp and have spread out in small groups throughout the city. They are afraid of the Germans, who know their hiding places. We hid two of them during the day in the weeds in the garden, gave them civilian clothes and hats and some food, although there is hardly anything left to eat. Late at night, new air-raid warnings. We remain in the shelter. Actually, very few people—just those who live farther away—have left. The heat is unbearable, but even more unbearable are the rumors that crop up every fifteen minutes. They all contradict one another, even the so-called official ones, which are unrealistic, since almost all means of communication are cut off. We have learned, nevertheless, that the Germans have been dislodged from many points in the city. The official radio communiqué, following the repair of the radio station, claims that the city is firmly in Romanian hands. The Germans have been routed from everywhere, the only remaining resistance being in the Băneasa forest. The news from radio London, however belated, does not correspond to the rumors here that impatiently trace the advance of the Russian motorized divisions toward our capital. The important fact is that Romania has declared war on Germany. From now on, the tempo of military action will be accelerated. We wait for the nightmare of one more night to be over, perhaps . . .

## September 1

I really have no idea why I go on jotting down things as I used to in the days of silent waiting when these trite pages were my consolation. I no longer have time now for personal thoughts, for sitting and contemplating people and events. Carried along on the impetuous wave of changes toward the labor awaiting me, I ought to give up these flimsy notes once and for all. Nevertheless, I was drawn again to the typewriter: a breathing space, a need to look around me. So many events have unfolded in a few days that it is impossible to tell them in any kind of chronological order. Many encounters, much running around, talks, undertakings—criss-cross feverishly, as in a hallucination.

*România Liberă* is shaping up into a first-class daily, competing for top place in the Romanian press. At the same time, a slew of other newspapers have made their appearance. An overwhelming outpouring. The tendency is for any malcontent to put out a paper, and, of course, the scoundrels of the former regime are also doing their best to cut out a virgin path for themselves so they can sneak into the new employment field. In the aftermath of August 23, all the established papers continue to appear, now innocently proclaiming their new political views. *Universul, Curentul,* renamed *The New Universul* and *The New Curentul,* as well as *Seara, Ordinea, Viaţa* are all trying to corner the market ("Who, me? I never touched the cookie jar"). Some papers feed their hungry readers with lies or misleading foolishness. The Jewish papers have also joined this frantic game whereby everyone overbids a hand of impeccable humanitarianism and the purest democratic Romanian honesty. A. L. Zissu,[13] who immediately reestablished the "national-Jewish party," issued *Mîntuirea,* just as *Renaşterea Noastră* reappeared promoting the same line. We are also promised *Curierul Israelit, Evreimea, Viaţa Evreiască,* and others. There are no names left for newspapers—they have all been used up.

Maniu is calling upon the Iron Guard in his decimated party. In a public letter, he appeals to his former Iron Guard friends with whom he admits he has been in touch for the last two years. A certain Iron Guard officer, Comaniciu, speaking of "the end of our mission," urges his comrades to join other political parties. The Patriotic Defense ought to increase its vigilance: the Iron Guard doctrine is still an abscess in the country's body. Last night, the Iron Guard call to arms circulated throughout Bucharest. They are still functioning freely, as are the Hitlerites. Maniu's dialogue with these people created a painful impression.

Meanwhile, nothing is known about the armistice negotiations underway in Moscow, where, it seems, the difficulties are very great.

A meeting at Maxy's[14] to get writers to form a union. Organizational decisions—hasty and unclear—under pressure of the many tasks to attend to. The difficult problem of barring fascists and collaborationists from the *Gazeta Evreiască.* A meeting at my home. Formation of a group, which appointed me and the writers Benador, Liman, Hervian, Călugăru, and Mircu, as a steering committee.

Several of my former colleagues from the Medical Association have asked me to reactivate the association. We got together at Dr. J.'s and decided to take action.

The Jewish writers have appointed a committee of three

13. Abraham Leib Zissu (1888–1956), a Romanian Zionist leader and writer.
14. See "1940," n. 38.

to make contact with a similar body of Romanian-Gentile writers. So far, no progress. It is difficult to find Romanian-Gentile writers untainted by a political attitude.

## September 6

Today I attended a large workers' meeting that took place in the yard and surroundings of the Malaxa factory. I went there on foot. Besides myself, the writers B. and M. were supposed to attend it. Indeed, I witnessed a most impressive spectacle. Twenty thousand people, a forest of placards and flags, a youthful, vigorous enthusiasm, just to protest Antonescu's and the Iron Guard's ceding of Transylvania. Unfettered, a spirit of freedom was blowing over the sea of heads, filling your lungs, restoring health, and galvanizing the participants.

Some Jews had an audience with Maniu to discuss the present Jewish problems. Maniu told them: "For the time being, the state has more important problems than the Jewish one. If nothing has been done so far, remember there are generals in the government, and they work slowly. Besides, what problems do you have? You've always gotten by on your money and your brains."

I contacted Şerban Cioculescu[15] regarding the writers' association. There is talk of unionizing. He has submitted to the SSR committee[16] a petition, signed by thirty members, to convoke a general assembly for the election of a new leadership. Another meeting will be called to discuss the inclusion of Jewish writers. The strange part is that we three, delegates of the Jewish writers, who are supposed to get in touch with the SSR group, do not belong to this association. We will discuss the matter at some other meeting.

Unchecked chaos. The Iron Guard does as it pleases. At this time of democratic victories, of successful underground

15. A Romanian critic and essayist.
16. See "1938," n. 7.

struggle against the Red Army, it was possible for a group of hooligans to beat up Jewish students who went to the university offices asking for information. If these hooligans are not punished quickly and in an exemplary manner, things will go badly. So far, we don't know whether any measures have been taken against them.

## September 10

An Iron Guard colonel was saying: "What foolishness! What the Russian soldiers are doing is normal. It doesn't begin to compare with what our soldiers did when they went on field maneuvers: no girl was left unloved, and we left not a pig, not even a chicken in any village!"

## September 13

Yesterday, at last, an armistice was signed. There are twenty conditions, and none is as harsh as we had expected. The damages caused by the Romanians in the Soviet Union are officially estimated at fifteen hundred million dollars. This established figure is very moderate. Naturally, it is unlikely that the various provisions for reparation and control will weigh lightly on the Romanian people, but we must not forget that we, under Antonescu's shameless rule, violated the Russians' way of life and pitilessly trampled on their villages, without a thought of any possible future compensation. It is to be hoped that after the armistice is signed, more sensible changes will take place here. But we don't quite see them. The fight to consolidate our liberation is yet to be fought, with fresh energy but under difficult conditions. Everything is in limbo.

The Romanians have not realized as yet that they have lost the war and that they must earn peace. They are still lost in the fog of old ideas, and as they lazily wake up, they would like to pick up life as it was of old, before it was interrupted. They are still unaware of the storm ahead.

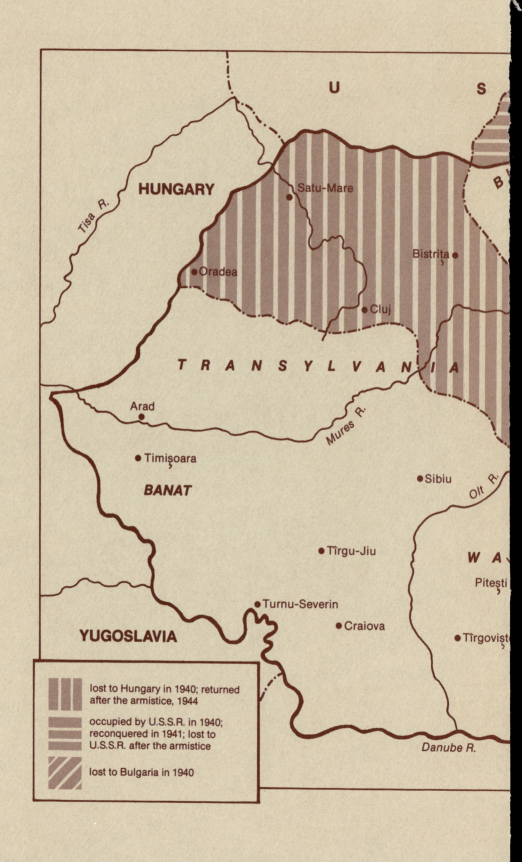

U

S

B

HUNGARY

Tisa R.

• Satu-Mare

Bistriţa •

• Oradea

• Cluj

T R A N S Y L V A N I A

Arad

Mures R.

• Timişoara

• Sibiu

BANAT

Olt R.

• Tîrgu-Jiu

W A

Piteşti

• Turnu-Severin

• Craiova

• Tîrgovişt

YUGOSLAVIA

Danube R.

lost to Hungary in 1940; returned
after the armistice, 1944

occupied by U.S.S.R. in 1940;
reconquered in 1941; lost to
U.S.S.R. after the armistice

lost to Bulgaria in 1940